AFRICAN ETHNOGRAPHIC STUDIES OF THE 20TH CENTURY

Volume 45

SUKUMALAND: AN AFRICAN PEOPLE AND THEIR COUNTRY

SUKUMALAND: AN AFRICAN PEOPLE AND THEIR COUNTRY
A Study of Land Use in Tanganyika

D. W. MALCOLM

LONDON AND NEW YORK

First published in 1953 by Oxford University Press for the International African Institute.

This edition first published in 2018
by Routledge
2 Park Square, Milton Park, Abingdon, Oxon OX14 4RN

and by Routledge
711 Third Avenue, New York, NY 10017

Routledge is an imprint of the Taylor & Francis Group, an informa business

© 1953 International African Institute

All rights reserved. No part of this book may be reprinted or reproduced or utilised in any form or by any electronic, mechanical, or other means, now known or hereafter invented, including photocopying and recording, or in any information storage or retrieval system, without permission in writing from the publishers.

Trademark notice: Product or corporate names may be trademarks or registered trademarks, and are used only for identification and explanation without intent to infringe.

British Library Cataloguing in Publication Data
A catalogue record for this book is available from the British Library

ISBN: 978-0-8153-8713-8 (Set)
ISBN: 978-0-429-48813-9 (Set) (ebk)
ISBN: 978-1-138-59567-5 (Volume 45) (hbk)
ISBN: 978-0-429-48817-7 (Volume 45) (ebk)

Publisher's Note
The publisher has gone to great lengths to ensure the quality of this reprint but points out that some imperfections in the original copies may be apparent.

Disclaimer
The publisher has made every effort to trace copyright holders and would welcome correspondence from those they have been unable to trace.

Due to modern production methods, it has not been possible to reproduce the fold-out maps within the book. Please visit www.routledge.com to view them.

SUKUMALAND

AN AFRICAN PEOPLE AND THEIR COUNTRY

A study of Land use in Tanganyika

BY

D. W. MALCOLM, M.A., Agric. (Oxon.)

Published for the
INTERNATIONAL AFRICAN INSTITUTE
by the
OXFORD UNIVERSITY PRESS
LONDON   NEW YORK   TORONTO
1953

Oxford University Press, Amen House, London E.C.4
GLASGOW NEW YORK TORONTO MELBOURNE WELLINGTON
BOMBAY CALCUTTA MADRAS KARACHI CAPE TOWN IBADAN
Geoffrey Cumberlege, Publisher to the University

PRINTED IN GREAT BRITAIN

PREFACE

THIS study of rural problems in Sukumaland began towards the end of 1936 as an investigation into the circumstances of population maldistribution in the four Sukuma districts of Mwanza, Maswa, Kwimba, and Shinyanga, in the Lake Province of Tanganyika. During the progress of the inquiry into the Sukumaland systems of cattle ownership and land tenure, a considerable amount of information was obtained concerning such matters as grazing rights, indigenous systems of pasture reservation, resettlement, and agricultural practice, which are component factors in the problems arising from the maldistribution of population and stock.

By the end of 1938, when the first edition of this study was submitted to the Tanganyika Government, the field investigation, in conjunction with the combined experience of several officers who had served in Sukumaland for many years, provided much information covering a wide field in the sphere of rural economy. It was therefore possible to compile a preliminary survey and to submit recommendations on the beneficial utilization of natural resources in Sukumaland under the title of the Sukuma Land Utilization Report.

In that first edition of this study extracts of the information obtained from all sources were included in the appendix. The text was copiously referenced to this selection of evidence which amounted to 100,000 words. In preparing this revision I feel that the reader would find so many footnotes and so much detail in the appendix tiresome. Thus the extracts of information have been almost entirely omitted. Copies, however, exist in the Colonial Office library and in the Secretariat, Dar-es-Salaam, Tanganyika.

Since the end of 1938 Sukumaland has seen many changes, some of which have profoundly affected the fundamental problems facing the people in this area. While the basic structure of Sukuma society has remained unchanged, not only is the problem of soil fertility deterioration ten years more urgent but also new factors have arisen which accentuate the need for drastic remedial measures if parts of this country are to be saved from becoming semi-desert areas subject to endemic famine conditions.

Of these new factors, perhaps the most important is the virtual elimination of rinderpest, which was carried out by the Veterinary

Department in a widespread and highly successful campaign in 1942. With the practical disappearance of this cattle-killing disease, natural biological control of the increase of stock has been seriously upset. On the other hand, as a war-time measure, it became necessary to introduce the compulsory marketing of cattle in order to provide a steady supply of tinned meat for the Forces in the Middle and Far East. This increase in the consumption of male cattle does not, however, counter-balance the natural herd increase caused by the uncontrolled multiplication of females, and consequently further measures, beyond those recommended and accepted by Government in 1938, have now to be considered.

In southern Sukumaland dust storms at the end of the dry season indicate the spread of desiccation. The food shortages in Sukumaland in the last few years, which have necessitated the importation of thousands of tons of grain, show the difficulties the people now have, in years of tricky rainfall, as a result of great stretches of the more easily cultivable land having been reduced to a low level of fertility; though, in some years, it may be said that any food shortages are induced as much by stalk-borer damage, *striga* damage, and bird damage, as by the other factors; the heavy soils are difficult to farm using only hoe cultivation. Further, it can be seen that newer areas at present still fairly fertile are being exploited as were the older areas. These facts give us warning of what we must expect if the seriousness of the situation and the urgency of remedial action is not fully appreciated. It has taken about forty-five years, since the first fields were cut out of the bush in Nyashimba[1] village, for the population to multiply and to reduce soil fertility to a point which has caused all but three villagers to move elsewhere. Those who have gone are doubtless repeating the process elsewhere, but within the congested cultivation steppe there is not enough space to permit this long-term rotational use of land to continue indefinitely, as it will take some time for such ruined land to regain its fertility under grass and bush fallow. Until this destructive process is stopped, recurrent food shortages and famines will inevitably becomes more frequent, more widespread, and more serious.

Besides these factors, which affect the urgency of the problem rather than its intrinsic quality, another development has taken

[1] Nyashimba village, Busiha, Shinyana District, of which detailed surveys were made in 1936–1937 and in 1945.

Preface

place which influences the organization designed to undertake the task of rehabilitation in Sukumaland. This development is the federation of all the chiefdoms of Sukumaland to form a single unit of African local government, with central headquarters at Malya. Previously the existence of four separate districts in Sukumaland, each with its federation of chiefs and its separate Government staff, led me to recommend the appointment of a special development team of officers who would control and co-ordinate reconstruction and development work throughout the whole area. Now, this inter-district and inter-departmental team is in being at Malya and, as a result of the federation of Sukumaland, they have the advantage of being connected with the new federal African government (with headquarters at the same place) with which they work in close collaboration. To make this federal development intelligible to those who are not acquainted with the structure of native administration in Sukumaland, it is therefore necessary to add some brief notes on the history, development, and functions of the federations of chiefs, their courts, and treasuries.

Another point affecting the recommendations submitted in 1938 is that some of them have already been tried and found inadequate for various reasons which I will explain. Others have been tried and have been found so successful that arguments to prove their value are now redundant and have therefore been omitted. Thus in place of recommendations which are no longer required I have simply discussed some of the facets of the problem for those who are not intimately acquainted with the work of rehabilitation which has already begun.

Now I must mention briefly two difficulties. The first is orthography. Some Sukuma words and names have come under Swahili influence which has affected their spelling in official correspondence though not amongst missionaries. For example, the Sukuma term for a village headman is usually written *mwanangwa* but in Kisukuma it should properly be spelt *ng'wanangwa*. While it is doubtless legitimate to anglicize names in common use, I feel that there is less justification for debasing a language spoken by over a million people and, as the majority of Sukuma words in the following chapters have not come under Swahili influence, I have decided, for the sake of uniformity, to adhere throughout to the orthography used by the Africa Inland Mission. The second difficulty is the use or translation of Sukuma terms. If I translated *nsumba ntale* as the viii *Preface*

'village trade union leader' it is almost inevitable that some English-speaking readers would invest the *nsumba ntale* not only with a pair of trousers he never possessed, but also with attributes or functions which only belong to trade union leaders as they exist in industrial countries, and so would obtain an erroneous impression. It is clearly impossible to repeat the very considerable descriptive circumlocution necessary to convey an adequate impression of what an *nsumba ntale* really is, each time he is mentioned. Therefore I have the choice of using the Kisukuma name, translated as adequately as possible in the glossary, or of trying to invent the closest possible abbreviated title in English. In the following chapters I have not found it feasible to adhere rigidly to either alternative, but I trust that in this study such terms as it has proved necessary to retain in their indigenous form are adequately explained when they first make their appearance on the stage of Sukuma social structure.

In the chapters devoted to fact it has been found impossible to include every variation of relevant custom within a reasonable compass. Consequently the risks of generalization must be run. The selections of evidence originally included in the appendix afforded some elucidation of the complexities of Sukumaland, but in their original form they represented less than a tenth of the information obtained and, for the reasons given, they have now been practically eliminated. A full survey of such a large and varied group as the Sukuma would occupy not less than five years,[1] but, provided that the unavoidable limitations imposed by generalization are borne in mind, I trust that the impressions conveyed by this synthesis of the numerous technical subjects involved give, in their true perspective, the salient points of Sukuma rural economy and land tenure, in so far as these matters are relevant to the main issue of the beneficial utilization of the land.

In all, I have spent some twelve years in Sukumaland. This period began with two years in the Mwanza District followed by two years spent in the intensive study of land utilization, which resulted in the first edition of this book. At that time I was based on the Shinyanga District while my research extended over the whole area. Later I spent six years as District Commissioner of the Maswa District and a year as Executive Officer of the

[1] A settlement report in India takes not less than three years to produce and statistics there are far more advanced than in this country.

Preface

Sukumaland Development organization at Federal Headquarters. I am, therefore, perhaps more intimately acquainted with the southern Sukumaland districts, but what I have written is, I believe, true of Sukumaland as a whole and where there are relevant differences between the north and the south I have pointed them out.

Throughout the progress of this investigation and its subsequent revision, the closest possible co-operation has been maintained with officers of the administration and of those departments which are concerned with this subject. Consequently, while the responsibility for the accuracy of facts is mine alone, a very large number have been checked by other officers to whom I should like to take this opportunity of expressing my gratitude for the extensive assistance I have received.

I am very much indebted to the following people for their generous assistance with the preparation of this work and in the following list their names are shown against the subjects in which they are expert and with which they so readily gave me particular assistance.

NATIVE ADMINISTRATION: J. Cheyne, Secretary for African Affairs. G. F. Webster, C.M.G., Provincial Commissioner. R. de Z. Hall, Provincial Commissioner. C. I. Meek, District Officer.

AGRICULTURE AND ANIMAL HUSBANDRY: R. B. Allnut, Senior Agricultural Officer. J. E. Peat, Empire Cotton Growing Corporation. A. N. Prentice, Empire Cotton Growing Corporation. M. Lunan, Agricultural Officer. J. G. M. King, Agricultural Officer. E. F. Peck, Senior Veterinary Officer. H. J. van Rensberg, Pasture Research Officer. Capt. Tremlett, Senior Veterinary Officer.

FORESTRY: C. J. W. Pitt, Assistant Conservator of Forests. H. R. Herring, Assistant Conservator of Forests. M. S. Parry, Silviculturist.

WATER: L. L. R. Buckland, Director of Water Development. W. P. Steele, Superintending Engineer, Water Development. P. Fadden, Works Foreman, Water Development Department.

SOILS AND GEOLOGY: J. G. M. King, Agricultural Officer. The late G. Milne, Soil Chemist, E.A.A.R.S., Amani. Dr. D. R. Grantham, M.C., Geologist. Dr. G. J. Williams, Geologist.

VEGETATION AND GRASSLAND: The late C. Gillman, Water Consultant. The late B. D. Burtt, Botanist, Tsetse Research Department. The Tsetse Research Department, Old Shinyanga. H. J. van Rensberg, Pasture Research Officer. E. F. Peck, Senior Veterinary Officer.

RAINFALL: British East African Meteorological Service.

ORTHOGRAPHY: Rev. W. J. Maynard, Africa Inland Mission, Nkola Ndoto. H. S. Senior, Administrative Officer.

GENERAL: E. F. Peck, Senior Veterinary Officer. J. G. M. King, Agricultural Officer. J. F. Spry, Registrar General. P. M. C. Clarke, Secretary, particularly in connexion with the revision of all maps and plans.

A very large number of Africans whose patient co-operation is most gratefully appreciated.

D. W. MALCOLM

DAR-ES-SALAAM, 1949

I am also indebted to Dr. H. Meinhard and to Mr. J. H. M. Beattie for advice and assistance prior to publication, to the International African Institute for sponsoring publication and seeing the book through the press, and to the Tanganyika Government for a generous grant towards the cost of publication.

CONTENTS

PREFACE	v
LIST OF ILLUSTRATIONS	xvii
LIST OF MAPS AND PLANS	xix
I. ENVIRONMENT	1
TOPOGRAPHY	3
GEOLOGY	3
SOILS	4
VEGETATION	5
RAINFALL	6
WIND	7
SOME COMPARISONS	8
II. POPULATION	9
STATISTICS	9
DISTRIBUTION AND DENSITY	11
MOVEMENTS	14
The Process of Transfer	17
III. THE PEOPLE AND THE LAND	20
HEREDITARY AUTHORITIES AND THE LAND	20
The Origin of Chieftainship	20
The Origin and Position of Subordinate Authorities	22
The Council of State	22
The Transmission of Chieftainship	23
The Chief's Rights	25
Subordinate Authorities	29
The Rights and Duties of the Village Headman	29
Water	32
ELECTED AUTHORITIES AND THE LAND	33
The Village Societies	33
The *Basumba Batale*	34
The Rights and Duties of the *Basumba Batale*	37
The *Banamhala* or Village Elders	40
The *Malika ga Mbina*	41
THE PEOPLE	43
The Family	43
Marriage	44
Inheritance	45
House Property and Reasons for Movement	47
Religion	50

xii   *Contents*

THE LAND	50
Land Acquisition	50
The Produce of the Land	51
Bush Products	53
Trees	53
THE USE OF THE LAND	55
Rotation of Crops and Fallow	55
Field Names	57
ANTI-FAMINE MEASURES	58
The Collective Village Sorghum Field	58
The Cassava Plots	58
Manuring	58
The Reasons for Scattered Holdings	59
THE ABUSE OF THE LAND	60
Soil Erosion and Fertility Losses	60
ECONOMICS	61
Cash Incomes	61
IV. CATTLE RIGHTS AND GRAZING	**62**
STATISTICS	62
CATTLE POPULATION	63
RIGHTS IN CATTLE	64
Acquisition and Disposal of Stock	64
REASONS FOR STOCK-OWNING	67
Religion	67
Marriage and Family	69
By-products	70
Famine	71
LENDING CATTLE	72
Cattle and Resettlement	72
GRAZING AND RESERVATION	73
Heavy Stocking	73
Reservation	73
WATER RIGHTS	78
FARMYARD MANURE	79
Manure and the Village Headman	79
Manure and the *Bahabi* (who have no stock)	80
SLAUGHTER	81
LAW AND CUSTOM	81
V. THE ADMINISTRATION OF LOCAL AFRICAN GOVERNMENT IN SUKUMALAND TODAY AND TOMORROW	**83**
The Legislative and Administrative Functions of the Native Authorities	87

Contents

Subjects Discussed at the Meeting of the Binza Federation Council of Chiefs, August 1945	90
Finance	91
Justice	93
Chieftainship and Democracy	95
General Considerations	98

VI. SUKUMALAND PROBLEMS. . . . 107

INTRODUCTORY NOTE	107
POPULATION, LAND, AND PRODUCTION	107
LAND POLICY AND LAND TENURE	110
African Land Rights	110
Land Policy and Production	110
Land Policy and Social Organization	111
Individualization	112
Sukuma Land Tenure Development	114
LAND UTILIZATION	119
Land Occupation	121
Improved Husbandry	122
Methods	123
Means	124
The Hand-hoe	124
Implemental Tillage	126
Mechanical Cultivation	127
Transport and Manure	130
RESETTLEMENT	131
Redistribution	131
Cattle and Water	133
Internal Redistribution	135
External Redistribution	136
Methods of Effecting Redistribution	138
Land Resting	140
CONCLUSIONS	142

APPENDIX

NATIVE ADMINISTRATION	146
EXTRACT FROM *Through the Dark Continent*, BY H. M. STANLEY	146
EXTRACTS FROM MINUTES OF FIRST PLENARY SESSION OF SUKUMALAND FEDERAL COUNCIL, OCTOBER 1946	146
SUKUMALAND SURFACE-WATER CATCHMENT WORKS	149
POLICY	150
ORGANIZATION	150
DEFINITIONS	152
SPACING	153

Contents

CAPACITY	154
CATCHMENT AREA	154
DEPTH	154
MAINTENANCE	155
General	155
Leaks	155
Breaches	157
Sealing Dam Basins	157
NEW WORKS	160
Dams	160
Siting	160
Layout	160
Instalment System	162
Spillways	162
Hafirs	165
Tanks	165
Size of Excavations	165
Intake Furrows	168
Check Dams	171
Sub-surface Dams	171
CONSTRUCTION	171
Tools	171
Earth Transport	171
Working Party Strength	172
Mechanical Assistance	172
Grass Planting	172
LEAKS AND BREACHES IN SURFACE-WATER CATCHMENT WORKS	173
SUKUMALAND SOILS	**174**
THE HILLS AND ROCKS	175
THE SANDY SOILS	176
THE RED FOSSIL (LATERIZED) SOILS	178
IBUSHI	179
THE HARDPAN GROUP	181
THE *MBUGA* SOILS	183
MINOR SOIL TYPES	186
WATER AND SOILS	190
SUITABILITY OF VARIOUS SOILS FOR CROPS	190
VEGETATION	**191**
SOME SUKUMALAND GRASSES AND PASTURE PLANTS	191
USEFUL INDIGENOUS SUKUMALAND TREES	193
BIBLIOGRAPHY	**194**

Contents

GLOSSARY	198
INHERITANCE TABLE	209
PLANNED GROUP FARMING	210
INDEX	213

LIST OF ILLUSTRATIONS

Sukuma sunset. Cattle tramping home from water in a cloud of dust . . . . . . *facing page*	16
Cattle by the old Malya Dam	16
'Slow-flowing meandering streams' (p. 4), Ndala river, Maswa District	17
The Sukuma cultivation steppe in *Adansonia digitata* (baobab) country, Shinyanga District	17
Busule, Shinyanga District	32
A pool in the upper reaches of the Shimiyu river . . .	32
The sorghum harvest of one family in *mbuga* country, Manonga Valley, Shinyanga	33
'. . . the vast majority of the regular agricultural work is done without assistance by each family on its own holding' (p. 38). .	33
The stream which runs all the year round from the Talaga springs, Shinyanga	48
Where the drinking-water is obtained from springs or wells, water must be drawn for washing	48
'Houses are even built in the neighbourhood of some new water catchment works which have not yet held water' (p. 33) .	49
such as this tank in the Ng'wabalumbaga *mbuga*, Busule, Shinyanga District	49
The *Badrilili* Snake Society Dance	64
A gum collector with spear, forked stick, and collecting gourd .	64
The owner of 300 head of cattle with part of his herd, as they start for home after watering in the Tungu river . . .	65
A Sukuma homestead in the plains	65
Well-grazed village commonage in the foreground with an even stand of fine grass in the village *ngitiri* reserve beyond . .	80
The boundary marks of village reserved grazing in Nyashimba .	80
'The village well or tank in which all the members of the village dig is sometimes used for cattle' (p. 78)	81
All along the stream-beds pools of water can be seen in twos and threes surrounded by piles of sand. Here three men dig together. Note the small sand-bar partitions	81
The water-holes at Ng'wajijenge in Busule . . .	128

List of Illustrations

Maldistribution of water leads to cattle-tracks . . . 128

The late Chief Makwaia and one of his surface-water catchment tanks 129

Panicum and *cynodon* pasture in rich flat land . . . 129

Cattle, sheep, and goats congregating at mid-day for water in the plains of central Sukumaland 160

The construction of the 200,000,000 gallon Ng'wamapalala Dam opened up some thirty square miles of hitherto waterless and tsetse-infested bush 160

The excavation is at right angles to the bank, thus increasing the transport of soil 161

The people are not carrying on the shortest haul, though consolidation on top should be relatively good 161

Heavy tractors at work raising the level of the Malya Dam bank . 176

Potatoes must be hoed beautifully clean. Note the rows of hoed weeds prior to burial under the ridges 176

'... both sorghums and maize give heavy yields....' (p. 184). This large crop of maize was grown in an *mbuga ya milala* . . 177

Sagia speaking at a meeting of Nyashimba villagers during the preliminary investigations for this study 177

MAPS AND PLANS

Due to modern production methods it has not been possible to include the fold out maps within the volume. Please see routledge.com for more details.

PLANS AND DIAGRAMS

Diagrammatic Representation of a Village	p. 35
Sukuma Systems of Pasture Reservation and Rotational Grazing	74
Water Supplies	153
Plan No. 1. Stopping a Leak	156
Plan No. 2. Repairing a Breached Dam	158
Plan No. 3. Dam Sites	159
Plan No. 4. Laying out a Dam	161
Plan No. 5. Layout on the Instalment System	163
Plan No. 6. *Hafir*	164
Plan No. 7. *Hafirs* and *Hafir* Layouts	166
Plan No. 8. Tanks	167
Plan No. 9. Intake Furrows	168
Plan No. 10. Check Dam	169
Plan No. 11. Sub-surface Dams	170

I

Environment

SUKUMALAND proper comprises the three districts of Shinyanga, Maswa, and Kwimba, in the Lake Province of Tanganyika, together with that part of the Mwanza District which lies to the east of Smith Sound. For administrative purposes, however, it is now convenient in some contexts to include under the term the adjacent Zinza and Ngambo groups of chiefdoms to the west of Smith Sound, in what is now the Geita District, for although the indigenous inhabitants of these areas differ both ethnically and linguistically from the Sukuma, their chiefs and people have elected to join the recently formed Sukumaland Federation, and so they together with the Sukuma chiefdoms constitute one political unit. Further, their country is, and has been for some time, subject to a continuous immigration of Sukuma from the overcrowded areas to the east of Smith Sound.

It will, in the following pages, be clear from the context in which sense the name 'Sukumaland' is used: it will as a rule be applied only to Sukumaland proper, the other areas concerned being referred to as Zinza or Ngambo, as the case may be. The discussion of Sukuma land tenure, marriage customs, political structure, &c., will be concerned with the forms found in the four districts of Sukumaland proper, east of Smith Sound.

Sukumaland, in the wider sense defined above, comprises an area of some 20,000 square miles, lying to the south of Lake Victoria and containing a population of about 1,000,000 people and 1,900,000 cattle units.[1] The area of this country is approximately twice that of Palestine.

In order to give a clear picture of land utilization and rural economy as a basis for the study of the major rural problems, it is necessary to include some account of the country itself. Everyone who has visited the Sukuma Districts of Mwanza, Kwimba, Maswa, and Shinyanga is familiar with the general appearance of the landscape seen from the railway or from the road, but the impression

---
[1] A cattle unit is either 1 head of cattle or 5 sheep or goats. Small stock units represent some 14 per cent. of the total.

created varies widely with the season. There is perhaps no better illustration of the great difference which exists on account of the long period of dry weather than Stanley's two descriptions of Sukumaland, the first of which was written in February during the heavy rains and the second in September at the height of the dry season.

February 17th 1875. Usiha (Busiha Chiefdom, Shinyanga District) is the commencement of a most beautiful pastoral country, which terminates only in the Victoria Nyanza. From the summit of one of the weird grey rock piles which characterise it, one may enjoy the unspeakable fascination of an apparently boundless horizon. On all sides there stretches towards it the face of a vast circle replete with peculiar features, of detached hills, great crag-masses of riven and sharply angled rock, and outcropping mounds, between which heaves and rolls in low broad waves a green grassy plain whereon feed thousands of cattle scattered about in small herds . . . the verdant downs of Sussex.[1]

But with the end of the rains 'the delicious smell of cattle and young grass' which reminded Stanley of 'home farm memories' fades away, and the 'thirsty and sere aspect' spreads, to become the background of his second description written $15\frac{1}{2}$ years later.

September 20th, 1889. Ikoma.[2] Before us, in the centre of a plain which three or four centuries ago, perhaps, was covered with the waters of Lake Victoria, there rose what must have been once a hilly island, but now the soil had been thoroughly scoured away, and left the frame of the island only in ridges of grey gneissic rock, and ruined heaps of monoliths and boulders and vast rock fragments, and under the shadow, and between these narrow levels, were grouped a population of about 5,000 people. . . . Every half mile or so there was a large cluster of hamlets, each separated from the other by hedges of milk-weed. The plain separating these clusters was common pasture ground and had been cropped by hungry herds as low as stone moss.[3]

This picture of Sukumaland, drawn by Stanley more than half a century ago, could hardly be improved upon today. This fact might tempt one to believe that no deterioration had taken place in Sukumaland during that time, but such a deduction would be incorrect. The inhabited area was much smaller then than it is now.

[1] H. M. Stanley, *Through the Dark Continent*, vol. i, p. 137.
[2] Then capital of Nera Chiefdom in Kwimba District.
[3] H. M. Stanley, *In Darkest Africa*, vol. ii, pp. 397–8.

TOPOGRAPHY

As Stanley indicated, the topography of Sukumaland is much reduced and the country is one of wide undulating plains interspersed with low ridges, hill blocks, and ranges, few of which rise over 1,000 feet above the general level of 3,500–4,500 feet above the sea. Large areas are *mbuga*[1] flats of which only those parts which the propinquity of permanent water makes available for arable agriculture and stock are at present in use. In the cultivated areas the practice of mixed cropping encourages a ground cover which usually appears fairly quickly after the first rains have fallen on unprotected earth. This cover then helps to retard the run-off on the upper slopes.

The map of physical features[2] read in conjunction with the vegetation map[3] shows the low relief obtaining throughout the majority of the cultivated lands, but within this area western Maswa, the neighbourhood of Mwanza to the east of Smith Sound, and the south-west corner of Shinyanga are the most hilly parts.

GEOLOGY

The greater part of the country is underlain by granite, part of the huge granite mass which composes the centre of Tanganyika. In some areas there remain relics of the older rocks, the Upper Basement Complex, lava flows, volcanic ashes, sediments, and banded ironstone, which the granite invaded. Through all these were injected dolerite dykes and finally kimberlite (diamond-bearing) pipes. Long periods of erosion reduced these rocks to a peneplain with a relief only slightly greater than that of the present day. Then followed the period when the surface of East Africa was ruptured and warped by the movements causing the great rifts, including the Eyasi depression in the south-east. This trough filled with water (possibly from the Lake Victoria basin), which rose till it flooded the valleys as far as Shinyanga: in it calcareous lake beds were deposited over the earlier terrestrial sands. Desiccation of the area, or an alteration of the outflow of Lake Victoria, reduced Lake Eyasi to its present size, and the deposits it left are now being removed by streams flowing into the Manonga river. *Mbuga* flats have formed where the gradient is too

---

[1] *Mbuga* is a very gently sloping area of dark clay alluvial soil, some of which is liable to flooding during the rains. See pp. 183–6.

[2] Facing p. 3.   [3] Facing p. 5.

4 *Environment*

gentle for active erosion and some are in the process of formation. In no *mbuga* is sheet erosion by water significant in terms of human occupation, though gully erosion is occurring in several places where the slope is steep enough for the rivers to eat back.[1]

Those of us who have had to build and maintain roads in this area know only too well that, where the roads cross rivers early in their course, the river-beds are constantly being cut deeper, and drifts, which were level with the sandy river-bed, are exposed within a few years and may be destroyed by the spate during the rains. On the other hand, where the roads cross rivers low down in the *mbuga* valleys, the sandy river-beds are rising and burying the drifts as more and more sand and silt are deposited by the slow-flowing meandering streams. Perhaps the best-known example of this is the so-called 'sandy river' on the Kwimba–Mwanza boundary, where the Shinyanga–Mwanza main road crosses it. In 1934 there was a pronounced river-bed crossed by a drift. Now the deposition of sand and silt has filled up the river-bed, and the pools, on which I used to shoot duck, have been replaced by fields of maize and other crops through which the shallow flood water flows gently over a wide area.

SOILS

The soil types of Sukumaland resulting from the geological structure outlined above show numerous varieties, largely of granite derivatives, and the late Mr. G. Milne's reconnaissance report gives some account of their characteristics. A knowledge of the soils is essential to a comprehension of the desiderata of resettlement and therefore the information on this subject obtained during my investigations has been co-ordinated with his work and with that done by other authorities, and the resulting collective contribution to the ecology of Sukumaland is included with a telluric table in the appendix.[2] Here it is only necessary to give a generalized account as a background to the study of the maldistribution of population which is endangering the productivity of the peasant's only source of wealth, his land. As the granitic outcrops of Sukumaland are characteristic, so the soil catena[3] from their base to the valleys below may be taken as typical. On the top of the rocky

---

[1] From 'Notes' by Dr. D. R. Grantham and Dr. G. J. Williams, geologists.
[2] See pp. 174–91.
[3] A catena is the sequence of soil types following topographic levels.

granite hills the slightly acid soils are dark grey-brown friable gritty loams containing some plant debris. Immediately below the rocks themselves, on a moderate slope, there is a broad zone of warm brown sandy soil grading into a gently sloping area of leached pale-coloured fine sandy soil. In some parts a belt of red sandy loam may be interposed in the catena. Lower down, on a very gentle gradient, the sandy soils pass imperceptibly into grey sandy 'hardpan', or rather, 'cemented' soils which, in the larger valleys, may occupy a wide zone. In the valley bottom the *mbuga* clays vary in colour from black to grey. The deep wide cracks associated with many of these *mbuga* types are not found elsewhere.[1] While the catena associated with granite is the most prevalent in Sukumaland, there is a red loam produced from the metamorphic rocks and, on lacustrine marls, a calcareous chocolate or dark grey loam, which shows lime nodules. These soils occupy considerable areas in southern Sukumaland. Both the lower hardpan soils and the *mbugas* in their natural state are clothed with a relatively sparse bush; *mbugas* normally have a thick grass cover and both soils are resistant to heavy grazing. Sheet erosion by water has some effect on the former but, as I have mentioned, some of the latter are actually being augmented by the deposition of silt from the higher levels. It must, however, be remembered that in contra-distinction to the higher lands, these lower soil types often require drainage. Experience has shown that, where arable agriculture is made possible by the existence of drinking-water supplies, the better drained *mbuga* soil types though difficult to work can, with suitable cultivation, produce heavy grain crops. The multiplicity of soils and their varied suitability to the numerous crops grown by the Sukuma tend to militate against an entirely compact holding in the present state of economic development.

VEGETATION

The vegetation of Sukumaland is shown in outline on the accompanying map, and it is only necessary to note that, while much of the cultivated area contains the *Acacia-Adansonia* (baobab) community, the areas of dense population cannot be rigidly associated only with this type of vegetation. Baobabs are rare for

---

[1] A similar catena occurs in the case of soils derived from the metamorphic rocks. The varieties are discussed on pp. 175, 176–89.

instance between Bubiki and Mwanza, and conversely blocks of them occur between Shanwa and Kimali in relatively uninhabited country. On the other hand, it would be fair to conclude that the centres of dense population generally follow either the *Terminalia-Combretum* or the *Acacia-Adansonia* and *Acacia* thorn country as opposed to the *miombo* or *Brachystegia-Isoberlinia* woodland to the west which, as in other parts of Africa, seems to avoid calcareous soils and is now relatively sparsely inhabited. In this connexion it is, however, noteworthy that the greater part of the *miombo* country contains secondary vegetation with indications of previous occupation. Experience has shown that the roots of many types of bush are practically indestructible by cutting down the trees, by cultivation and by grass burning, so that even after many years of cultivation an area of bush fallow will regenerate with unexpected rapidity. This fact is of no small importance in connexion with grass-land management and land resting and will be mentioned again.[1]

It should be emphasized here that, in the densely populated parts of Sukumaland, there are very few trees or shrubs left, other than those planted by the Native Authorities as wind-breaks or fuel plantations and also regenerating bush on hill-tops, which is reserved under Native Authority legislation. The Sukuma do not like some species of trees in the neighbourhood of their arable fields on account of the extensive damage done to their millet and sorghum crops by weavers and other graminivorous birds, but the Sukuma never fell trees simply to get rid of birds. They cut trees for firewood or for building poles or for stock-yard fences; hence in the open plains such trees as baobabs and figs remain because they are useless for fuel or for building; tamarinds also are untouched as their fruit is very popular, as are both the fruit and leaves of the baobab. Consequently central Sukumaland presents a picture of wide rolling almost treeless plains which, when the grass cover is removed by heavy grazing and when the top soil is pulverized by the cattle and desiccated by the scorching dry-season sun, are susceptible to aeolian erosion, particularly on the fine *ibushi* soils and on some of the dark clay *mbuga* flats.

RAINFALL

The rainfall map[2] indicates that the average annual rainfall of Sukumaland is in the neighbourhood of 30 inches and the percent-

---

[1] See pp. 76, 140-1.   [2] Facing p. 7.

Rainfall

age diagram shows the division of the seasons, which the short dry period between December and February almost separates into four. It is noticeable that the main dry season becomes progressively more pronounced inland from Lake Victoria. Statistics do not tell the whole story of precipitation and they must be amplified by mention of the increased humidity which exists near the shores of Lake Victoria and in the rocky country of the Nyanza Federation near Mwanza. It is noteworthy also that the small percentages of the annual rainfall recorded both at the beginning and at the end of the dry season are of negligible importance in Sukumaland from the point of view of general aridity. Broadly speaking, it may be taken that this period of desiccating sun, characterized by a haze of dust and smoke, is hardly interrupted from the middle of May to the middle of November. Experience has shown also that the rain tends to fall in localized storms rather than in a generalized downpour and so may be unevenly distributed in quite a small area. This fact has been erroneously adduced as an explanation of the local habit of borrowing fields at some distance in preference to using more land in the block already allocated by the village headman.[1]

It is interesting to note that rain falling on Sukumaland drains from the south-western area of the Ngambo Federation to the Atlantic via Lake Tanganyika and the Lukuga, Lualaba, and Congo rivers, from the central plains and the north to the Mediterranean via Lake Victoria and the Nile, and from the south and south-western area into the dischargeless basin of Lake Eyasi.

WIND

The prevailing wind of Sukumaland blows north-westwards from the dry area of the Central Province and across the salt pans of Lake Eyasi. The velocity of the wind is generally very low, but in some years dust storms make their appearance towards the end of the dry season. These dust storms are like the *haboobs* of Egypt and the Sudan and while the actual amount of fine dust particles removed from the soil, during a few weeks in some years, may not cause appreciable damage to the land in any one season, there can be no doubt that the appearance of these dust storms is an indication of desiccation.

The monthly average wind velocity measured in m.p.h. as the

[1] See pp. 59–60.

mean of each twenty-four hours by the Tsetse Research Department at Old Shinyanga for the years 1931 to 1940 is as follows:

Nov.	Dec.	Jan.	Feb.	Mar.	Apr.
3·3	2·2	1·7	1·5	1·4	1·8
May	June	July	Aug.	Sept.	Oct.
2·5	2·9	3·2	4·0	4·2	4·1

During this period the highest monthly average of the twenty-four hourly means was 6·4 m.p.h. in September 1940. It should be noted, however, that the wind here tends to blow in gusts and squalls before the beginning of the rains, so that for short periods in the day the wind may attain fairly considerable velocities, which are not reflected in these figures, as subsequent calms reduce the daily average. It would perhaps be fair to estimate that there may be half a dozen dust storms in south-east Shinyanga towards the end of the dry season in a normal year and these storms may be some ten to twenty miles wide and perhaps 60 to 100 feet high, though it is difficult to assess how far they travel.

SOME COMPARISONS

This brief description of Sukumaland, besides providing an outline in which to set in perspective the people and their problems, will also suffice to show that the conditions prevalent here are not entirely peculiar to this area. Large parts of the central Sudan, through Kordofan to the Kassala Province, with their granite tors, wide stretches of *mbuga*, and a large percentage of the flora to be found here, are remarkably similar to parts of Sukumaland. Northern Nigeria also has certain similarities; over 50 per cent. of the natural vegetation is common to both places, though, while the rainfall is similar, the *harmattan* is perhaps a more powerful desiccating agent than the winds of East Africa and soil types tend to be more sandy. In some ways the similarities of soil, vegetation, and climate are vitiated by the dissimilarity of other factors, yet many of the fundamental aspects of land utilization are comparable, as they are with such areas as the Punjab, a study of which area would do much towards an appreciation of future problems likely to arise with further increases of production and population in Sukumaland.[1]

[1] Cf. *The Punjab Peasant in Prosperity and Debt* and *Rusticus Loquitur*, by M. L. Darling (Oxford University Press).

2
Population

SUKUMALAND POPULATION STATISTICS

Chiefdom	1934	1944	1947	1948
Mwanza District				
Mwanza	33,400	32,400	38,200	31,866[1]
Busukuma	27,200	24,000	23,400	27,658
Bujashi	5,000	4,400	4,000	5,892
Beda	4,000	3,400	2,800	3,789
Nyamhanda	800	1,000	800	1,178
Iwanda	1,000	800	600	1,044
Nyegezi	2,200	2,000	1,800	1,915
Bukumbi	14,600	15,000	13,600	17,806
Burima	33,800	34,800	35,000	36,913
Nassa	10,000	24,200	27,600	34,075
Masanza I	12,800	12,600	12,000	14,552
Masanza II	1,800	1,600	1,200	1,506
Karumo	10,000	28,800	36,200	47,833
Busambiro	3,400	4,200	11,000	10,801
Buchosa	14,600	21,600	32,600	37,126
Msalala	17,800	24,400	17,400	27,245
Mwingiro	1,200	800	600	614
Buyombe	4,000	3,800	5,800	8,143
Bukoli	4,600	3,600	4,600	5,072
Total	202,200	243,400	269,200	315,048
Kwimba District				
Nera	78,000	80,000	..	88,962
Buhungukira	13,200	18,000	..	20,812
Busmao	79,600	74,800	..	90,884
Sima	9,600	10,600	..	13,644
Magu	8,400	9,000	..	12,054
Ndagalu	2,800	7,200	..	11,519
Total	191,600	199,600		237,875

[1] Does not include Mwanza township, the population of which is shown in the 1948 census as 8,885.

Chiefdom	1934	1944	1947	1948[1]
Shinyanga District				
Buduhe	19,200	25,800	19,800	25,853
Busiha	34,000	48,800	40,400	43,605
Buchunga	7,400	5,600	4,800	6,205
Ng'wadubi	7,800	7,800	7,200	12,612
Mondo	5,200	6,000	6,000	6,982
Seke	13,600	10,400	9,400	11,730
Shinyanga	12,400	15,400	13,400	18,979
Samuye	3,000	9,200	6,600	9,254
Busanda	10,800	15,200	14,000	15,696
Tinde	8,600	9,800	9,000	10,752
Busule	6,400	8,600	8,000	8,411
Lohumbo	16,200	21,600	22,800	26,292
Nindo	400	1,200	1,600	2,284
Salawe	7,600	10,000	8,400	11,390
Total	152,600	195,400	171,400	210,045
Maswa District				
Dutwa	4,600	6,200	6,800	8,858
Kimali / Sanga	4,800	10,400	15,600	19,307
Kanadi	15,600	20,000	20,600	27,695
Ntuzu	46,800	25,000	34,200	42,730
Itilima	8,600	24,000	26,400	35,265
Sengerema	13,400	15,400	19,800	19,769
Badi	6,200	4,800	5,800	5,788
Ng'unghu	19,800	18,800	19,600	22,247
Kigoku	12,800	8,200	8,600	9,166
Ng'wagala	71,600	43,800	46,400	53,936
Bugarama	2,000	1,200	1,400	
Total	206,200	177,800	205,200	244,761

BEFORE discussing questions connected with the distribution of population, a brief description of some of the characteristics of the people of Sukumaland will provide an indication of the human factors involved in the problems of this country.

The African of the Sukuma[2] or northern branch of the Nyamwezi tribe, by far the largest racial group in Tanganyika, who form the vast majority of the inhabitants of this area, are a Bantu people of medium height and dark brown in colour. They are generally undernourished, but they are happy, phlegmatic, industrious, and law-abiding. Unlike such tribes as the Masai, they are not primarily a cattle people. They treat the possession of stock as an invest-

[1] These figures do not include Shinyanga township which in 1948 was 2,103.
[2] *Sukuma* means 'north' in the Nyamwezi language.

ment at a very high rate of interest, as it undoubtedly is, particularly since the virtual elimination of rinderpest. With very few exceptions, which are usually reflected in the records of the native courts, the Sukuma are kind to their animals and go to immense trouble to ensure that their cattle obtain adequate pasture and water. One might almost say that the Sukuma looks upon his cattle, of which all the adults are named, with the same affection shown by an Englishman for his dogs. This attachment, however, is not so marked as in some other tribes.

As is often the case in other peasant communities, their language is very rich in relation to rural matters. For example, each different type of rain at each different period of the year has a special name. There can be no doubt that we still have a very great deal to learn from them of the knowledge which they have accumulated during many generations' residence in this area. Both the men and women take part in the agricultural work of the household. Men, women, and children look after the cattle and small stock and there is no question of an idle sex or class in this contented and largely undifferentiated peasant society.

DISTRIBUTION AND DENSITY

The population map,[1] compiled from various sources and available statistics, gives a general picture of the distribution, density, and movements of the people during the last thirteen years, though in a few cases movements out and back within this period are naturally cloaked. It will be seen that in most chiefdoms the total area is greater than that which is actually in use, though the margin of land which is capable of settlement varies widely, not only in size, but also in carrying capacity.

In considering the questions connected with the more congested parts of Sukumaland, it is necessary to examine the factors which have led to the present distribution of the inhabitants and their livestock. Besides considerations of soil, rainfall, game, and water supply, which influenced the location of the earlier settlements, it is easy to forget that as recently as sixty years ago the distribution of population was still controlled to a considerable extent by considerations of security. Most independent chiefdoms were isolated units, and the people, however concentrated in certain areas, were unable to move into the neighbouring lands on account of inter-

[1] Facing p. 9.

necine warfare. Even today the justified fear inspired by the Masai undoubtedly limits expansion eastwards. The traditional Sukuma village was usually situated on high ground if not actually under the shadow of a granite tor. It was roughly circular in shape and protected by euphorbia and thorn hedges or even stone ramparts, which are still to be seen amongst the granite outcrops, particularly in the south-west where the reputation of Mirambo, the raider, was no myth.[1] Within these fortifications lived the whole village community with their stock, and the present organization of collective labour is a natural result of conditions in which it would have been dangerous to hoe alone. The arable and pasture lands of the village were in its immediate vicinity and were often limited to the area in which the alarm could be heard. Stanley's description of Nera in 1889,[2] which is corroborated by the elders of the late chief's court (one of whom carried a load for Stanley), indicates the conditions of congestion which were largely attributable to the necessities of defence. Clearly a very large percentage of the population was then concentrated in the neighbourhood of Chief Kumaliza's headquarters at Ikoma at a density equal to, if not greater than, that to be seen today.

Then came the German Administration and with it the practical cessation of tribal warfare. It became safe to settle farther from the centre of the village. The German authorities are said to have prohibited the system of land sales between individuals, which had been evolved in some places during the period of extreme congestion, and people, anxious to obtain good land, began to move farther afield and clear new areas such as the present site of Ngudu, the headquarters of Kwimba District, which was at that time bush country inhabited by buffalo and other game. The spread appears to have been rapid and in a period of about twenty years the occupied area must have been very considerably extended. This process of expansion also removed the necessity for manuring which had been started in the south-west.

The next historical factor was the famine of 1900. It is remembered by its Nyamwezi name as the *nzala ya mitundu*, which means the famine of the *Brachystegia Spiciformis*, better known as *miombo*, as the people of the south-west were so hungry that they chewed the phloem or inner bark of these trees. This famine further assisted

---

[1] The old stone fort at Busule in Shinyanga is an example.
[2] H. M. Stanley, *In Darkest Africa*, vol. ii, pp. 397–401.

Distribution and Density

the reduction of density and the redistribution of population. Some died in the overcrowded areas, while others scattered in search of work and food with their more fortunate neighbours. Another factor with more local influence was the construction of the Tabora–Mwanza road in 1903 which had the effect of depopulating the adjacent villages owing to the impositions, such as forced labour and food levies, which were placed on them. The personal character of individual regional headmen and their good or bad administration has influenced the density of population of many areas to a marked extent. Thus, after the period of tribal warfare, which had tended to maintain concentrations of population, the various factors mentioned above began to assist redistribution.[1]

This process continued until about 1914 when the tsetse fly, which is the vector of *trypanosomiasis* (sleeping sickness in men and *nagana* in cattle), is said to have become of accentuated importance, particularly in the south-west. Although the epidemic of rinderpest in 1897 had greatly reduced the number of cattle, they were still a very important factor in the life of the people and therefore the advent of the tsetse fly[2] may have accelerated the abandonment and depopulation of some sparsely populated areas, thus increasing the population density of other parts.

This brings us to the present day. Though in some small areas the tsetse may advance where the population is not sufficiently concentrated to maintain an open cultivation steppe or where land has been abandoned to a regenerating bush fallow, elsewhere the people have recently reclaimed and resettled large areas of bushland where adequate water supplies exist, leaving their stock with friends until clearing operations have reduced the dangers of residence in the bush to a minimum.[3] For example, the movements to Zinza, North Maswa, and elsewhere show considerable expansion in conformity with the increase of population.

The fundamental problem is, however, *trypanosomiasis* both of human beings and of their livestock, and it is the optimum density of population in relation to protection against these diseases and to the preservation of soil fertility and not the actual area won from, or lost to, the tsetse which is of importance when considering land utilization.

To maintain an open cultivation steppe which cannot provide

---

[1] The age of trees in the bush gives some indication of the date of previous settlement.   [2] *Glossina* spp.   [3] For fuller details of reclamation, see p. 137.

a habitat for the tsetse fly, a population density of between fifty and one hundred to the square mile is necessary according to the type of natural vegetation. A population density below this minimum may result either from the partial abandonment of land to a bush fallow or from the infiltration of people into the bush. In either case a suitable habitat for the tsetse fly will exist in this partly occupied country. It is therefore essential that the line between the bush and the inhabited area should be well defined. It is immaterial whether the fly has penetrated into a cultivated area left to rest or whether an expanding population has penetrated into fly-infested bush. In either case the resulting low density occupation lays the people and their stock open to the dangers of sleeping sickness, an outbreak of which may well throw the low density population back on to fully occupied areas thus causing undue congestion and soil degradation there. It follows that both retreat and advance of population should be orderly. The expansion of the occupied areas should take the form of clean bites, as from a piece of bread and butter.

While the tsetse flies may be looked upon as some of the guardians of our reserves of good land which cannot be won from them without effort, yet the whole relationship to man and stock of the diseases which the tsetse flies carry is an intricate and important problem, which has been engaging the attention of scientists in this territory since 1921.

MOVEMENTS

The earlier movements of population appear to have come from both the south and west, but never to or from the east where, apart from the warlike Masai, the maldistribution of dry season water supplies is one of the more important factors constituting a barrier to human occupation. The earlier inhabitants of Sukumaland are said to have been primarily hunters who also practised arable agriculture. As their first requirement would be a well-watered country abounding with game they would seek bush- rather than grassland, and consequently they would not be attracted by the dry thorn savannah in the east. It seems probable that the subsequent influx of people from the west, including the pastoral Huma,[1]

[1] Cf. E. C. Baker, *Administrative Survey of Uzinza*. *Huma* is the local form of the more general term *Hima*. These people, who are Bantu-Hamitic pastoralists from the Nyoro-speaking countries of Uganda and north-west Tanganyika,

introduced cattle and provided many of the ruling families. Waves of immigration followed by invasion are said to have come round the southern end of Lake Victoria, culminating in the Ganda invasions, but the Huma left the greatest mark on Sukumaland, including many words in the language and the tall light-coloured men with fine features and beautiful hands still to be found in certain important families.

As with immigration so with the only major exodus which has begun from Sukumaland proper. This movement at present flows from the congested Nyanza Federation to northern and eastern Zinza. It was at first composed of a large percentage of Zinza returning to the land of their fathers, though in many cases a sojourn of one or two generations in the Mwanza area had rendered them almost indistinguishable from the earlier inhabitants of the Nyanza Federation.[1] The remainder are what one might call true Sukuma and they are seeking a new land for economic reasons.

Besides the flow of population westwards across Smith Sound to the shores and valleys of Zinza, a general tendency to move downhill is noticeable in many parts. A good example is the ridge of hills running east and west through South Maswa covering some 200 square miles of country which was very densely populated some thirty years ago. Today it is practically uninhabited. Amongst the granite rocks and regenerating thorn scrub numerous clumps of *Euphorbia tirucalli* which Stanley called 'milk-weed' (now commonly known as *manyara*) mark the sites of abandoned homesteads.

Besides such upland areas, which on abandonment have reverted to bush fallow, other areas have been depopulated not only on account of the exhaustion of the soil but also as a result of serious infestation of witchweed.[2] But there can be no doubt that food shortage is by far the most important immediate cause of population movement, whether the shortage is due to witchweed, or to erosion, or to soil exhaustion from overcropping without replacing fertility, or to a local failure of the rains, or to any of the other ills to which arable agriculture is heir in Sukumaland.

are sometimes mistakenly referred to as *Tusi*, a term restricted by ethnographers to the related but culturally and linguistically distinct pastoralists of the Rundi-speaking countries of Ruanda-Urundi and the Buha District of Tanganyika.

[1] Chiefdoms in Mwanza District to the east of Smith Sound. See political map facing p. 83.

[2] *Striga helmonthica*, a semi-parasitic weed on sorghums, maize, and grasses (a very serious factor reducing sorghum yields in the heavier soil areas).

During the last decade there have been numerous inadequate local food harvests. In other countries some of these would have caused serious famines, but the social structure and co-operative loyalty of the Sukuma have assured food for all, while there was food for any. It is a criminal offence in Sukuma law to refuse food to a traveller. This fact is eloquent of the customary mutual aid which exists here. The complete absence of cases in the native courts for such offences is even more eloquent. It must also be remembered that the Sukuma have other wealth, particularly their cattle, so that while a family may have a very poor food harvest they are not therefore necessarily destitute.

From the areas where the food crops failed come cattle which are bartered for grain; one heifer for one to three sacks of sorghum according to the current rate of exchange. This fact was a contributory cause of the redistribution of stock from the previously densely populated areas on the Shinyanga–Maswa border towards the rich grain-lands of the Shimiyu river valley. The grain returns on donkeys and sometimes even on lorries. In more serious cases of food shortage considerable quantities of food are imported by the Native Authorities for sale to the people and for distribution on loan or free to a small percentage who are not in a position to pay for their requirements. The Native Authorities also import seed stocks of quick-maturing grains and take other action such as the construction of grain stores to help the people.

Those Sukuma who have lived in an area where soil productivity has been reduced by constant cropping, witchweed, or the like, soon tire of having to go in search of food each year. So they tend to move to new areas which they saw to be producing large grain crops when they sold their cattle there for grain. Thus the population of Ng'wagala Chiefdom, Maswa District, was reduced from some 71,600 people in 1934 to about 43,800 in 1944, rising again to some 46,400 later. Some went to increase the population of the new areas of Busiha Chiefdom, Shinyanga District, where in the same decade 1934–44 the population increased from some 34,000 to 48,800 largely as a result of the water-tanks constructed by the late Chief Makwaia. Between 1944 and 1947, however, the Busiha population dropped again to 40,400. Chief Makwaia's tanks had been the only ones constructed in Sukumaland at that time, so that they attracted too many settlers and the resultant overcrowding was followed by the exodus of 8,400 people, some of whom returned

Sukuma sunset. Cattle tramping home from water in a cloud of dust

Cattle by the old Malya Dam

'Slow-flowing meandering streams', (p. 4) Ndala river, Maswa District

The Sukuma cultivation steppe in *Adansonia digitata* (baobab) country, Shinyanga District

home to Ng'wagala causing the increase there mentioned above. Others from Ng'wagala moved to Sanga and Kimali Chiefdoms, Maswa District, where the population, based mainly on the pools in the Semu and Sanga rivers and on the Shibiti river, has increased in the last thirteen years from 4,800 to 15,600. Yet others moved from South Ng'wagala to the fertile new lands on the banks of the Shimiyu river, mainly in Itilima Chiefdom. Similarly, as the population map shows, there has been a very considerable exodus from Ntuzu Chiefdom in the north of Maswa District mainly to swell the population of Itilima to the south, where much new land has been opened up as a result of two large dams at Ng'wamapalala and Nhomango and smaller ones elsewhere. Other people from Ntuzu have gone to Kanadi, in spite of a very real fear of the Masai, and still others have gone north to the Nassa Chiefdom of Mwanza District which has gained some 17,600 people compared with 12,600 lost to Ntuzu. Such examples need not be multiplied, as the map facing p. 9 gives some indication not only of the distribution and density of population but also of the larger movements which have taken place during the last thirteen years. It must be remembered that although expansion to the east is limited by the Serengeti National Park and by the Masai, to the north by Lake Victoria and to the west by the less satisfactory *miombo* soils, yet to the south and south-east beyond the Manonga and Shibiti rivers there is no barrier to emigration. In fact, of recent years quite a considerable number of Sukuma have crossed the southern boundary of Sukumaland to settle amongst their Sukuma and Nyamwezi neighbours to the south.

The Process of Transfer. Provided a family can continue to extract a subsistence from their land, they will not usually move until famine, death, or disease provides a more tangible reason than the gradual reduction of crop yields. When an explanation of a sudden fatality is sought, an African doctor may sometimes ascribe it to environment and recommend a change. During the period before a vague dissatisfaction with decreasing yields is translated by some event into a definite decision, the man of the house may borrow fields in a village some distance away to plant cotton and perhaps other crops in order to improve his economic position. During his visits to his distant farm he will have stayed with friends for whom he works, and he will then have had an opportunity to attend the local court to study customary law, and also to look for a suitable place to live. Then, when the move is made he may again stay with friends or relations and complete the move prior to the planting rains. If his move was across Smith Sound to Zinza he will have time during the first year to examine the country farther inland or along the coast, asking for information concerning its potentialities from the inhabitants of neighbouring settlements, until at length he finds a locality which meets his requirements from the point of view both of available area and soil types. Then, or just after the harvest, he and his wife will build their new house[1] with the assistance of the young people of the village of which they are becoming members. The second stage of the move will thus be completed before the planting rains.

Naturally there is nothing hard and fast about this procedure and a family may complete a sudden move in one season, if there happens to be adequate land or an empty house and the fields which go with it available in the village which they first visit. On the other hand, the whole process may take several years. Some of those who are now crossing Smith Sound have grown cotton in Zinza for some time before actually deciding to go and live there, while many young bachelors without wealth marry into families in Zinza where the large bride-price of cattle customary in Sukumaland proper is not demanded.[2] On the average it would perhaps be safe to say that, from the first visits of investigation, the move occupies at least two years. In this connexion it is important to note that no individual, whatever the ostensible cause of his move from a densely populated part, will be content with an allocation of land of a similar productive capacity to that which he has left. The majority moving to Zinza, while they will borrow fields in the crowded coastal strip as a temporary measure, are now moving to the less crowded areas farther inland following water, soils, and grazing, or if possible to the less densely populated villages farther along the coast, where, besides advantages of rainfall and the like, the supply of fish provides an additional attraction.

It has been suggested that the new settlers will not be allocated sufficient land for the cultivation of economic crops, but this does not appear to be the case, as the settler himself is responsible for obtaining an area adequate to his requirements, which now

---

[1] In Zinza the women collect the thatching-grass.

[2] There is some doubt as to what form of bride-price, if any, is customary among the Zinza.

constitutes a considerably greater acreage than he would have needed for the production of subsistence crops only. No sane human being, with large unoccupied areas to choose from, will be content to remain where he is unable to obtain a more productive farm than that which he has abandoned.

The process of transfer from such areas as the strip of hills in South Maswa to new lands opened up by the provision of surface-water catchment works, or to the country watered by the pools in the upper reaches of the Shimiyu river, is substantially similar to the process of transfer from the Mwanza area to Zinza, except that the movements which are taking place in other parts of Sukumaland have not the water barrier of Smith Sound to complicate and delay the process. As I have mentioned, the people move ahead of their stock, which only follows when the new clearings are sufficiently consolidated to reduce substantially the danger from lions, tsetse, and vermin.

3

The People and the Land

HEREDITARY AUTHORITIES AND THE LAND

'THE chief is the absolute owner of all the land.' This is the answer of chiefs and people alike, but to appreciate its full meaning it is necessary to examine the rights and nature of chieftainship in relation to the social structure and rural economy of the people. Any reconstruction of the past, in such an area as Sukumaland, in order to assess the rights of the present, necessarily leads us into 'a shadowy world of legends and guesswork and we must content ourselves with the conclusion—that the truth is known only to God'.[1] Nevertheless there are indications and, as it is impossible within a reasonable compass to give in detail the known history of each chiefdom in Sukumaland, the following account is an attempt to draw a generalized picture.

The Origin of Chieftainship. In or near Sukumaland we have examples of almost every stage of social and economic evolution. At the lower end of the scale there are the little Bahi people[2] in Kimali (Meadu) Chiefdom of south-east Maswa, who number only some 98 individuals and *inter se* are administered by their clan elders under the final authority of the Sukuma chief of Kimali. 'They are a surviving example of a way of life which is estimated to support one human family to every forty square miles.'[3] The 'elders' are in fact still in the prime of life as no old or sick people can survive the hard life of these hunters. The Bahi have not yet begun to practise agriculture or animal husbandry but live entirely on wild fruits, roots, and the spoils of the chase.[4] In the non-Sukuma tribes of parts of Musoma District to the north, we have examples of larger groups where, before the beginning of European

---

[1] M. Perham, *Native Administration in Nigeria*, p. 163.
[2] These people are not, of course, of Sukuma stock, being a branch of the Tingida hunters, who are centred at the eastern end of Lake Eyasi.
[3] Cf. *The Earth's Green Carpet*, by L. E. Howard (Faber & Faber), p. 36.
[4] On several occasions the Bahi have been given cows, hoes, and maize seed by the chief. They keep the cows for a few days but cannot resist the temptation to eat them! They also eat the maize seed and use the hoes for making arrowheads. They prefer their own way of life. They are not taxed.

Hereditary Authorities and the Land

rule, local administration was carried out by the family and clan elders. With closer administration the need for fewer and more effective local authorities arose, and the institution of chieftainship was thus the result of a comparatively recent change in circumstances. In most of Sukumaland, however, there have been chiefs for a considerable period, the length of which is indicated by the number of names of former chiefs which can be recounted by the elders and which may be supposed to indicate a period of perhaps 150 to 200 years even allowing for the fact that, before the advent of European Administration, a chief's tenure of office was always precarious and often short. *Inter alia*, a local failure of the rains would probably have assured a chief's deposition by his Council of State.

The language, customs, and institutions of the Sukuma people are so similar to those of the Nyamwezi of Tabora and Nzega in the Western Province that there can be little doubt of a common origin.[1] Thus we can follow, even though only conjecturally, the fortunes of hypothetical families of Nyamwezi hunters who may be supposed to have come to Sukumaland many years ago following reports of abundant game. In the early days each small group would move within a large area in pursuit of food, but gradually arable agriculture replaced hunting as the primary activity of the people. Law and order would be maintained by the elders within the now extended family groups in much the same way as the senior members of the family now exercise responsibility for the distribution of heritable wealth. This period of gerontocratic rule could only continue as long as the number of families was small and the population scattered. With an increased population there would come a time when inter-family or clan disputes, which could only be settled by force, would become more troublesome. The usual method, employed even today, of laying the responsibility for important decisions either on the supernatural or on the hidden vote of a number of elders, may well have proved unsuccessful in the more serious cases between the families of one village and another. Thus the time would be ripe to place the ultimate decision in the hands of a final authority and the necessity for chieftainship would have arisen. This period may be supposed to have coincided with the arrival of Hamitic families from the north-west.

There would be obvious objections to choosing a chief from one

[1] Cf. R. P. Fridolin Bösch, *Les Banyamwezi*, 1930.

of the indigenous families in a given area, for he would lack the impartiality requisite to the exercise of his functions as a final arbiter. Consequently as 'a prophet is not without honour save in his own country', the choice would tend to fall upon a stranger.[1] One method is exemplified in the history of Nera Chiefdom, where the son of an unmarried daughter of the chief of Busuma is said to have been selected; another in that of Bukumbi Chiefdom, where Ilago, a hunter who came from the south-west with a few followers, is said to have been the first *ntemi* or chief, chosen primarily to make equitable division of the spoils of the chase. The necessity having arisen and having been met in this way, full final powers would become vested in the chief without reservation. With everything else, the demarcation of boundaries and land allocation which was of no great importance at that time, would come within his ultimate jurisdiction.

The Origin and Position of Subordinate Authorities. It would be difficult for the chief of an extensive area to fulfil his task without assistance, and consequently he would appoint his sons to the charge of villages wherein they would be his representatives, and would exercise subordinate judicial and executive powers delegated to them by him. They would exercise these powers in collaboration with the pre-existing organization of village elders.[2] Thus the rights of the *ng'wanangwa* or village headman in relation to land allocation or the hearing of cases are derived from the chief whose representative he is and by whom he can be appointed or dismissed.[3] The powers of the chief were originally derived directly from the people and do not constitute encroachments on the rights of the village headmen[4] who, being his sons and his representatives, did not exist prior to the institution of chieftainship.

The Council of State. In Sukumaland succession to the chieftainship was usually matrilineal, although exceptions existed as in the chiefdom of Bukumbi in Mwanza District and possibly in other littoral chiefdoms. Since the advent of European rule,

[1] Cf. O. Guise-Williams, *Memorandum on Village Organisation*—'impact of newcomers in a higher stage of development was accepted, not imposed upon them; the newcomers became leaders'. See also Thomas and Scott, *Uganda*, chapter 1.
[2] Cf. O. Guise-Williams, *The Village Constitution in Maswa*.
[3] Cf. W. E. H. Scupham, Letter to Provincial Commissioner, Lake Province, from District Officer, Mwanza, 101/1/49 of 30/4/31.
[4] Cf. a parallel question in English land tenure outlined in *English Farming Past and Present*, by Lord Ernle, p. 4.

Hereditary Authorities and the Land

however, patrilineal succession has undoubtedly become more general for various reasons, particularly on account of the advantages which accrue when the heir is known and so can be given particular educational attention. However the custom of selecting the new chief from amongst the sons of the late chief's sisters was until very recently prevalent throughout much of Sukumaland. The duty of selecting a new chief is discharged by the Council of State or *banang'oma*, a body of elders known in the Nyamwezi language as *bang'hong'hogong'ho*. The sons of a chief are called *banangwa*, whether they are given charge of villages or not. His grandsons are called *bizukuru*; great-grandsons *banangwa*; great-great-grandsons *bizukuru* again, and so on. The Council of State of the present chief is selected from the *banangwa* and *bizukuru* of former chiefs, and vacancies are filled by selection from amongst these eligible descendants. This process of selection is carried out by the existing body of state councillors and the chief himself. No *ng'wanangwa* or *nzukuru* would be chosen who had not reached mature age. Thus the Council of State of today is selected from the grandsons and great-grandsons of the present chief's great-great-great-uncle, the sons and grandsons of his great-great-uncle, and perhaps a son of his great-uncle. His first cousins, the *banangwa* or sons of the last chief, cannot become his state councillors but he may appoint them to be headmen of villages.

The functions of the state councillors are largely religious, and perhaps the most important is participation with other tribal notables such as the queens, *ngole w'ihanga* and *ngole ntale*, the sacerdotal sub-chief *ntemi nhoja* and others,[1] in the annual ceremony of seed benediction; they also play the principal part in ancestor worship at the graves of former chiefs in times of misfortune. Besides their sacerdotal functions they are a very real Council of State, and exercise considerable influence over the chief in matters affecting the government of the country. Further, the personal power of the chief is limited by them in certain spheres; for example, he must obtain their permission to dispose of heritable wealth such as cattle belonging to his office.

The Transmission of Chieftainship. Besides transmission through selection by the Council of State from within a wide inheritance group, the office of chief could be transferred to an alien dynasty by force. In such cases all the powers and rights of the office were

[1] See glossary for fuller description of these notables, pp. 206, 207.

immediately assumed by and vested in the new ruler. In accounts of ancient wars there are few traces of a chief whose power happened to be in the ascendant gaining blocks of inhabited country from his weaker neighbours, and thereby extending his boundaries. The conflict usually amounted either to an internal war in which the ruling family was ousted, possibly with the assistance of mercenaries such as the Masai, or to a conquest in which the whole conquered chiefdom became tributary and retained its chief, unless he gave constant trouble, in which case he might be replaced by a son of the conqueror.[1] A change of royal house for any of the above reasons often entailed a change of village headmen,[2] as naturally the new-comer could not delegate his powers with confidence to relations of the dynasty which he had replaced.

The majority of the chiefs in Sukumaland trace their origin to Huma invaders or hunters from the west and, as Omukama Alexander of Karumo has pointed out, the recurrence of village names gives some indication of the lines of migration from Ruanda, Urundi, and Bukoba. Almost without exception the royal families were originally strangers to the people over whom they came to rule either by election or force.

Today a change of royal house can be effected, and the influence of the European Government behind its nominee has become the modern equivalent of the spears of the Masai or of other allies. Besides the fact that some chiefs are the sons of their predecessors in chiefdoms where this could not have happened prior to European rule,[3] the chiefs of Karumo and Buchosa in Zinza are examples of the appointment of recently arrived strangers. There is no doubt whatever that they are in every respect possessed of all the rights of chieftainship, which they hold as a result of the power of Government and their acceptance by the vast majority of the people, exactly as they would have held them as a result of war.[4]

In areas where external contracts have been few or where the scattered nature of the population is such that the necessity for chieftainship had not arisen at the time of European penetration, administration remained in the hands of a gerontocracy. Attempts

[1] The chief of Kimali (Meadu) was a son of a chief of Ng'wagala.
[2] Cf. E. C. Baker, *Administrative Survey of Uzinza*.
[3] It took the Council of State of Ng'wagala Chiefdom, Maswa District, ten years to accept the Government nominee and to invest him with the insignia of chieftainship.
[4] Cf. E. C. Baker, op. cit.

Hereditary Authorities and the Land

to take the next step in evolution by the appointment of a chief chosen by the people from amongst themselves have seldom proved really satisfactory. There is naturally a tendency to choose a weak man who could be easily ruled, instead of a stranger whose impartiality might command that unanimous loyalty which would give him strength to maintain internal order and impartial justice.[1]

The Chief's Rights. When the people gave their chief the powers of final arbiter over all matters, there were no reservations and in effect he then acquired rights analogous to full control, if not ownership, of the lands of the community. In the exercise of these rights, as in all others, the chief was of course subject to the general control of the Council of State which could, did, and still does, depose a chief should he abuse his position or fail to rule his people wisely and well. Ordinarily the ultimate right of external disposal of land was not conceivable and was therefore non-existent. Rights of disposal were confined to those concerned with the creation of new rights of use, by bringing bush-land under cultivation or by admitting strangers, and these were gradually delegated to the village headmen. As the populations grew and occupied larger areas of country, the administrative chain containing only two links, the chief and the village headman, became too short and a chief's son, instead of becoming a village headman, was sometimes given a block of country of which he became the *ntemi ndo*, or small chief, under the paramount authority of the parent chiefdom. As inheritance usually passed through the female line and as (except in a few cases such as that of Meadu) no direct contact was maintained with the parent house, these subordinate chiefdoms soon ceased to feel bound by ties of blood which had become attenuated, and the majority are now independent. Besides appointments of sons or other near relations there are, however, rare instances of gifts of territory as a reward for services rendered, such as the reputed cession of Mwingiro by Mugabe Muyahabi to a doctor called Mwowa; these seem to be exceptional cases indicating the

---

[1] In such circumstances it seems that the Belgian Administration of the Congo often install a stranger as chief over a number of families or clans, maintaining that on historical precedent 'an innovation supported by strength will soon become a valued institution'. This would appear to be a reasonable solution in some cases where existing structure is too fragmentary to be capable of adaptation to the requirements of modern administration, though experience in Southern Nigeria illustrates the necessity of a full knowledge of existing organization prior to any attempt to influence or accelerate evolution.

existence of a power of external disposal. This, however, cannot be looked upon as a right in view of its condemnation by the people. Clearly the instance quoted amounts to abuse of power rather than the due exercise of even a potential or contingent right. There is in any case nothing to show the nature of the alienation which in the first instance may have consisted only of hunting rights in uninhabited bush or the like.

The rights of cultivation control and disposal attaching to the position of chief have now all been delegated to the village headman and will be described later.[1] There was, however, one exception, and that was the right of eviction which remained in the hands of the chief himself. In a village community an individual found to be practising malignant witchcraft or other activities seriously prejudicial to the common weal was accused before the chief. After hearing the charge the chief would send some of the state councillors to investigate on the spot. If this inquiry substantiated the allegations, the chief would give an order for the expulsion of the offender. While today such action may seem indefensible, there was something to be said for the expulsion from the community of one who had attempted murder by supernatural means, if only on the grounds that he might be expected to use a spear should those means prove unsuccessful. This then was the procedure of expulsion from the village, which naturally entailed eviction from the land, though ordinarily standing crops could be harvested by the evicted person. As the strength of the family, village, and chiefdom was a matter of supreme importance, expulsion was naturally rare and was only used in extreme cases. There are no indications that it was ever used as a weapon against the chief's enemies, and the investigation by the state councillors precluded the possibility that it might be used for personal gain. In this connexion it must be remembered that the Council of State could break as well as make a chief, so that his position was none too secure. Unconstitutional acts of tyranny or injustice could and still do assure the deposition of the offender and the selection of one of his brothers or cousins. Thus, movement from one village to another could be said to have been either voluntary or just. The right of expulsion from a chiefdom now no longer exists though, where there is a federation of chiefs, as is now the case in each of the Sukuma Districts, the Federal Council can order deportation from one chiefdom to

[1] Pp. 29–32.

another within the jurisdiction of the Federation. As the right of expulsion was never delegated by the chiefs to their subordinates, it is safe to conclude that, even if it is still occasionally exercised, it is so rare that it cannot be considered a matter of even the smallest importance from the point of view of land tenure. Therefore, normal movement can now be considered entirely voluntary and, subject to the overriding needs of the community, unless an individual wishes to move he cannot be disturbed in the occupation of his land. Even with shifting cultivation, under customary law he had complete security of tenure in that no one could reduce the period of cultivation in one area or accelerate his transfer to new land. The only reasons for which a village headman can legally take away a field which is normally in use is in order to adjust a cattle track to grazing or water or to form a grazing reserve. This he can only do after harvest and he should find a new field of equal value for the late occupier before the time of planting. It is, however, not unknown in some parts where population pressure is severe for a headman to evict a man by indirect means with a view to reallocating the vacated land to someone who is willing to pay him a consideration. The indirect means most commonly used are either the picking of a quarrel or the spreading of rumours that the man is a malignant wizard; rather than face constant unpleasantness the man emigrates. The customary law I have quoted is, however, honoured more in the observance than in this type of breach which would eventually cost village headmen dear.

The origin of *sekule* or tribute is obscure but it is clear that these dues, which almost amounted to a voluntary contribution towards the maintenance of the institution of chieftainship, could not be looked upon as in any sense comparable to a rent payable for use of the chief's land. Tribute varied with the harvest, but in normal years it amounted to one basket of grain weighing not more than 20 lb. per household,[1] or the equivalent in other food crops or small stock if the family had insufficient grain. These supplies served to replenish the chief's stores from which his household

---

[1] The ratio of this amount to the food supplies of a household can be envisaged when it is realized that in *mbuga* land a homestead of two men and their wives can harvest up to 4 tons of sorghums, of which they would require about twenty bags for a year's food. A fair sized *ifuma* grain store holds about 2½ tons, and there are many families in the marginal *mbugas* of Sukumaland today with as much as two or three *mafuma*, which contain the surplus grain from the last four or even five harvests.

and retainers were fed. Invariably the chief has a great many mouths to feed. The state councillors are often at his headquarters, as are village headmen, litigants and other visitors, including travellers. In many cases after meeting such liabilities, chiefs employ all the means at their disposal for the benefit of their people. A good example of this was the expenditure by the late Chief Makwaia of Busiha Chiefdom, Shinyanga, in 1937 of large sums on surface-water catchment works to which his lorry ran daily during construction with food and other supplies for the labour. Similarly Chief Alexander of Karumo pays a bounty for the destruction of lions which are sometimes troublesome in the interior of his chiefdom.

The tribute is now represented by the rebate payable to the Native Administration by Government from the Native Tax, but the chief still receives the customary tokens of loyalty, which are usually cattle payable on the death of a state councillor or village headman and the appointment of his successor. He also receives small presents of food, particularly in Zinza, where the quantity thus furnished is sufficient to remove the necessity for the chief to hoe any considerable area. In Sukumaland, however, it is necessary for the chief to obtain large supplies of food to replace the grain tribute, and in consequence the majority make contracts for cultivation with the village societies in the same way as anyone else can do who has cattle or cash with which to pay for the assistance of collective labour.[1]

The contract rates for labour on a chief's fields are usually lower than those current in the same area, but this is both voluntary and just, as much of the grain is used for the benefit of the community. The fields in which these crops are grown are set aside for the chief by the village headmen, and according to the type of soil in the area, groups of villages will combine to grow the crop which is most suitable to local conditions.

After the annual benediction of seed the state councillors and others hoe in the chief's fields on two days. When the token handfuls of blessed seed have been distributed to the villages, the people hoe likewise in the village headman's fields. This has given the impression of two days' free labour for the chief and village headmen, but in fact it appears to be only ceremonial as the work only lasts for an hour or so each day, and the area thus cultivated is negligible.

[1] See pp. 37, 41-2.

Hereditary Authorities and the Land

Subordinate Authorities. As spreading populations in earlier periods necessitated the creation of *batemi bado* or subordinate chiefs, who have now become independent, so increasing populations have in more recent times necessitated additional links in the administrative chain between the chief and the village headman. In the Shinyanga District the first of these additional posts became necessary during the period of German rule and the *ntwale*, whose rank was previously a purely military one, was given administrative functions in a group of villages known as a *butwale* and became an authority superior to the village headmen but subordinate to the chief. The *ntwale* as such usually held no court. Within the last few years it became apparent in certain of the larger chiefdoms that the chief must receive assistance with judicial work, which was increasing. To fill this need posts of sub-chief evolved and these officials are known as *mlamji* in central Sukumaland and *ng'wambilija* in Ng'wagala and other chiefdoms in southern Sukumaland. The former term means 'arbitrator' and the latter 'assistant'. In both cases the functions of the sub-chiefs are largely judicial and they have elders attached to their courts. Thus the full administrative and judicial hierarchy can be shown as follows:

The Chief	*Ntemi*
The Councillors of State	*Banang'oma*
The Sub-chief	*Mlamji* or *Ng'wambilija*
The Court Elders	*Banamhala ba Ibanza*
The regional headman	*Ntwale*
The village headman (senior)	*Ng'wanangwa (Ntale)*
The village headman (junior)	*Ng'wanangwa (Ndo)*.

With the exception of the *banang'oma* all are appointed by the chief and hold office at his pleasure. With the chief's consent, which is often tacit on his acceptance of the token of loyalty, the post of headman is now often hereditary through the male line if brideprice was paid by the deceased and the heir happens to wish to live in the village in question.[1] In some cases a village headman may also fill the posts of *ntwale*, *munangoma*, and *ng'wambilija* though the circumstances enabling one individual to discharge all these duties are obviously exceptional.

The Rights and Duties of the Village Headman. For the sake of brevity I will trace the village headman's rights in relation to the

[1] See p. 30.

growth of a hypothetical village. There is an old *ng'wanangwa*, the son of a former chief, and the village of which he is in charge consists of a cleared area, in which his people and their cattle live, and a block of bush-land which is not yet inhabited. In the inhabited part, the village headman as the chief's representative hears all the cases with the *banamhala* or elders of the village, decides a large percentage of them,[1] and discharges other administrative functions which will be outlined below. In the block of bush country he only exercises a general supervision, settles any quarrels which may arise over grass or building-poles and protects the chief's interests. For instance, if an elephant was killed or died in his territory he would formerly have received a tusk on behalf of his chief and today he would forward the ivory to Government. But the population of the inhabited part of his village is increasing and it becomes apparent that the bush must soon be settled, as it is good country and well watered. The village headman himself is not young and the area is large. While he can look after the bush as bush, he could not fulfil the functions of village headman in the whole area when settlement had taken place. His son is just married and goes to the chief to ask if he may be given the post of village headman in the bush area which has hitherto been in his father's sphere of influence. If the chief has not promised the new village to anyone else, he will be appointed. He will become the *ng'wanangwa ndo* or junior village headman, while by that time his father may have reached the position of *ng'wanangwa ntale* or senior village headman. *Ntale* means great, and this rank is not necessarily connected with the actual number of 'offspring' villages. The boundaries of the new village will be defined by the elders of neighbouring settlements with a view to incorporating an adequate range of soil types, grazing lands, water supplies, and the like. Here it must be emphasized that custom is fluid and will be related to the necessities of each case. Usually the new village headman is the first inhabitant of his bush village, but occasionally a hunter will have settled there first. In such a case the hunter will have put up his house and begun to clear and cultivate with the tacit consent of the old village headman, who may have visited him and approved the allocation of land during an expedition into the bush. After the new village headman has settled, friends and relations will follow him. They will choose house sites and fields

---

[1] Compensation is the basis of village justice.

themselves and clear the bush, but the village headman as the chief's representative is responsible for land allocation and will indicate the available areas to them. In the early days the arable land will probably have to be fenced against animals and so each settler makes one large clearing in order to economize fencing. This fact accounts for the large compact blocks of land which are often still allocated with each house or site. While the population of the new village is still small, the village headman can combine the work of administration with his own farm work. Later, as his village grows, he may co-opt an assistant known in some parts as *nsweda*. Land allocation may now become more difficult as the whole village is cleared. There may be no bush left for a new-comer to clear and occupy, and so the village headman must consider whether all his people are making full use of the land allocated to them. One of the families which arrived early in the history of the village became large and occupied a considerable area of land. Now the children have grown up and gone to live elsewhere and the old man is no longer using all the land allocated to him. The village headman and elders discuss the matter with him and arrange to give the unused portion to a new-comer. Ordinarily this is a matter of arrangement, as the old man knows that should he require more land he can obtain it without difficulty, but, in any event, the village headman has the right to withdraw land for reallocation if it is not in effective occupation. In another family two children died, and consequently the remaining members moved to another village, leaving their house and fields. No new-comer required the farm at once, so the village headman permitted neighbours to borrow fields. Later the holding was required for allocation to a new settler and the borrowed fields were automatically returned after harvest. Should a man go away on a journey leaving his wife and family, they will remain in possession of his land until his return. If his wife accompanied him and no one remained to cultivate his farm, but his food stores and household goods remained in the house, indicating an intention to return, his holding would not be reallocated, though fields could certainly be lent by the village headman for a period of years, the length of which would depend upon the density of population and the demand for land in the village. Eventually, however, his possessions would be handed over for safe keeping to his relations or friends and the farm would be given to a new-comer. (In parts of northern Sukumaland families which have emigrated and are now living many miles away, have been known to maintain their rights to arable land in the village which they left years before. Sometimes they even refuse to lend such fields though they are not in use, but the exercise of such rights *in absentia* will lapse if the land is not reoccupied within a reasonable period.) Later, should the absentee return, an arrangement would be made: either he would resume occupation after harvest or he would accept another house and fields, probably the latter. In any event the matter is of little importance to the African and would be adjusted without difficulty. Thus it is clear that the village headman as representative of the chief has full rights of control and disposal of land within the village.[1] The exercise of these rights is, as usual, related solely to convenience and necessity.

Before describing the village collective organizations it must be emphasized that the village headman holds the lowest office in the chief's administrative and judicial hierarchy, and is therefore the smallest cog in the existing machine with which the Government can deal. He is the final agency for the transmission of instructions emanating from Government or from the chief to the individuals in his village. In many areas he collaborates closely with the village associations (which will be described later) whose officers give him much assistance.[2]

Water. During the rains water is free for all, but the village dry-season water supply, like the land, is usually controlled by the village headman who gives the word to have it cleaned or enlarged. Water may be obtained along a river-bed, in which case no organization is necessary, but in many villages on the higher land of the lighter soil groups water for domestic purposes is obtained either from a well tapping a shallow ground water-table, or from a spring. These are sometimes supplemented by pits, which are situated in impervious soil for the catchment of surface water. As with other types of work, one person from each household must come to help clean out the village well or to build up a bank to form a catchment tank below a spring. Where cattle also water at the village spring or well the *nsumba ntale*, or village labour leader, will fine a defaulter from work, and his cattle will not be allowed to drink there until the small fine is paid, and eaten or shared by the villagers. This practically amounts to the payment of, say, a sheep in lieu

[1] Bukumbi Case No. 59/32 for appropriating land without being given it by the village headman (fine 10s.).   [2] p. 38.

Busule, Shinyanga District

A pool in the upper reaches of the Shimiyu river

The sorghum harvest of one family in *mbuga* country, Manonga Valley, Shinyanga

'... the vast majority of the regular agricultural work is done without assistance by each family on its own holding.' (p. 38)

Hereditary Authorities and the Land

of labour. This village turn-out applies to any new work, including catchment tanks, but there is an ingenious system which can be seen in operation near Bubiki for increasing the capacity or cleaning a catchment pit. The first pit is dug as described above and it fills with water. During the next dry season each person who goes to draw water from it must dig or remove a specified quantity of earth from a new excavation nearby. The men do the digging and the women remove the spoil, so that by the end of the six months' dry season a new catchment pit is ready. Next year one pit is used and the other reserved. When the water is finished in the former, the same organization is used to clear out mud and silt and then to deepen it. Thus after the construction of the first pit there is no further interruption of normal daily routine beyond a little extra time spent digging while drawing water.

The new tanks, *hafirs*, and dams which are being constructed in various parts of Sukumaland are attracting settlement especially if they are situated in a waterless area near to a dense population. Houses are even built in the neighbourhood of some new surface-water catchment works which have not yet held water. It is therefore of great importance that these new catchment works should be properly constructed so that they will hold water and not disappoint the new settlers who are relying on their efficiency. Naturally it is not possible for the Sukuma to wait and see if the tanks will fill, unless a whole year is to be lost, as houses must be built and thatched before the rains. If, after all the work of building a new house, the tank fails or is too shallow to last throughout the dry season and the settler has to move back to a congested area, others will be less ready to take the same risk and resettlement will be retarded. Consequently some suggestions are put forward in a later chapter in connexion with tank and dam construction,[1] including a discussion on the utilization of the existing labour organization and the multiplication of village water supplies.

ELECTED AUTHORITIES AND THE LAND

The Village Societies. When the village is small, the needs of mutual assistance are met by personal arrangement. The village headman and the elders help with such small matters of organization as may arise. Later, if the village area is considerable and the population increases to a number sufficient to preclude the

[1] pp. 134, 138, 150-1.

possibility of making all arrangements for mutual assistance by personal contact, some organization becomes necessary. To meet this need the age grades into which the people are divided have produced age societies or associations. It is not necessary to enumerate all the various age groups of both men and women, and the following list shows only the more important, including those which have produced associations for mutual assistance, which are marked thus ‡.

 ‡*Bayanda*. Boys, up to puberty[1]
 Baniki. Girls, up to puberty
 ‡*Basumba*. Young men of the working age group
 ‡*Banhya*. Young women
 ‡*Bashimbe*. Women who have been married and had children, but who have left their husbands, or whose husbands have died
 Bajaha. Men aged about 40 to 50
 Bashike. Women aged about 40 to 50
 ‡*Banamhala*. Old men
 ‡*Bagikulu*. Old women.

Of these, from the point of view of the land, the *basumba* are the most important. The number of associations of young men within a village will depend on the size of the village. Taking an example in Busiha, Shinyanga District, such as that represented in the plan, p. 35, there are three associations in the village, each in a section known as a *kibanda* which might contain perhaps 100 people. In such a case the young men of each section, with the advice of the elders, select one of their number to be their leader and representative. He is called the *nsumba ntale*. Of the three *basumba batale* in the village one will be the senior, so that the other two will actually be *basumba batale balonda* or 'followers'. This, however, makes no difference to their relationship to the other young people in the associations of their own sections. Many smaller villages have only one association of young men and so only one *nsumba ntale*.

 The Basumba Batale.[2] Even a short acquaintance with Sukumaland reveals the fact that in some areas *basumba batale* do not exist,

---

 [1] The society amongst *Bayanda* is not common. It exists, however, in parts of Salawe, Shinyanga District, where collective work on *shilaba* (children's personal fields) is paid for in chickens.
 [2] The final *e* of *ntale* or *batale* is sounded, i.e. *batalé*.

Elected Authorities and the Land

whilst in others they have considerable influence. An example of the former state of affairs occurs in Shinyanga west of the Nhumbu river where the functions of *nsumba ntale* are now discharged by the *kanumba* (whose only duty in Maswa District is to cook the

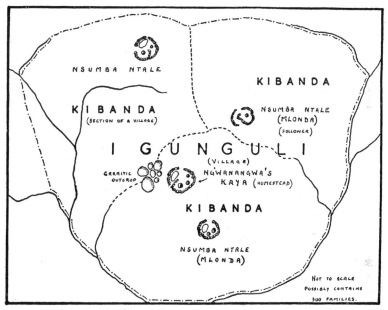

Diagrammatic representation of a village (Igunguli) showing—1. The area of the village headman's (*ng'wanangwa*) authority, i.e. within the village boundary. 2. The area of the *nsumba ntale's* authority, i.e. within the village boundary, or if there is more than one *nsumba ntale* within the boundary of a '*kibanda*'.

NOTE. *Basumba batale balonda* (followers) are of lower rank than the *nsumba ntale* but have full powers, each with the members of the *nsumba ilika* in his own *kibanda*.

meat paid for collective labour, though in Busiha, Shinyanga District, he assists the *nsumba ntale* in other ways as well). An example of an area where the *basumba batale* have considerable power is Maswa District, where they are of much more importance than in Shinyanga east of the Nhumbu river. The variations in the position occupied by these leaders, or representatives of the village associations of young men, are largely attributable to historical influences. In the first place, the institution may be of recent origin in areas where the villages have only reached a stage of population density necessitating its introduction. Secondly, in the western

Shinyanga area at least, the *basumba batale* acquired considerable power some sixty years ago and used their position and influence in ways which were detrimental to the chief's authority. Muzzle-loading guns reached Shinyanga early and were obtained by the chiefs, who used this accession of power to break the influence of the *basumba batale* who appear to have shown a unity which is rare today. It was after this suppression of the *basumba batale* that the *kanumba*, or cook to the association, took over their duties which were, of course, still necessary. It appears probable that in Maswa both the *basumba batale* and guns arrived at a later date, when the presence of a European Administration made it impossible for the chiefs to deal summarily with these village labour leaders. As the *nsumba ntale* is the elected leader and representative of the young men in a section or village, and beyond the power of the chief, who can neither appoint nor dismiss him, there is no doubt that some chiefs resented this potential check on their authority. If the *basumba batale* in a given area come to an agreement to resist an order which appears to them unreasonable, they can call a strike and make the enforcement of the order difficult. The *nsumba ntale* may say 'My people whom I represent refuse to comply, as they do not consider your instruction either just or reasonable'. In such a case the chief cannot punish a mouth-piece or deal with a body of men who are not known to him except through the channel of his village headman.[1] While this check on the power of the chief might conceivably prove a hindrance to progress in certain circumstances, there is no doubt that the institution of village associations is of considerable value as a counterpoise to the chief's power from which European support has withdrawn some of the customary restraints (though it has imposed others). For example it is no longer possible for the Council of State to replace an unsatisfactory chief without using the unfamiliar and awe-inspiring machinery of Government. As will be seen, the *nsumba ntale* occupies something of the position of a 'trade union leader', and through this organization the villager has a method of collective bargaining which protects the individual from labour exploitation by his more influential neighbours.[2]

[1] e.g. The Chief of Ng'wagala had over 70,000 people and could not know them all personally.
[2] These societies could never be forced to work for remuneration which the members considered inadequate.

The Rights and Duties of the Basumba Batale. The primary function of the *nsumba ntale* is to organize collective work amongst the men of the working age group, who have chosen him to be their leader. At the time of hoeing, for example, someone may require assistance. He can inform the *nsumba ntale* that he has a sheep or ox with which he is willing to pay for cultivation in a certain field. The *nsumba ntale* with his assistant (who is called the *ngati* in Bukumbi, Mwanza District, or the *kanumba* in Busiha) and one or two members of the *ilika* or association (which is known as *bisanzu* in Bukumbi) will inspect the sheep or ox, settle the contract, and then call out the members of the association. At a full turn-out one person from each homestead comes to answer the call to collective work, while the others continue with the work on their own farms. There are no definite rates for labour and each contract is concluded on its own merits. The variable factors include soil (which ranges from cement-like *ibambasi* hardpan and viscous clay *mbuga*, to the soft and easily worked *isanga* types), the number of people, the size of the beast to be slaughtered for payment, and whether or not the hide will be retained by the owner or will be distributed with the meat amongst the labour. In southern Sukumaland the beast is usually killed before the work begins so that the *kanumba* can cook the meat for the evening meal. In the north the *nsumba ntale* often keeps the receipts for collective work until the total justifies a feast or the distribution of the contents of his goat-skin bag in which cash receipts are collected. It is unheard of that the officers of a society should conclude a contract which would not prove acceptable to the members. Were such a thing to happen the people would either (*a*) stop early, (*b*) refuse to work, or (*c*) tell their representatives to fulfil the contract alone!

Besides this agricultural work, which is called *isalenge* in the south (from the collection of hoes which used to precede the commencement of cultivation or weeding), the associations of the young men construct the majority of new houses. Some materials may be collected by the man for whom the house is to be built, but usually he will receive considerable assistance with the collection of poles, grass, string, and the like as well as with building. In consequence the houses in the village are looked upon as the property of the community and are controlled by the *nsumba ntale*, particularly as regards destruction and the use in new buildings of sound poles from old houses. In some parts, such as Bukumbi, Mwanza District, the village headman has the right to break up old disused houses and to dispose of the materials. In Nera, Kwimba District, however, he may not sell poles but can use some himself. The quantity and type of materials provided by the occupant at the time of building and the source of food and drink for the labour during construction are taken into account when a house is abandoned, if the late occupant wants to remove some of the poles. Within these limits the routine control of building and house property is in the hands of the *basumba batale*, and in some parts this has led naturally to the delegation to them of the village headman's powers of land allocation as a matter of convenience, though in cases of dispute the headman remains the higher authority. As a definite block of land goes with each homestead it is the *nsumba ntale* who shows the new-comer the fields which are attached to the house which has been allocated to him with the village headman's knowledge and consent. Similarly the *nsumba ntale* will make inquiries concerning the character and antecedents of a new-comer and assist the village headman and elders to decide whether or not he is a fit and proper person to be admitted as a member of the village community. At this point it must be stressed that, while an efficient system of collective labour and collective bargaining exists in the village associations, the vast bulk of the regular agricultural work is done without assistance by each family on its own holding. After family labour the most usual type of agricultural assistance is that of friends and neighbours called personally by the homestead which requires labour, and it is paid for in beef or beer at somewhat lower rates than are usual for the labour of the village association. Besides the activities mentioned above, the young men's association is responsible for organizing burials, arranging house removals, with the transport of food stores for new arrivals in the village, and the like.

With such a collective organization as the village associations the members must obey the orders of the officers whom they have elected, and it is necessary to support them with certain sanctions which can be imposed for wilful default. Ordinarily if someone fails to turn out to collective cultivation or to assist with such activities as house building, he will get no share in the meat or beer. If the omission is repeated the association may refuse to work for the delinquent, or may exact a small fine (called *mchenya* in

Maswa),[1] and this will be collected by the whole body at the end of work, thus making refusal to pay impossible in face of such numbers. Finally, repeated and serious breaches of the social code are punished by ostracism, which, however, is the last resort and consequently rare. This sanction is known as *bubiti* in the south and *ihyu* in northern and central Sukumaland. Anyone who is ostracized may cause the ban to be lifted and regain his normal position in society by making a payment, such as a sheep or a goat, which is acceptable to the association. This fine is killed and eaten at once, whereupon the delinquent is reinstated. Theoretically, if payment is not made, ostracism will continue indefinitely. In practice this is impossible as the individual is largely dependent on the community for assistance in numerous little ways which, in the aggregate, are of considerable importance. For example, the Sukuma do not as a rule make fire, so the refusal of neighbours to supply fire in the event of its extinction would stop all cooking and seriously inconvenience the ostracized family; consequently the fine is paid at once or the delinquent moves to another village.

There is no such thing as a society of *basumba batale* embracing these elected authorities from a number of villages. Each *nsumba ntale* is the final authority in the working age association of his village or section. Thus at present there is no one who can set in motion the power of these co-operative bodies over a wide area. The *nsumba ntale* does not as a rule hold office for long. It would perhaps be safe to estimate that the average period is somewhere in the neighbourhood of five years. His term of office is brought to an end by an invitation from the senior age grade to join their ranks. This short term of office has the advantage that injustice and favouritism are precluded by the knowledge that in a short while the junior members of his family will be subject to the authority of another *nsumba ntale*, even though he himself has become a member of the elders' society. The above description of the young men's association does not yet apply to Zinza where there is little collective work, and the senior age grade alone, the *abanyampala*, seems to have developed a form similar to that of the old men's 'clubs' of Sukumaland proper.

As I have already mentioned, the village associations and their

---

[1] This fine may be a small number of arrows, or such a thing as a roll of tobacco.

officers are absolutely distinct from the organization subordinate to the chief, and the two organizations are summarized as follows:

Salaried posts in the Native Administration Civil List	Honorary appointments (unpaid)	Elected Village Authorities (unpaid)
Ntemi (pl. Batemi) = Chief	Munang'oma = Councillor (pl. Banang'oma) of State	Nsumba Ntale = Labour leader (pl. Basumba Batale)
Wakili = Chief's Deputy		Kanumba or Ngati = Cook and General assistant
Ng'wambilija = Sub-chief (pl. Bambilija)	Banamhala ba Ibanza = Court Elders	
Ntwale = Regional Headman (pl. Batwale)		
Ng'wanangwa = Village Headman (pl. Banangwa)	Banamhala ba Igunguli = Village Elders	
	Nsweda = Village Headman's Assistant or Messenger	

The Banamhala or Village Elders. When the *nsumba ntale*, or indeed anyone, is invited to join the association of village elders, an entrance fee is payable which varies widely but may be taken as the equivalent of a goat which the old men eat. Thereafter his rank in the elders' club is usually determined by the number of animals he has slaughtered or the amount of beer he has brewed for their consumption! The work of the elders consists of such activities as the clearing of small regenerating bush and the sowing of seed ahead of the advancing hoeing party of the young men's association. Some of the elders are co-opted by the village headman to assist him with the judicial work of the (unofficial) village court of which they are the backbone; also they have both religious and medical work which they sometimes perform as members of extra-village societies.[1] As the institution of chieftainship is believed to have been superimposed on the gerontocratic organization of early Sukumaland and did not wholly replace it, these village councils of elders have probably altered little. Consequently, apart from their specific functions the old men's association and to some extent the old women have very considerable influence in connexion with such modifications of custom as may become necessary from time to time. As the Council of State influences the chief in matters of importance to the chiefdom, so the village elders influence the village headman in matters of local importance. Naturally there is

[1] See p. 41.

a tendency towards caution and conservatism, but this is by no means invariable. When convinced of the advantages to the community, the village elders have supported innovations such as the pasture reservation system in Busiha, Shinyanga, and collective grain cultivation. This aspect of the position of the old men in village life is of considerable importance from the point of view of Government, as the *basumba batale* and the associations generally cannot be approached direct, and it is only through the channel of the chief and his subordinate authorities ending with the village headman and the elders, whose ancient organization has been fused with his, that effective contact can be made with the working age group which provides the man-power for agriculture and labour generally. Thus from the angle of social influence the village elders are the key to the co-operative body of the junior working party.

The Malika ga Mbina. These associations, which are often referred to as dance societies, have numerous primary objects. Some are purely religious, such as the *Bufumu* and *Bumanga*, which embody the cults of ancestor worship. The *Nyangogo* of the *Bufumu* is perhaps the nearest approach to a priest to be found in Sukumaland. Other societies have utilitarian objectives such as the *Bagoyangi* or *Badrilili* and the *Bayeye* of some parts, who know a great deal about snakes, their poisons, and the antidotes. The *Banunguri* dig out porcupines, display them at the dance and subsequently eat them. As the porcupine does a great deal of damage to crops, this society is distinctly useful. With the exception of *Bufumu*, *Bumanga*, and one or two others of minor importance, most of these societies do collective agricultural work. The parent societies which are perhaps the most important from this point of view are the *Bagika* and the *Bagalu* or *Bagumha*. Each has its own officers and many borrow their titles from the chief's hierarchy. Thus a dance society will often have its own *ntemi*, *batwale*, and *banangwa*. These societies have no geographical limits and consequently members can be called out to do society labour from considerable distances. The extent to which this labour organization is used varies greatly, and in the south of Sukumaland it is distinctly unusual to hear of the members of such a society being called out to fulfil a cultivation contract. In the north, however, it is more common, and in certain parts it is said that the leaders of some of these associations are becoming more powerful than the village headmen, as they can command a following unlimited by political boundaries. It is extremely doubtful whether such power could conceivably become subversive or undermine the authority of the Native Administrations, and I am inclined to think that it has been exaggerated, in that collective labour cannot occupy more than a small fraction of an individual's time or he would be unable to complete the agricultural activities on his own holding. The Sukuma, as a general rule, has too much sense to permit contract work with his dance society to jeopardize his own food reserves; further, the elders, knowing that they would have to find cattle to make good a grain shortage, would not permit it. On the other hand, even if work for a society will never reduce the members to starvation, those who have no property with which to pay for agricultural assistance may be called out sufficiently often to reduce their own harvests to a bare subsistence level, while those with wealth get assistance with cultivation at rates which are low in comparison with the increased yields which they obtain. One other aspect of this matter must, however, be borne in mind. Collective labour, whether it is for the dance societies or for the village associations, is the direct cause of the slaughter of a large number of stock each year.

The labour rates, besides varying with the factors mentioned above,[1] also vary in different localities with the number of cattle. Thus in areas where stock are scarce the amount of work for one beast will be considerably greater than in parts where domestic animals are plentiful, and vice versa. Therefore it would appear that while the village associations are of undoubted value from numerous points of view, the dance societies in certain parts of northern Sukumaland might do more harm by an unduly rapid differentiation of a hitherto undifferentiated society and by the exercise of wide powers, than the good they do by increasing the consumption of meat. This, however, is not a matter of great significance, as the effects of each society in each area are by no means constant.[2] No generalizations are possible and any wholesale condemnation of the dance societies followed by a general attempt to

---

[1] See p. 37.

[2] The characteristics of a dance society are by no means uniform, and it would be possible to make serious mistakes by supposing that a society carefully studied in western Shinyanga would necessarily be exactly the same as the societies bearing the same name elsewhere in Sukumaland. For example, the *Iginya* dress and do their hair like Swahili women in South Busiha, but this fashion is seldom found elsewhere.

Elected Authorities and the Land

control or limit their activities in the economic sphere could only lead to their becoming secret, and consequently both more powerful and more dangerous. Even the secret society *Baswezi* is of little or no importance, and it would be a grave error to take any action which might lead to societies being driven underground. Under a policy of *laissez-faire* they will maintain their own level in the rural economy of Sukumaland.

THE PEOPLE

The Family. From the point of view of land tenure as well as of general considerations of agriculture and land utilization, it is necessary to examine the structure of the village group. As we have seen, the village has a definite boundary within which the chief's land rights of control and disposal are delegated to the village headman who exercises them personally, or with the collaboration, in some areas, of the *basumba batale*. If within the village area the joint or extended family group[1] existed as a definite unit, it might be possible to make use of this smaller group as a basis for the introduction of necessary agricultural improvements. This, however, is not the case, as the dispersed Sukuma or Zinza family is by no means confined to one village or even to a group of villages. The family is scattered over a large area and today members are to be found not only in numerous villages but also in various chiefdoms and districts. Not only is the family widespread in Sukumaland but also tribes and clans are both numerous and inextricably mixed. The first inquiry will elicit the reply 'I am a Sukuma' but the second will show that this is used only as a generic name for the inhabitants of a country of which the ethnological antecedents are heterogeneous. Thus the words 'alien native' can hardly be used in Sukumaland and Zinza,[2] as any African who settles in the country becomes a Sukuma or a Zinza, though he may be referred to as 'Mganda', or whatever his tribe may be, for some time. In any event an African coming to live here will probably marry locally, his children will speak their mother's tongue and will be indistinguishable from their neighbours. Chief Alexander of Karumo, Zinza, asserts that there are

[1] By 'joint or extended family group' is meant a corporate group of lineally related kinsfolk with their spouses and children, living either in a single homestead or in separate ones, and being subject to the authority of a single head.
[2] Cf. E. C. Baker, *Administrative Survey of Uzinza*.

about thirteen languages spoken in Zinza 'and besides these languages there are many tribes represented by too few people to keep a language alive'. This indicates the settlement of men with their wives and illustrates the amount of intermixture in this area, although most of the individuals concerned will consider themselves Zinza whatever their origin. The largest type of residential family group to be found in Sukumaland villages consists of a man with two or three wives and their children. When the children are full-grown, sons-in-law may come to live in the homestead and a son may stay at home, though these new families will usually move to found new homesteads elsewhere unless there is abundant land in the village. In any event the Sukuma values freedom, even from parental authority, and so full-grown sons seldom remain at home long after marriage.

Marriage. There are two types of marriage in Sukumaland which are of importance on account of the alternative lines of inheritance which result from them. The first and perhaps the more usual is the marriage with payment of bride-price known as *kukwa*. Bride-price varies with the number of cattle in the area but the average is in the neighbourhood of ten head. The children of this type of marriage belong to the father's family and will inherit movable property from him. Until recently, the chieftainship was apparently an exception and, in spite of the payment of bride-price, followed the alternative line or method which is undoubtedly the older, as cattle and other forms of wealth are no doubt a recent innovation compared with marriage. The second type of marriage is known as *butende* or *kubola*, and no bride-price is payable. The children of a *butende* marriage belong to their mother's family from which they may inherit such wealth as cattle. Until recently there have been very few cattle or other forms of wealth in northern Zinza amongst the Nyaisanga[1] and consequently the idea of a bride-price paid in cattle is new. This provides an example of the relation of the *kukwa* form of marriage to the cattle population; as a rule in Zinza no payment of cattle is made, the children nevertheless remain members of their father's line. A cattle bride-price is only now beginning to appear with the influx of people and cattle from

[1] The two lake-shore swampy soils are called *isanga*. Thus Nyaisanga or Banyaisanga are the shore dwellers. Cf. E. C. Baker, *Administrative Survey of Uzinza*. The Rongo of the Zinza hinterland are iron-workers, and have long used the hoe as wealth which is transferred as bride-price.

the Nyanza Federation across Smith Sound. This matter is of some importance and will be mentioned again in connexion with the reasons underlying the keeping of cattle in Sukumaland.[1] While, as we have seen, no bride-price is payable in a *butende* marriage, a payment called *nsango* must be made on the birth of each child, so that even in this case a transference of stock takes place and here again the rates appear to vary in accordance with the cattle wealth of the people.

Inheritance. To a European the rules of inheritance are exceedingly complex. As I have mentioned, the issue is governed primarily by the payment or non-payment of bride-price. The inheritance table of a concrete case included in the appendix[2] gives some idea of the lines followed, but it is necessary to note that, for the sake of simplification, this instance deals with monogamous marriages. As with other aspects of the lives of the Sukuma it is almost impossible to use a European language including such words as 'rights' when dealing with the fluid and flexible customary law of the African. There is no doubt that each case is decided largely on its merits rather than on immutable rules, and the two guiding principles behind each decision would appear to be convenience and necessity.

In the first place, as regards inheritance, division of heritable wealth does not automatically follow death, and it is unlikely that any survivor will have more than a vague idea of the number of cattle which he may receive on the death of a near relation. This is due to the fact that in many cases, particularly in connexion with a polygamous marriage where the survivors are at all numerous, the whole onus of division devolves upon the senior members of the family whose decision is usually final. Dissatisfied parties can, however, appeal to the village headman and elders of the deceased's village and thence of course through the assistant chief's court to the chief. The court records show that this is rare. Cattle are undoubtedly the most important heritable property, and this aspect of inheritance will be mentioned again in the next chapter.[3] Neither houses nor land are strictly speaking heritable in the European sense. Generally when a man dies the senior remaining married member of his *kaya* (or family group of houses) may continue to occupy his house and hoe his land. Thus if an old man who had paid bride-price for his wife died, leaving two sons both

---

[1] See pp. 65, 68–70.   [2] See p. 209.   [3] See p. 65.

resident in their father's homestead, the elder being unmarried, the younger would occupy the house and continue to use the arable land. The elder, being the heir, would however receive the majority of the cattle, goats, and sheep. He would almost certainly leave the animals with his younger brother to begin with, and only take possession after marrying and settling down elsewhere, and then only when his family had become sufficiently numerous to look after the animals. If on the death of the old man both sons were married but the elder had moved to live in another village, much the same procedure would be followed, the younger taking over the homestead and land and possibly retaining the cattle for some years. If the old man's death aroused any suspicion of witchcraft it is quite possible that the remaining son might not wish to stay in the village; then the farm would revert to the village for reallocation by the village headman. Even if the relation remaining in the homestead on the old man's death was only a son-in-law who could not inherit, it would be unheard of for the village headman to give him notice to quit in order to make room for a nearer relation. On the other hand a residual married relative has a prior right to both house and land as against a complete stranger, particularly if the land in question had been cleared of bush in the first instance by his ancestors. Therefore, if on the old man's death no relation remained in the homestead or village and the holding remained unoccupied, it would be allocated to a relation coming to live in the village in preference to a stranger, though first come would be first served. The strongest right of use or occupation is gained by first cultivation[1] which is heritable to the extent indicated above; but movements are such that there are not many areas where members of the family which first cleared it still remain in possession of their ancestral land. This, however, does not apply to areas in which human occupation is of recent origin, such as Nyashimba village in Busiha, Shinyanga, where the first holdings were cut out from the bush only about fifty years ago, though even here in 1938 there were only two families occupying land cleared by their forbears.[2] Whether the land and homestead is taken over by a relation or abandoned and reallocated to a new-comer, it is

[1] See *kusenga* and *kutindula* in glossary, p. 203.

[2] In 1945 there were only three people left in the village (though six lepers from the settlement in the neighbouring village of Nkola Ndoto live and cultivate small fields in Nyashimba). No one now in Nyashimba is related to those who first cultivated.

The People

important to note that it is never divided between two sons or in any way subject to fragmentation. One man will take the holding. If his dependants are few in comparison with the previous occupant he will certainly agree to lend land; probably he will give some away, or if the congestion in the village is considerable the village headman may reduce his holding by reallocation of land in excess of the area which he and his family are able to hoe. Were the headman to reduce the area further a good case would lie to the chief, though in all probability such action on the part of the village headman would indicate a quarrel, and the aggrieved party usually prefers to leave a village in which he cannot get on with the headman rather than waste time on a case.[1] Even if his case were successful the atmosphere of antagonism would be enhanced. Such a state of affairs is, however, exceptional as, on the one hand, the headman has the power of refusing admission to the village in the first instance, and, on the other, he is not anxious to cause umbrage and reduce the population of his village. Unjust headmen are soon known and their villages naturally empty rapidly. As I have already mentioned[2] sales of land existed in the more congested areas of central Sukumaland. The land sold at that time was *mbuga* soil only, as this rich dark valley land, when within range of water and therefore capable of exploitation, produces the heaviest sorghum crops. These transfers of land for a consideration, which usually consisted of one or two cattle, were only sales of the right of use. While it is understood that the German Administration put a stop to these land sales, it is also clear that they became unnecessary, as owing to the cessation of tribal warfare the population was able to spread and obtain new *mbuga* lands without payment. In any event these sales were confined to lands in the occupation of those who had first cultivated or their successors, a class which owing to movement is now comparatively rare.[3]

House Property and Reasons for Movement. The introduction of mud-brick houses necessitated by the increasing difficulty of obtaining poles and other building materials is making little difference to the village ownership of house property and its administration by

[1] For example Tungu *nsumba ntale* left Nyashimba in 1940 because the village headman Machiya died and the village was amalgamated with another village and Tungu could not get on with the new village headman.
[2] See p. 12.
[3] See Karumo case No. 2/29 for a judgement stating that land cannot be sold in Zinza, 'only crops can be sold'.

the *basumba batale*.[1] Assistance is now given more particularly with roofing, and on moving house the mud-brick walls which are of little value are abandoned. As we have seen a house or house site goes with a block of land which, though it may have been slightly reduced in size, is substantially the same as that which was first cut out of the bush and surrounded with a fence to keep out marauding game. The house site is not necessarily within this area, and particularly when a new house is built it may be erected almost anywhere within the village commonage. Wherever possible, house sites are selected on top of the ridge, so that the compound is only affected by direct rainfall and does not receive the drainage water from higher ground. Some years ago the chiefs of Sukumaland understood that the Government considered an individual should have the right to sell his house as an encouragement to improved building. While in many areas little notice has been taken of this suggestion, its effects on a small scale elsewhere have been somewhat unexpected. In the first place a man leaving a village retained the right to sell his house so that the village headman and *nsumba ntale* could not allocate it to the new-comer who took over the land. A house was therefore built for the new settler if he did not wish to pay the price asked for the vacant building. Later this abandoned dwelling might be sold and the purchaser could then take up his residence in the village without passing the customary 'entrance examination' concerning character and the like. While this could be prevented by a categorical refusal to allocate land, in some cases the village headman felt bound to find fields. If the village were already full, this might mean the division of the block of land which originally went with the house, between the purchaser and the other new-comer to whom the land had first been allocated. Thus fragmentation was introduced. In practice, however, this is not a matter of great importance in an area of annual crops, since if the resulting farms were too small to support a reasonable standard of living, one new-comer or the other would move again and settle elsewhere. There is, however, a second consideration. A man who has worked as a mason and has some money comes to live in a village; he is given an abandoned house and fields; the house is in a state of disrepair and the mason decides to build himself a good new house with the help of the young men of the village. He builds a mud-brick house and receives practically no help

[1] See p. 37.

The stream which runs all the year round from the Talaga springs, Shinyanga

Where the drinking-water is obtained from springs or wells, water must be drawn for washing

'Houses are even built in the neighbourhood of some new water catchment works which have not yet held water' (p. 33)

—such as this tank in the Ng'wabalumbaga *mbuga*, Busule, Shinyanga District

The People

beyond that for which he pays on contract. When he makes his decision to build a good house he has lived for some time in the old one; he knows and likes his neighbours and has found the crops good. He is looking forward to spending the rest of his life there and leaving his property to his children. The considerations which have affected his decision are almost entirely financial. He knows that he has the means to build a good house which most Sukuma, with an average annual cash income of about Shs. 70/- and such commitments as tax, have not. The thought of moving later does not enter his head. An increased family will only mean additional buildings. Five or ten years later, however, a wife and child die and he is advised by his doctor to move. Now if he can sell his house and any other improvements he may have made, he will probably go. If, on the other hand, he knows that on leaving the village his house will revert to the community and he will incur the expense of building another elsewhere, he will think twice about leaving on grounds of health only, and he may decide to remain and follow a static agricultural practice. But if he has not sufficient land or the receipts from his farm are not adequate to permit him to maintain his family at a reasonable standard of living, he will move to an area where the increased productivity will more than counterbalance the loss he has incurred in abandoning his house.

Thus, the causes of movement mentioned above can be summarized as follows:

1. Eviction for witchcraft by the chief.
2. Ostracism, due to a quarrel with his neighbours.
3. A quarrel with the village headman.
4. Illness or misfortune.
5. Decreased crop yields due to over-cultivation or witchweed.
6. Insufficient water or grazing for an increasing herd of cattle.

As we have seen the first no longer exists; the second and third are rare and if a man moves for these reasons he does so voluntarily; the fourth is perhaps one of the commoner ostensible causes, while the last two are the only sound economic considerations governing movement and are unaffected by the village ownership of houses. Thus the right of sale encourages uneconomic movement, postpones a general static agricultural practice, introduces the possibility of fragmentation, and upsets the chief's rights of land allocation which are delegated to the village headman and which form one of the most important pillars of the Native Administrations as well as of village social structure.

Religion. The connexion between religion and land rights is mainly negative. The religion of the Sukuma and the Zinza is ancestor worship. The rites and ceremonies are not related to particular localities except in the case of chiefs whose graves are actually visited. A pilgrimage to an ancestor's grave or village may be prescribed in a case of illness, but the existence of the grave gives no prior right to the land in which it is situated. In Sukumaland people are buried in the cattle-pens, or within the home compound, both of which places become what are known as *matongo* in the south or *shilugu* in northern and central Sukumaland. For the first three years after a stockyard is abandoned nothing can be planted on account of the quantity of manure; either the manure is spread, as in parts of northern Nzega, or later maize and other crops are grown. This *kilugu* remains in the possession of the family which abandoned the house or stockyard so long as they remain in the village. When they move to another village it reverts to the community for reallocation by the village headman with all the other fields, no matter how many ancestors are buried there. In parts of south-western Shinyanga and north Nzega the abandoned cattle kraal is taken over by the village headman who cultivates it himself if he wishes to do so, and this illustrates the fact that graves give no rights to land. This question of the village headman's rights in manured lands is of some local importance and will be mentioned again.[1]

THE LAND

Land Acquisition. Though legal sale of the right to use land no longer exists, reserved grazing on fallow in central Sukumaland can be rented. As this primarily concerns cattle and grazing rights it will be described more fully in the next chapter. To summarize the position we have the following methods of land acquisition:

1. Inheritance, or rather continued occupation.
2. The rent of personal grazing reserves in grass on arable land in central Sukumaland. (This practice has many serious

[1] See p. 79.

disadvantages and has been superseded in several chiefdoms of southern Sukumaland[1] by a more efficient system.)
3. Field borrowing.
4. Allocation on movement to a new village.
5. Clearing new land in a bush area with the consent of the village headman.

As regards the fourth method it must be borne in mind that an individual will not go to a village and just ask for land. First he examines the available holdings and, having found one of adequate acreage and soil range for the requirements of his household, he applies to the village headman for that particular farm. If no vacant holding is available he will get the village headman to show him the unused arable land, and only when satisfied will he make a definite application which will then be rejected or approved after investigation into his character and antecedents. Incidentally, just as the collaboration of the village headman with the *basumba batale* and the delegation to them of some of his duties, tend to veil the actual source of authority and rights in certain areas, so also the sale of standing crops sometimes simulates land sales, which as I have mentioned do not now exist.[2]

Uninterrupted possession gives permanent rights of use, and so a man with a good house and manured land has no fear of eviction either for himself or his descendants, though an unscrupulous headman might engineer a man into reluctantly abandoning possession. Further, the reallocation of cultivated land to the descendants of the first occupier restores all previous rights. *Basa ya ndugu wane yatema kunu*,—'My family's axe cut here', is the phrase often used to indicate these original occupation rights which, however, are not automatically restored on return to the village in which land first cultivated by an ancestor is situated. If the farm has been allocated to someone else during the period of absence its return to the original owner might be arranged by mutual consent after harvest.

The Produce of the Land. The wealthiest man is the man with the largest family. A large family meant power in war or the chase. Those days are over, but the large family is still an asset of

[1] Busiha, Ng'wadubi, Buchunga, Buduhe, Mondo, Seke, Shinyanga, Ng'wagala, &c.
[2] The late Chief Masanja stated that land sales no longer existed in Nera in 1938.

unequalled value as it means many hoes, and hoes spell grain which is the most important material wealth today. With grain, cattle can be bought as can all other necessities or luxuries of life, so that the fundamental measure of riches in Sukumaland and Zinza lies in food.

Land can be allocated either to a man or to a woman if she is a widow or divorced or a member of the old women's association and head of her household,[1] but a married woman who is living with her husband hoes in his fields, as do all other dependants. She acquires from him *shilaba* or personal plots to cultivate for her own benefit; so do the children. While the main food crops such as grain are the property of the man, a number of other crops used as vegetables, condiments, and herbs are looked upon as the property of the woman in Sukumaland proper, though in Zinza all food crops are the property of the man.[2] One of the women's crops in Sukumaland is groundnuts and in this case a change has been brought about by the spread of a cash economy. As direct taxation is often met from the proceeds of the groundnut crop, as well as from sales of cotton and the like, the men now have groundnut fields and in certain circumstances the ownership of seed is now the principal factor governing possession of the crop and its division in case of divorce.[3] The spread of a cash economy has influenced Sukuma custom in other ways. Cotton is the property of the man, but in Zinza, for example, the courts are recognizing an inevitable change due to the alteration of economic circumstances. Some men in Zinza marry at the time of planting and, after obtaining a season's labour on cotton as well as other crops, refuse to give the women any share in the form of clothes, &c. The courts are upholding the women's rights to a share in the fruits of their toil, though food crops remain the property of the men. Crop residues are treated in the same way as the crops themselves, though if left long in the fields after harvest they are eaten by the cattle of the village. In the more densely populated parts which lie at some distance from the bush, firewood is scarce and the stalks of sorghums, millets, and maize are stacked. Like stored grain, any such fuel supplies which are in excess of requirements can be sold.

[1] A woman can also inherit or take over land as head of a family in certain circumstances.

[2] Karumo cases Nos. 5/33 and 39/33, 'The hoe belongs to the man'.

[3] In Bukumbi if the groundnut seed belonged to the man the crop will now be divided.

Bush Products. In villages near the bush, finding is keeping, and it is not until well into the cultivation steppe that such bush products as may remain begin to assume a value. Honey and beeswax are perhaps the most important bush products, and the latter commands a high price. In parts of the cultivation steppe where the baobab tree exists it harbours bees, but it is not everyone who wishes to take honey and wax, so that collection presents no problems of competition. Ordinarily the nearest household will collect from the baobab if they want to do so; otherwise some neighbour will note the position of the hive and let it be known that he wishes to collect the honey. He will make and drive the pegs which are often used for climbing baobabs, and the execution of this work appears to give him the right of collection in the eyes of the community. To generalize it might be said that labour is the origin of ownership, and the expenditure of physical energy gives the right to revenue accruing as a direct result. Where the baobab is absent, as in the north of Sukumaland, honey and wax are obtained in hives, the making of which fills the same position as the pegging of the baobab. Besides rights originating with work, others appear to be established by force. Thus in some areas the village headman will lay claim to the fruit of the baobab or the tamarind, though as a general rule these fruits are not in sufficient demand to have produced personal ownership, and are collected at will by any member of the village community. Strangers, however, would usually be expected to ask permission of the village headman before picking them. The collection of gum, which is only undertaken in bush areas, is free for all, and this product is the property of the finder.[1] Grass and building-poles come into the same category in bush country, though in the more densely populated parts they have both acquired an enhanced value. Grass will be referred to again under animal husbandry.[2]

Trees. I will deal first with indigenous species which are used for building-poles, bark rope, and the like. These are of value in the cultivation steppe where they are scarce, but even so trees are seldom planted as they take up some space and, if only a small number are sown by an individual in or near his compound, he considers that they take an unreasonable amount of time and trouble to protect from cattle, goats, and sheep. Usually it is thought

---

[1] D. W. Malcolm, *Report on Gum and Gum Arabic*, pp. 19 and 20. Government Printer, Dar-es-Salaam. [2] See pp. 73-75.

simpler to make a three or four days' journey to the nearest bush and cut poles or string rather than to attempt to plant individually. In this connexion it is noteworthy that many species are required. Wooden utensils, house-wall uprights, string, withies for baskets, toothbrushes, and the hafts for hoes all require different trees or shrubs, so that a considerable number of species are required if the best material is to be used for each purpose. This has usually been overlooked in the past when establishing plantations or shelter belts.

There is no superstition which lays an interdict on the planting of indigenous trees, though in one part near Shinyanga it is said that if a man plants mangoes he may die before they fruit. This does not apply to any other tree or to collective planting. The Sukuma do not connect the planting of trees with rainfall. In certain cases a doctor may warn an individual not to touch tree seed, in the same way that a man may be warned not to touch cow-dung. A personal prohibition against touching the seed of certain trees is perhaps more common than recommendations concerning manure, as plants are the basis of African medicine. Some species of trees, such as mangoes and pawpaws, have been planted at various times. Fig-trees often mark the site of old villages where they were planted as cuttings for gateposts to stockyards. *Cassia Siamea* are sometimes planted in compounds to give shade. In the densely populated villages of central Sukumaland, the remaining bush trees are often appropriated. This usually constitutes acquisition by force, and the claim to the trees is often supported by the assertion 'I prevented people cutting them'. In many cases such trees will consist of a clump of regenerating bush close to a homestead, though groves of *Acacia Fischeri* and the like may be claimed by individuals who have protected the young trees in arable land or even in pasture at some distance from human habitation. Apart from shelter belts and fuel plantations of *Cassia Siamea, Acacia Arabica*, &c., established by the Native Authorities, exotic trees (and bananas) are almost all the result of personal planting. The trees include mangoes, citrus, coffee, and in Zinza some eucalyptus. Here again, as labour is the parent of ownership, these plants, which include even sugar-cane, are looked upon as the personal property of the individual who cultivated them, exactly as annual crops like sorghums are the personal property of the planter. The difference is only one of time. This, however, is of great importance in connexion with the land upon which they grow, as the rights of use under annual crops lapse after harvest, whereas fruit-trees, being perennial, perpetuate the right to a return from the initial expenditure of labour. Sale and purchase of banana groves and exotic trees exist in Sukumaland and Zinza but the rights of ownership are not looked upon as of great value, and in many cases people move from one village to another in Zinza cheerfully abandoning their banana patch which reverts to the village and thereafter can never be sold, as the rights acquired by planting have lapsed, and, like the other fields of the emigrant, it remains in the hands of the village headman; when reallocated no payment is made beyond a present of beer to the village headman or his representative who actually showed the grove to the new-comer. Personal ownership of exotic trees, with the right claimed by force over blocks of regenerating bush, have caused considerable trouble along lines analogous to those concerned with house property. With bush in the middle of pasture or arable land the management of village grazings becomes difficult when there are any number of these little clumps dotted about, and clearly it would be much simpler to reserve one area for tree planting or regeneration in each village. With exotic species in which, unlike the above, ownership was retained even after leaving the village, the maintenance of a right to enter the compound of the house which had been allotted to another family caused difficulties.[1] Clearly, as with the house itself, the ability to sell to someone other than the new-comer admitted by the village authorities was an equally undesirable feature of individual ownership in trees, as it entailed the removal of another potential check on uneconomic movement. Thus the withdrawal of the right of sale of trees would not check planting and, as I have shown in connexion with house property, it would also tend to encourage a static agriculture, by which I mean good farming *in situ* without complete abandonment to a long term bush fallow.

THE USE OF THE LAND

Rotation of Crops and Fallow. Broadly speaking the Sukuma and the Zinza have no fixed or preconceived system of crop rotation, but in most parts there is a long term cycle including bush fallow.[2]

[1] Purchase of bananas gives no rights to the other fields in the same holding as the banana grove. Buchosa case No. 3/37.
[2] See maps facing pp. 9 and 63.

In place of a system of crop rotation they practise the interplanting of several crops of different growth and habit often including a legume.[1] Each mixture is related to the type of soil, so that it is not possible to give an example of a mixture generally suitable to Sukumaland. This system of mixed cropping has been highly commended elsewhere:

It has always been supposed that plants were compensatory to each other in what they took out of the soil, but it has been left to the Chinese to draw the logical consequences from this idea, to imitate Nature's confusion as far as can be done, to plant as many different things together as can well be managed; our own practice of the rotation is clumsy by comparison. The Chinese system implies a vast amount of hard labour, but it is, at any rate, highly successful.[2]

While systematic crop rotation as we know it does not exist, the Sukuma do use grass fallow but, in many of the densely populated parts, fallowing is practised only in a somewhat sketchy fashion, which is probably of little benefit in the cropping cycle. Each cultivator in his block of arable land has usually a percentage in excess of his annual requirements which remains unhoed and under grass. This area, which is called *ikela* in the south and *ilale* in the north, is exchanged periodically with the cultivated fields according to the condition of each. The period under fallow of a given piece of land will depend on its position and fertility and on the area of land available for cultivation in the village. Thus, on account of the pressure on land in the more densely populated areas, the periods of rest will be shorter and at greater intervals than in less congested parts. The extension of cotton planting may have reduced the periods of fallow by extending the average annual acreage under crops, the progressive impoverishment of the soil at the same time reducing the yields from the food crops, all of which increased the acreage required under cultivation. As the fallow in arable land is also grazing land, it is possible that cotton and to a less extent groundnuts may have slightly reduced the available pasture, though the crop residues and weeds are cattle feed. But where this reduction in pasture is most serious, the land is mainly so exhausted that the fallow-grass cover is of little value as grazing. Another factor which has already shown signs of making further

---

[1] Rice and cotton are planted as single crops and Bambarra groundnuts are often grown alone, though maize is occasionally interplanted with them.
[2] *The Earth's Green Carpet*, by L. E. Howard, Faber & Faber.

The Use of the Land 57

reductions is the plough. Admittedly there are only a few ox-drawn ploughs in Sukumaland, but many of those who used them stated that they left no grass fallow within the land allocated to them, and some plough owners noticed consequent deterioration on the lighter soils, which they attributed to the loss of resting periods which were usual under the grass fallow left by a hand hoe.[1]

Besides arable fields under grass fallow there is another reason of recent importance for the periodic alternation of crops grown on a particular piece of land. The semi-parasitic *striga* weed has become a serious menace to agriculture in some areas. Either the African moves to a new village and to uninfected land, or he transposes as far as possible his bulrush millet or cotton, which are not affected by *striga*, with his sorghum plots for a number of years. At first sight this alternation may give the appearance of a fixed rotation, but in every case it is related only to necessity born of the actual condition of the fields in question.

Field Names. To those who are concerned with the development of African agriculture, a knowledge of field names is of great importance. In England during the Middle Ages the lines of unploughed turf between field strips had not less than ten different names used in various parts of the country. Perhaps the commonest was 'balks'. The field strips themselves had as many if not more names, and in Cambridgeshire they too were known as 'balks'. Similarly in Sukumaland there are many dialect variations, and just as a generalized use of the word 'balk' in England could have led to confusion, so the generalized use of the word *itongo*, which has various meanings in different localities, has led to some misunderstandings here.[2] Moreover, just as it is necessary to appreciate the difference between a 'ham', a 'dole', a 'fother', and other types of fields in order to understand English land rights and rural economy, so it is necessary to distinguish between the *itunu, kilaba, kilugu, idimilo, ngitiri*, and the other land names in Sukumaland. The majority of these terms are explained in this survey and are included in the glossary for easy reference,[3] but further linguistic research is needed to complete the list of dialect variations.

[1] Plough cultivation legislation is now under consideration by the Sukumaland Federation.
[2] 'Put manure on your *matongo*' would mean 'on your home fields' in north and central Sukumaland but in the south it would mean 'put manure on your manured land'!
[3] See pp. 200, 202, 203, 206.

ANTI-FAMINE MEASURES

The Collective Village Sorghum Field. In a number of the chiefdoms of northern and southern Sukumaland many of the villages have a sorghum field which is cultivated by one representative from each household. This collective field originated as an anti-famine measure supplementary to the cassava plots. The idea caught on and is spreading slowly, though it has not proved popular in central Sukumaland. In the north, the collective labour is arranged by the village headman and elders, and in southern Sukumaland it is the *nsumba ntale* who calls the people for cultivation, the two weedings *ngese* and *nzubile*, and later for harvesting and threshing. He keeps the grain in his house and arranges distribution to those who are in need or who have to go to Government or Native Administration work. Gifts of grain are made only to old people. Young men who are in need on account of sickness are given loans which must be repaid; this is done to avoid the encouragement of idleness. Ordinarily sorghums are planted alone without the usual interplanting of other crops, as it would be too difficult to arrange for collective work at all stages of a number of different crops, and undue interference with the normal agricultural routine of the village would result. Grain which is not used before the next harvest is either distributed to each household or exchanged for an animal or beer to be consumed by the villagers.

The Cassava Plots. These are run on a different system (except in Mwanza) as each household in southern Sukumaland, where suitable light soils exist, has a small field of cassava. These fields are often all situated in one block in the village, as are the cotton plots. It appears that this concentration of the majority of the village crop into a single area originated in order to facilitate supervision, though in many villages the particular suitability of a small area of soil seems to have influenced the site selection. Naturally, however, anyone who wishes to have a second cassava field on his own land elsewhere in the village may do so, but the crop is not generally popular in southern Sukumaland and very little is planted.

Manuring. The rights in manure and manured land will be mentioned in the next chapter. Here it is only necessary to note that the enhanced yields due to manuring are well known to the Sukuma, as its effects are constantly demonstrated by the crops harvested in *matongo* or *shilugu* which are the abandoned stockyards.

Anti-Famine Measures

When this is realized it is at first difficult to understand why the Sukuma, who knows the value of manure, does not make better use of it by spreading it on his other fields. The answer is sometimes a question of labour in relation to the fertility of the soils at his disposal. Thus if his field is still productive and at some distance from the stockyard, it will usually pay him better to spend more days hoeing a larger area at the ultimate expense of fallow and fertility than an equal time carrying manure in head loads. But this does not apply to fields near stockyards. The probable explanation is that Africans know that in a really favourable season they will obtain plenty of food even from semi-exhausted fields without manuring and, being by nature optimistic and fatalistic, they trust to fate to provide a good season. Lacking in ambition, they are loath to undertake the work of manuring with the object of securing a maximum crop. In the case of those few men who habitually use manure there is the further difficulty that the amount available is often small. Moreover, in the densely populated parts where fuel supplies are short, manure is used for burning in conjunction with stover, as well as in the stockyards where a smoky manure fire is thought to be a prophylaxis against cattle disease and a protection against flies. Thus the main obstacles to manuring are transport and lack of fuel other than manure and stover. This will be discussed later.[1] Because there are no roads in villages and because the space between arable fields is often only sufficient for pedestrians, the use of oxcarts or sledges is difficult and furthermore these implements with their necessary harness are too expensive for the average Sukuma. Even the use of basket panniers has not been successful; pack transport is not ideal for short hauls. The introduction of the wheel into Sukumaland economy, beginning with the wheelbarrow, bids fair to meet this transport difficulty.

The Reasons for Scattered Holdings. Even where an individual has been allocated a compact block of land, it will often be found that he has lent fields in it and has borrowed others elsewhere in the village. As I have already mentioned,[2] this fact has been attributed to the maldistribution of rainfall, but the Sukuma do not consider this. Ordinarily if a man has land with a soil suitable for, say, white sorghums he will not borrow another field of the same soil type unless he has planted up his whole acreage and has time to spare. As a rule it will be found that an individual with

[1] See pp. 79-81, 130-1.   [2] See p. 7.

a compact block of land has not got the complete range of soils. The fields he has borrowed will therefore be on soil types other than those which he has, and suitable to crops which cannot grow well on his own land. The table showing the soils of Sukumaland in relation to typical vegetation and crops gives some indication of the range required to supply an adequately varied diet and to occupy the whole planting season.[1] In the early stages of settlement farms tend to be compact but later land allocation follows soil types more closely. In this connexion it is noteworthy that in England during the reign of Henry VIII 'the same care was taken to make the divisions equal in agricultural value, so that each man might have his fair proportion of the best and worst land. To divide equally the good and bad, well and ill-situated soil, the bundle of strips allocated in each of the three fields did not lie together, but was intermixed and scattered.'[2] Similarly the village headman in Sukumaland or Zinza will try to find a full range of soils for all the crop requirements of a new-comer to the village.

THE ABUSE OF THE LAND

Soil Erosion and Fertility Losses. The views of the Sukuma on these subjects are partly explained by reference to the list of soils.[3] They fear two things in relation to contour cultivation. First, they are afraid of a general order applicable to the whole country that all fields must be cultivated on the contour, as on the lower and heavier soils drainage is necessary if water-logging is to be avoided. Propaganda on this subject has not always differentiated between soil types. Secondly, they are afraid of large concentrations of water from contour furrows on the lighter soils, as their only general experience is of indigenous incomplete efforts with unprotected discharges which have sometimes made deep cuttings. These *sluits* or *dongas* eat back into the surrounding fields and may do considerable damage. Moreover, sporadic contour cultivation has sometimes met with unfortunate results. The contour ridges have been badly damaged by water from the flat cultivation or downhill ridges of neighbouring fields. Thus, of the two evils it would appear that they consider sheet erosion modified by the weed aftermath in arable land to be less dangerous than *donga* erosion. This

[1] See pp. 190–1.
[2] The Rt. Hon. Lord Ernle, *English Farming Past and Present*, p. 25.
[3] See pp. 174–89.

The Abuse of the Land

prejudice can only be overcome by the encouragement of a contour cultivation system including tie-ridging which gets over these difficulties. There is, however, a good deal of successful contour ridged cultivation which is generally beneficial.

ECONOMICS

Cash Incomes. In several parts of this study it has been necessary to mention that the average cash income of the adult male taxpayer in Sukumaland in 1938 was about 30 shillings per annum. This figure was arrived at both by Mr. H. S. Senior of the Administrative Service and myself, working on the incomes of various individuals and families. Further, the average total cash receipts for the whole area worked out to almost exactly the same figure. It is now estimated that this figure has increased to about 70 shillings owing to increased prices of produce and increased sales of cattle. Government has long been looking for a way to raise the standard of living, because much that could be suggested to improve the material conditions of the people in the way of better housing and the like is precluded by their limited monetary resources. The introduction of cotton as a cash crop succeeded in raising the standard of living in many parts within the limits of the available land, but in a faulty system of husbandry it requires to be adjusted to soils and cultural conditions. Thus the next step towards a further expansion in the cash economy of Sukumaland must clearly be co-ordinated with the requirements of the land by increasing production without decreasing fertility, by inculcating better husbandry and a wiser use of the land.[1] In recent years the cattle auctions have proved increasingly popular and it is likely that cattle will continue to be one of the main sources of cash for the people. At the same time, with the better use of manure and stover, the cattle can be a means of increasing production without decreasing fertility. Cattle wrongly used are the bane of agriculture but rightly used they are her blessing.

[1] See pp. 122-30.

4
Cattle Rights and Grazing

SUKUMALAND CATTLE POPULATION STATISTICS

Chiefdom	Cattle units[1] 1934	Cattle units 1944	Cattle units 1947
Mwanza District			
Mwanza	19,800	22,000	16,800
Busukuma	25,000	30,000	23,800
Bujashi	8,600	7,400	8,400
Beda	3,000	3,400	3,000
Nyamhanda	1,400	1,400	600
Iwanda	600	600	600
Nyegezi	2,000	2,400	1,800
Bukumbi	17,800	19,000	14,800
Burima	40,800	40,400	45,600
Nassa	13,000	29,400	35,600
Masanza I	10,800	17,400	20,000
Masanza II	1,400	1,200	1,600
Karumo	15,200	32,200	43,400
Busambiro	3,600	3,800	8,000
Buchosa	7,800	30,200	50,800
Msalala	18,200	26,000	43,400
Mwingiro	1,000	800	1,000
Buyombe	1,000	1,200	1,400
Bukoli	1,200	2,200	2,600
Total	192,200	271,000	323,200
Kwimba District			
Nera	125,000	189,000	..
Buhungukira	16,400	38,000	..
Busmao	115,000	146,800	..
Sima	16,000	22,000	..
Magu	10,800	11,000	..
Ndagalu	1,800	3,800	..
Total	285,000	410,600	..

[1] 1 cattle unit = 1 head of cattle or 5 head of sheep and/or goats. Small stock represent some 14 per cent. of the total number of cattle units.

Cattle Population

Chiefdom	Cattle units 1934	Cattle units 1944	Cattle units 1947
Shinyanga District			
Buduhe	57,000	72,400	76,200
Busiha	130,200	127,800	130,400
Buchunga	23,600	16,000	15,600
Ng'wadubi	31,000	21,200	25,400
Mondo	15,200	14,600	15,200
Seke	25,400	34,600	37,200
Shinyanga	24,200	36,600	42,800
Samuye	11,000	31,600	33,000
Busanda	22,600	26,400	35,000
Tinde	18,600	20,200	21,200
Busule	12,600	13,200	13,600
Lohumbo	26,400	39,400	53,400
Nindo	2,000	3,200	3,400
Salawe	20,600	19,800	23,200
Total	420,400	477,000	525,600
Maswa District			
Dutwa	10,600	18,000	21,800
Sanga	6,200	13,400	18,800
Kimali	18,600	44,000	48,400
Kanadi	20,600	55,600	64,400
Ntuzu	86,200	95,400	108,800
Itilima	23,400	69,000	87,800
Sengerema	31,000	40,800	47,600
Badi	10,200	15,600	12,000
Ng'unghu	45,000	71,200	68,000
Kigoku	33,400	29,600	25,600
Ng'wagala	144,400	112,400	140,600
Bugarama	5,600	4,800	4,400
Total	435,200	569,800	648,200

PERHAPS the most important fact in connexion with animal husbandry in both Sukumaland proper and Zinza is that the people are primarily agriculturists and cattle are definitely adventitious to the original economy of this country. This is the fundamental difference between Sukumaland and such other areas as Masailand, which also contain large cattle populations. The Sukuma cattle are a breed of small hardy Zebu stock, which is well adapted to local conditions.

CATTLE POPULATION

The map of cattle population,[1] showing distribution, density, and movements during the last thirteen years indicates the

[1] Facing p. 63.

considerable redistribution of stock which has taken place in that period. It should be noted that each dot represents 400 cattle units as opposed to the 200 people represented by a similar dot in the population map.[1] The distribution of cattle shown indicates the position of stockyards rather than grazing areas, though there is little marked difference except in relation to seasonal grazing along the Isanga, Manonga, and Shibiti rivers in the south and parts of the central Sukumaland *mbuga* system, where cattle from the higher lands graze up to a maximum of about fifteen miles from permanent water. It should also be noted that during the dry season cattle are grazed into the bush on the margins of the cultivation steppe in such places as along the Sanga and Bariadi rivers.[2] The factors which have influenced the present distribution are substantially the same as those which influenced the people themselves and include tribal war, water, good grazing, and disease. At the termination of the tribal war period, it is probable that the decentralization of stock was less rapid than that of arable agriculture, as it still is on account of lions, tsetse-fly, and the necessity for clearing for cultivation in bush areas before they normally become suitable for stock. Remarks concerning the movements of human population[3] apply also *mutatis mutandis* to cattle. Here, however, there is no decrease in Ntuzu (27),[4] though excess cattle population was drawn off from Kigoku (37), Ng'wagala (32), Ng'wadubi (40), and Buchunga (44) towards the newly watered areas in north Ng'wagala (32), Ng'unghu (31), Itilima (29), and north Sanga (33). This process was accelerated by the food shortages along the Maswa–Shinyanga border in 1942 and subsequent years, as a result of which considerable numbers of cattle from that area (the then 'dust bowl') were exchanged for grain from Itilima (29). The slight reduction of cattle in the Nyanza Federation is intimately related to the movement of their owners across Smith Sound to Karumo (13) and east Buchosa (14).

RIGHTS IN CATTLE

Acquisition and Disposal of Stock. Cattle and small stock may be obtained by inheritance,[5] bride-price, exchange, purchase, and gift.

---

[1] Facing p. 9.

[2] A light infestation of tsetse does not preclude brief periods of grazing, but it always causes infection and some losses.   [3] pp. 14–17.

[4] The numbers in brackets are chiefdom reference numbers on the population maps.   [5] See p. 209.

The *Badrilili* Snake Society Dance

A gum collector with spear, forked stick, and collecting gourd

The owner of 300 head of cattle with part of his herd, as they start for home after watering in the Tungu river

A Sukuma homestead in the plains

Rights in Cattle

Of these inheritance and bride-price are the most important. The following are instances of inheritance. If a man dies leaving cattle and the eldest son (for whose mother bride-price was paid) takes them over, he should provide for the bride-price of his younger brothers. The sons of a second wife have a right to a share of the cattle, rather than to have bride-price paid for them, and the elders of the family will arrange the distribution of property. This applies to cattle obtained by the deceased by purchase, exchange, or inheritance. If the cattle were obtained as bride-price for the daughters of his two wives, the sons will inherit the cattle which were given as bride-price for their full sisters. Thus the eldest son of the first wife would get nothing if all the daughters belonged to the household of the second wife and were only his half-sisters. On the other hand, if the second wife had no sons he would inherit, though it would be his duty to hold the cattle until children were born to his half-sisters in case a return of bride-price were demanded, and to provide bride-price for their male children. Thus in these circumstances his rights in the cattle are somewhat similar to those of a trustee, though he might eventually retain some of the cattle. If a man dies without paying bride-price, then any property, such as cattle and small stock, which he may leave will not be heritable by his children but will be taken by his brother, whose children would inherit if he had paid bride-price, or his sister's children would inherit a share, if no bride-price had been paid for her. The deceased's sons would inherit from their mother's family if she has no brothers, who would of course have a prior right of inheritance over their sister's children, for whom they would, however, pay bride-price when required.

By the return of bride-price, the type of marriage and consequent line of inheritance can be changed. Thus if a man inherits the position of head of a family, and one of his nephews (brother's sons), on whose account he has paid bride-price, is consistently disobedient, the elders of the family may decide to return the young man to his mother's people. This, though it is rare, can be done by withdrawing two or three head of cattle originally paid on account of the bride-price of the delinquent's mother. After his return to his mother's family the bride-price paid on his behalf is also automatically withdrawn and must be replaced by his mother's family, or, if the girl is not anxious to continue her marriage with him, the bride-price may remain on account of another young man of her former husband's father's family, of which the retention of bride-price by her people makes her still a member. If a man paid bride-price and his sister was married without bride-price then her children count as his, but the share of inheritance which will be allotted to them by the elders on their uncle's death will be smaller than the shares of their cousins. Had they been girls their uncle would have received either the bride-price for them in marriage or the blood-price payable on the birth of each child in a marriage without bride-price.

In Zinza the customs of inheritance show some differences. If a Sukuma marries a Zinza he will not be required to make the payment of cattle customary among Sukuma, though he may give a present which would be returned at any time if the marriage were to be dissolved. His son would inherit according to Zinza custom, and his nephew, who would have inherited according to Sukuma custom, will not do so. Formerly in Zinza a widow could not inherit her deceased husband's property, which was taken to the chief with the woman herself and her small children. Now she can remain at home like the unattached women or *bashimbe* of Sukumaland. Generally speaking, in Sukumaland it is preferred that a woman should marry again after her husband's death. If bride-price was paid for her she may marry again without bride-price, as any children will remain members of her first husband's family. If no bride-price was paid, it is her own family's business to decide whether or not bride-price will be accepted. They may accept it or prefer to retain her children, a choice which is largely influenced by the number of male members of the family. While the eldest son is normally the heir in Zinza, it is the duty of the elders to decide if he is a fit and proper person to take over his father's duties and position as head of the family. If they do not consider him to be suitable the matter will be taken before the chief, who will decide which of the remaining sons should inherit. This applies also to the Rongo in Zinza, but as they demand bride-price for their girls, there is some variety of practice amongst the numerous tribes and clans west of Smith Sound. The considerable movement of Sukuma across Smith Sound has, however, increased the influence of Sukuma custom in Zinza, and as the Sukuma are now in the majority, it is probable that Zinza and Rongo customs will be gradually superseded.

These examples give some idea of the complexity due to the

Rights in Cattle

intermixture of matrilineal and patrilineal inheritance; and other instances to illustrate the numerous variable factors are included in the appendix.[1] Suffice it that the type of marriage has a controlling influence on the line of inheritance in Sukumaland. Thus the only means of acquiring stock which do not carry with them contingent or reversionary rights are purchase or exchange for such commodities as grain, in fact means which are the direct result of work. Cattle obtained thus can be disposed of at will, though in most cases the family elders resident in the neighbourhood are consulted where the sale of a large percentage is concerned. Similarly cattle obtained by purchase are the only stock which can be disposed of by most chiefs without the prior sanction of the Council of State. If cattle are acquired by inheritance the requirements for bride-price of the junior members of the family (wherever they live) must be remembered and provided for. If cattle are acquired as bride-price a similar number must be retained in case its return is required, while it is also advisable to keep a small number of unallocated stock in case of childbirth blood-price being awarded against a son or nephew. These contingent, latent, or reversionary rights however do not concern stock increases, and there is no bar to the 'trustee' selling oxen or barren cows, or slaughtering surplus bulls to pay for collective labour, provided a reasonable number, sufficient to satisfy the family elders, is retained to meet such needs as may arise, including food shortage. Cattle obtained by gift are usually required for immediate disposal for bride-price, for payment of labour, or to pay a doctor.

The practical conclusions which can be drawn from these complex rights in cattle will be discussed later. Meanwhile it is obvious that a man with say twenty head of cattle could not often dispose of the majority by sale or slaughter on account of contingent family needs. He could not surrender the family insurance policy; he might, however, dispose of the surplus by selling a few and lending others. In any event, as will be shown, the desiderata of mixed farming can be achieved, without interference with cattle rights, by grafting the necessary developments on to existing village organization.

REASONS FOR STOCK-OWNING

Religion. As we have seen, the religion of the Sukuma is ancestor worship and in cases of illness or misfortune a relation is sent to

[1] p. 209.

visit an *nfumu* doctor. These *bafumu* are not necessarily members of the *bufumu* societies,[1] and the term is applied to all doctors who lay the responsibility for their prescriptions on the supernatural by means of divination. After consulting the oracle (*kulagula*), which may be done by killing a chicken and examining its entrails, the doctor may prescribe 'a change of air' which entails moving to another village, or indeed he may prescribe almost anything. He may attribute the illness or misfortune to neglect of the patient's ancestors and advise ancestor worship either of the *babuta*[2] (father's ancestors) or the *bamigongo*[3] (mother's ancestors) regardless of the society to which he himself belongs, though his prescription may include his own dance if the patient is a member of his own dance society.

Ancestor worship does not appear to be determined by the side of the family of which the individual is a member, though if worship of the paternal grandfather is prescribed the members of the father's family will not be invited to attend if bride-price was not paid and the patient belongs to his mother's family. A man for whose mother bride-price was paid, who therefore belongs to his father's family, may be told that he must sacrifice a goat and brew beer for the spirits of his maternal ancestors. Similarly a man, whose mother was married *butende* and who is consequently a member of her family, may be informed by a doctor of the *bumanga* or some other society that neglect of his paternal grandfather is the cause of the trouble and that he must therefore perform the rites of ancestor worship and organize a dance to propitiate his spirit. Thus it would appear that the payment of bride-price and the consequent alteration of the line of inheritance from the female to the male, is not reflected in ancestor worship. I have suggested to many Sukuma that the real reason for the acquisition of stock is connected with ancestor worship, only to be met with this reply—'What? Pay wealth to gain grandsons to invoke my spirit? But I shall be dead and where is the profit in that? My grandchildren will invoke my spirit if the *nfumu* tells them to do so whether bride-price is paid or not. Even if bride-price is not paid and my grandchildren belong to their mother's family, they

---

[1] p. 41.
[2] From *buta*, a bow. Thus the left hand which holds the bow indicates the male line.
[3] From *ngongo*, the back. Woman carry children on their backs.

could not forget me because they are of my blood. The man is the author of life and women are only the carriers of the new life given to them.' Both ancestor worship and marriage are certainly much earlier institutions in Sukumaland than cattle culture which is said to have come with the Huma from the west. Moreover, it is not long since bride-price was paid in hoes and more recently in small stock. Anyone who has seen the Sukuma handling cattle will have recognized at once that they are not primarily a cattle or pastoral people, so it is not surprising that stock are not fundamental to their religion. While it appears that no religious grounds can be said to exist for the acquisition of cattle,[1] the importance of wealth to the perpetuation and increase of a family is quite another matter and must certainly rank as one of the primary considerations influencing the acquisition of stock.

Marriage and Family. The most important wealth, as we have seen, is children, because they will grow up and produce the most important material assets, which are food and cattle. Also it is not long since military considerations were of great importance, and every man looked forward to raising a large family for self-protection; to provide him with food in his old age and with women to cook it. While war and hunting may at one time have been the most important reasons for wanting a large family,[2] there is no doubt that economics and the desire for peace and security in old age are primary factors now. Consider the case of a man who has barely managed to pay bride-price for his wife and has no relations. As he has no more cattle his son must marry *butende*, and the grandchildren belong to their mother's family and are lost to him. If he has a daughter and she is married for bride-price, he will take the cattle to pay bride-price for his son's wife and thus regain the grandchildren. If his daughter is married without bride-price, her children will be his and his family will grow. Everything depends on the daughter, so that if he has no daughter both he and his son must do their best to acquire wealth in order to pay the latter's bride-price and regain the grandchildren. Thus in certain circumstances wealth, which was hoes or small stock and which is now cattle, can be vital to the very existence of a family.

---

[1] There is the sacred bull in whom the spirit of an ancestor resides and before whom oblations and prayers are offered, but this, as in the case of a sacrifice, involves one beast not 'cattle'.

[2] The fact that the male line is called *buta*, the bow, lends colour to this.

Apart from such cases there is no doubt that the *kukwa* form of marriage with the payment of bride-price is becoming increasingly common in some parts where cattle are more numerous, and in those areas the *butende* marriage tends to be despised. For example, the children of a *butende* marriage are sometimes referred to with a smile as *bana ba nda ya bu*, which means the 'children of the pregnancy of the bush'. Yet it must be remembered on the other hand that marriage without bride-price is still very common indeed in Sukumaland. Further, the alteration of the inheritance line from female to male, which as we have seen is a result of paying bride-price in a *kukwa* marriage, cannot be looked upon as a matter of universal importance and clearly varies with the circumstances of each family. For example, Jacobo *ng'wana* Mazinge's father withdrew the bride-price paid by him, thus handing his children over to their mother's family, and there are many Sukuma with sufficient cattle to afford bride-price who have nevertheless married *butende*. Further, the fact that cases exist where men with no cattle of their own look after a number of stock belonging to friends or neighbours, in which they can have no possible religious or family interest, seems to indicate the comparative importance of the economic reasons for acquiring cattle. Here I must draw a distinction between acquisition and retention. While particular circumstances of individual families may necessitate the acquisition of stock, the bride-price received for girls often counterbalances the bride-price payable for the young men's wives. The requirements of the family for bride-price and contingent needs, for birth blood-price and the like, are sufficient to preclude thoughtless disposal of existing family stock and to justify retention; but alone they are usually insufficient to stimulate the acquisition of stock, as contingent or reversionary rights in cattle do not come into existence until after the cattle have been acquired.

By-products. As grain, which is used for the purchase of cloth, hoes, and other things, is the currency of the country, so cattle are the capital, or the equivalent of grain, stored in another and more durable form. Besides calves, which are the most obvious interest on this capital, there are numerous other by-products which are of considerable value.

Milk and ghee or clarified butter[1] are perhaps the most important,

---

[1] Ghee = cream which has been heated to precipitate the proteins and so liberate the pure butter fat. The term ghee is very elastic and embraces all

and they are the property of the man who is looking after the cattle whether he is the actual owner or whether the animals have only been lent to him. The ghee exported from Sukumaland shows that this revenue alone is a not inconsiderable recompense for keeping cattle, especially as the open and settled nature of the country makes it possible for children to do most of the work of herding. The milk is looked upon as a valuable food for the children, and ghee is often used for food as well as for sale.

Manure is another by-product which is also the property of the man in whose stockyard the cattle sleep. At present it is mainly used for fuel, though some is used for lining grain stores, surfacing threshing floors, and an increasing quantity is being used for manuring arable land.

The animal alive or dead with its progeny, hide, and meat are the property of its owner, whether in his possession or in the stockyard of someone to whom he has lent it. When a beast dies the owner will give some of the meat to the man who was looking after it or, in cases where the two are far apart, the latter may sometimes take a fixed proportion; the rest will be dried for the owner.

Famine. Another important reason for acquiring and retaining stock is that they are an insurance against famine. As surplus grain rots in time, or may be destroyed by borers or other insects, it is sold eventually or exchanged for cattle. Later, in the event of a food shortage, the cattle are themselves food, or they can be exchanged for grain in neighbouring areas, so that a man with cattle will not starve. In south and south-east Sukumaland a few people have carried this exchange of cattle for grain a stage further. Their herds have escaped lightly from epizootics and, being in good pasture-land, they have multiplied to such an extent that in some thirty or forty cases individuals have over 1,000 cattle. In consequence their whole time and that of their families is spent looking after their stock, and each year a few head are sold or bartered to obtain food. Circumstances seem to be creating a small band of pastoralists, but this state of affairs is rare. Besides being exchanged for grain in times of food shortage, cattle are also widely used to pay for assistance with cultivating which, of course, means larger grain harvests and greater security for the cattle-owner.

products from a stinking mess of smoked and rancid cream to an excellent article which is barely distinguishable from butter. Clarified butter = grade 1 ghee of super excellence.

The use of the ox for work has started since the introduction of draught implements which has gained impetus as a result of Sukuma soldiers seeing oxen working in India and Burma during the 1939-45 war.

Finally the phrase *shillingi jitobialaga* is a common expression meaning 'shillings do not breed'; in the circumstances of Sukumaland it would be hard to find a more profitable investment than cattle. The rate of interest is high and, if the owner herds his own cattle, it includes hides, meat, milk, ghee, and manure, besides calves. Before the virtual eradication of rinderpest there were cases where disease wiped out whole herds or took a heavy toll, but on the other hand there are records of enormous increases even before 1942, for most of the short grass Sukumaland cultivation steppe is both suitable and healthy for cattle. In many parts the beasts remain in good condition even through long dry seasons.

LENDING CATTLE

The custom of *kubirisa*, lending stock to friends or neighbours, is very common. The most usual reasons are that the owner has not sufficient children to do the work of herding, or too few cattle to make the work worth-while. Another reason for lending cattle is that they can thus be sent to villages with better grazing. A water shortage or a move into tsetse bush where cattle cannot come during the first few years may necessitate lending, and also there was the obvious desirability of spreading stock over a number of villages so that an epizootic would not kill them all. Ordinarily, as I have shown, the herdsman or borrower gets only the milk, ghee, and manure, but in some cases, where cattle are lent to the quasi-professional herdsmen for seasonal grazing, an arrangement may be made for them to receive, say, a calf in payment. This seasonal movement to the large *mbuga* areas is known as *lugundiga*. Not only may these composite herds, containing stock belonging to several people, journey to the *mbuga* black cotton-soil plains during the rains when water is available in natural depressions, but also they may continue to pasture there during the dry season. If they do this on account of the shortage of grazing in their home villages, they will return to water every third or even fourth day.

Cattle and Resettlement. If there is good water and soil in the bush near to a crowded area, it is probable that a new village will

Lending Cattle

make its appearance as already described.[1] After the village headman, who is often the first inhabitant, others will follow, but these early settlers cannot take their cattle with them on account of lions, vermin, and the dangers of disease. Consequently they leave them with relations or lend them to friends or neighbours. As the settlement grows the cleared area expands, and eventually those in the middle begin to introduce livestock. First come the sheep and goats, next the calves. These feed near at hand and sleep in the houses. Last of all come the cattle when the size of the clearing makes it safe for them.

GRAZING AND RESERVATION

Heavy Stocking. Now, were the herds to range into the bush, lions are looked upon as perhaps the most serious danger.[2] Even where no tsetse fly exist the long grass harbours ticks which, in east coast fever areas, are a serious danger to stock; the cattle, therefore, graze near home until all the grass is eaten off or trampled down in a small area. This process of intentional heavy stocking to produce a short grass pasture is known as *kutobanga* and is practised to obtain a short sweet herbage inimical to ticks, to destroy inedible weeds, and (with goats) to prevent any considerable regeneration of bush. In some areas unduly heavy grazing, apart from pulverizing the soil and so making it susceptible to water and wind erosion, may also tend to reduce the vegetational succession to annual grasses which yield food for relatively few months of the year. However, some perennial grasses such as *Cynodons* are very highly resistant to heavy grazing and tramping, and on the heavier clay soils will survive almost any amount of damage above ground.

Reservation. When a village has been occupied for many years, the people will recognize that there is too little grass in the dry season to meet the requirements of an increased stock population within range of water. Each cattle-owner will then begin to reserve grass-land in the fallow of the arable area allotted to him, partly to supply thatching grass but mainly for reserve cattle fodder. This process of individual reservation began more than twenty-five

[1] pp. 30–32.
[2] If a cow is killed by lions the lions eat the meat; if a beast dies of disease the owner and his family eat the meat. Thus lions are the only cause of complete loss, though disease causes loss in condition.

Cattle Rights and Grazing

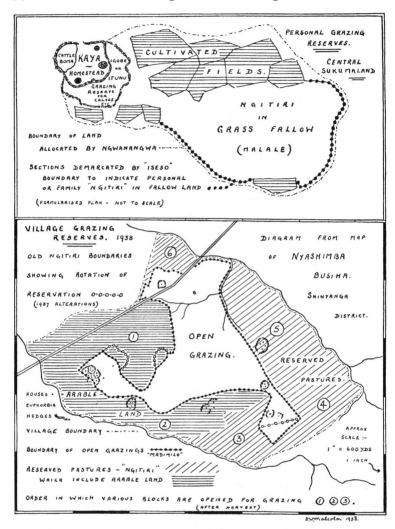

Sukuma systems of pasture reservation and rotational grazing.

years ago in some parts of Shinyanga and Maswa Districts, and is considerably older in Bukwimba District. Further north in the east coast fever lake-shore areas cattle population is less dense, the growth of grass is more luxuriant, and the dry season is less pronounced. Furthermore, long grass is a suitable habitat for ticks, so

Grazing and Reservation

that reservations in these parts are seldom found. At the same time there are relatively new villages in which reservation has only become necessary during the last two or three years, while in Salawe, west Shinyanga District, for example, the pasture is still so plentiful in relation to the stock population that reservation has not yet begun.[1] The accompanying plans[2] show the generalized layout of personal reserves as they exist in central Sukumaland. Good pasture to a Sukuma looks overgrazed to those who are accustomed to the permanent grass-lands of Europe. As we shall see, there is often much to be said for the Sukuma African's definition of good grazing in the circumstances of his country, but there comes a time in the stocking of the village when all the grass which has not been eaten is trampled down, and that which is not removed by the wind is washed away by the first rains. It is at this stage, when cattle lose condition and the older beasts die (partly of starvation and partly of the effects of eating sand while attempting to feed on broken-down grass), that the *ngitiri* grazing reserve becomes a necessity.

There is no doubt that the personal reserve on grass fallow, in conjunction with the loan of animals to people in better grazing areas, meets the case to begin with, by providing each herd with standing grass on which to fall back when the village pastures are finished. But it has several serious disadvantages. In the first place it is not long before the *bahabi*, or people who have no cattle, follow the example of the stock-owners or *basabi* and reserve plots of grass within a demarcated boundary. With a growing demand for grazing they soon learn to lease these reserves annually for a goat or a sheep. Two or three men who are herding together may rent one of these private reserves jointly. Personal *magitiri* grazing reserves can be lent but not rented in Maswa, just as one village may lend a village reserve to another village. A result of personal reservations, which can be seen in central Sukumaland, is that the whole village area is chequered with numerous blocks of reserved grazing. It is easy to visualize the difficulties of a herd-boy trying to pasture his animals in such a maze. These personal reserves do not vary in size according to the number of animals for which they are reserved but vary with the arable land and fallow of the family, which may have few or no cattle. This patchwork organization

---

[1] It is also noteworthy that there are few grazing reserves either in Mwanza, western Shinyanga, or in Zinza. [2] p. 74.

produces endless difficulties; quarrelling and litigation are natural corollaries which sometimes lead to bloodshed, and the village lands are not put to their optimum use in relation to the whole village stock population. Some areas can be over-reserved and become coarse and overgrown with regenerating bush, while others are heavily overgrazed and seriously damaged.

In Busiha matters came to a head in 1926 and the village headmen took the problem before the chief. He eventually decided with the advice of the elders that, as cultivated land is half-year land (similar to the Lammas lands of England), and the cattle of the village can eat the stover after harvest, so the whole arable area should be looked upon in the same way, whether it had been cultivated or put down to grass fallow. Personal reserves thus became a thing of the past in Busiha, and the management of the whole village area was left in the hands of the village headman, who is often assisted by the *nsumba ntale*. Ng'wagala Chiefdom followed suit the next year and there are signs that this solution to the difficulties inherent in private grass-land reservation is spreading.[1] Recently personal reserves were found in Busiha, but further investigation showed that they had been demarcated by a few people from Nera Chiefdom in Kwimba District who were not acquainted with the local custom.

The efficiency with which these village grazings are managed naturally varies with the capabilities of the numerous village headmen. There are no general rules defining either reservation or rotation; that is to say, there is no standardized technique and each area is manipulated in accordance with its condition. As usual the object in view is the maintenance of a short sweet herbage, free from inedible weeds and regenerating bush. Thus when an area which has been reserved for some years shows a marked weed growth or regenerating bush, it will be exchanged for a block of heavily grazed *idimilo* or open commonage which will then have a period of rest. Both arable land and pasture on the higher and lighter soils and in the valleys are included in one system of management. The actual method of opening sections of the arable, fallow, and reserved grazing areas after harvest is perhaps

---

[1] The village reserved pastures are managed by the *basumba batale* in Maswa where reservation is in a period of transition. Personal reserves still exist but may be included in a village reserve to which personal rights must give way.

most simply described by reference to the plan taken from the Nyashimba survey.[1]

From this it will be seen that the whole village area is divided into two blocks. In the case of Nyashimba village the one surrounds the other. The first block contains all the arable land including the areas under temporary grass fallow and a considerable stretch of pasture. The second block is the open commonage. At the beginning of the Sukuma year with the advent of the rains in November, the first block containing the arable land is closed to grazing. The village cattle and small stock are confined to the *madimilo* commonage. This division obtains until after the harvest when in July–August the arable land, interspersed with fallow, is opened up for the grazing of crop residues. This process of opening up is done in sections, one section being completely grazed and finished before the next is opened. The underlying idea is to maintain an area of standing hay until the next rains break so that the last section is never opened until perhaps November or even December. It is easy to envisage the results which would follow indiscriminate opening of the arable land and grazing reserves. The cattle would pick and choose and, in the process of wandering over the whole area, they would trample down as much or more grass than they ate. By September perhaps they would be faced with the task of licking up broken-down grass stems and would therefore suffer even more severely from eating sand than they already do in the densely stocked areas. It will also be seen from this plan that areas are exchanged between the first and the second blocks in accordance with the requirements of particular areas. This system has the advantages of securing protection during seeding for all the grass in the arable and reserved pasture block, of providing standing hay right up to, and into, the beginning of the rains and of protecting the growing crops from stock. Its main disadvantage may well lie in maintaining too much of the commonage area as open grazing for too long a period without a protected seed-time. This matter will be discussed further[2] but it is perhaps worth-while to mention here that the existence of a recognized practice of grass-land reservation and deferred grazing offers a valuable foundation on which to build such improvements as may be necessary to provide an adequate regimen for pasture improvement on a wide scale, which will be infinitely easier in relation to a

[1] p. 74.   [2] pp. 133–5.

system embracing the whole village area than it would be in relation to multitudinous petty individual reservations.

It is also noteworthy that the results of over-reservation could be seen, for example, in the village of Ng'wamagunguli, Shinyanga District, where a strong growth of inedible weeds existed while regenerating bush was gaining ground. Besides the weed growth another danger of over-reservation is long grass which harbours ticks. In connexion with the indigenous system of heavy stocking, it is interesting to note that similar methods are now in use in Great Britain to reclaim rough pastures and improve the grazing.[1] When a further increase of stock passes the limits of village capacity thus enhanced by the Busiha system of management, the cattle-owners have no alternative but to lend their surplus animals to friends in other villages where more abundant grazing is still available or to move and take their stock with them. While this is seldom necessary in most of southern Sukumaland, a glance at the map of cattle distribution and density[2] will explain why it is done farther north.

Attempts to organize wet season stock movements under Government auspices to the large plains of the Huruhuru and Shimiyu *mbuga* systems, in order to supplement the existing process and save the grass-land of the villages, did not prove successful, and were resented by the people. The Sukuma naturally reacts only to stimuli of immediate consequence to the well-being of his family or his stock, and therefore his idea of necessity lags behind the long-range view resulting from an appreciation of accelerated soil erosion and the consequent destruction of soil fertility.

WATER RIGHTS

The arrangements concerning domestic water supply have been mentioned, but as cattle drink more than men, their water supply must be more plentiful. The village well or tank in which all the members of the village dig is sometimes used for cattle;[3] at present the most important sources of water supply for stock are in the

[1] Cf. English practice: 'There remains a further method of technique that can be usefully employed in the improvement of derelict land—the massing of animals in a regularised manner on limited areas at a time can be used to great advantage to destroy roughage of all kinds (bracken and even small scrub) and to rough up the surface.' Sir R. G. Stapleton, K.B.E., *The Land Now and To-morrow*, Faber & Faber.

[2] Facing p. 63.   [3] pp. 32–33.

'The village well or tank in which all the members of the village dig is sometimes used for cattle.' (p. 78)

All along the stream-beds pools of water can be seen in twos and threes surrounded by piles of sand. Here three men dig together. Note the small sand-bar partitions

Well-grazed village commonage in the foreground with an even stand of fine grass in the village *ngitiri* reserve beyond

The boundary marks of village reserved grazing in Nyashimba

sandy river-beds. Here during the dry season nearly everyone digs to uncover a water supply for his own stock, though there are a few professionals who are paid in cattle. Along the stream-beds in places where water is held up in the sand, pools can be seen in twos and threes surrounded by large piles of sand. The reason why these ponds are in groups is the custom prevalent both in Sukumaland and Zinza for the cattle belonging to two or three homesteads to be herded and watered together. The herdsmen take turns of about six days, and the man or boy on duty will collect the cattle from several stockyards in the morning. When they come back after grazing and watering the animals will all return to their own stockyards. If a man has lent his cattle to someone else he takes no part in digging for their water, and in fact has nothing to do with them beyond visiting them occasionally; presumably the milk and ghee are sufficient recompense not only for the trouble of herding but also for the work of digging for water. The same arrangements apply to areas where a water-bearing stratum below sandy soils has been tapped and cattle are watered from springs; the water-holes in Busule, Shinyanga District, which are illustrated in the accompanying photographs, are managed in this way.

FARMYARD MANURE

Manure and the Village Headman. It has been suggested that a serious bar to manuring is the right of a village headman to take over the abandoned sites of houses or cattle-yards, which are known as *matongo* in the south, since it was supposed that the headman, having the right to the only known form of manured land, would naturally have the right to all manured lands. In the first place, in the greater part of Sukumaland or Zinza, the village headman does not take over these *matongo* (or *shilugu* as they are called farther north), and this custom is confined to south-western Shinyanga and northern Nzega. In the second place, while the village headman can reallocate abandoned cultivation as he thinks fit, he could not expropriate a man who was manuring his fields, in order to use them himself. And finally it is recognized that the fortuitous fertility of an abandoned cattle-pen is quite a different matter from land improved as a result of work, so that even in the area where the headman can and does take over the *matongo* (if he happens to want them—and he cannot use an unlimited number) he would reallocate manured land in just the same way as unmanured land, and relations or descendants would thus retain preference over all others.

Manure and the Bahabi (who have no stock). Another question which has arisen is the position of those who have no cattle, in relation to supplies of manure. This has already assumed some importance in the south-west. As I have mentioned, manure is the property of the person in whose stockyard the cattle sleep. But who are the *bahabi* or stockless people? Investigation shows that we are not dealing with two distinct classes of people or different clans, as the use of the two names might lead one to suppose. Perhaps in the majority of marriages bride-price is paid, and many young men are sufficiently closely related to a cattle-owner to obtain the stock necessary for bride-price. Thus it would appear that in many instances the cattle-owners are the elders and those who have no cattle are junior members of their families. While this is true of a large percentage, it must be remembered that the sons are sometimes resident in villages at some distance from their father's homestead and also that some families have few or no cattle. This is particularly noticeable in the Mwanza District. Generally speaking, however, those without cattle can beg manure from cattle-owning relations or friends. It can be pointed out that the cattle have eaten the stover on the arable land of stock-owners and others alike, and that in exchange it is only fair that their owners should give those who have no cattle permission to use some of the resulting manure, which will in any case increase the crop residues and thus the next dry season's fodder for the cattle of the donor.

At the same time it might be advisable to lay stress on bulking in order to assure a sufficient supply, and to this end the converse would be emphasized to encourage those who have no stock to help take crop residues or grass to the cattle-pens for bulking, so that they themselves may obtain a larger supply of better made manure which will repay their labour with increased food crops. Such well-balanced propaganda should lay the foundation of a practice beneficial to all. It is noteworthy that in parts of Northern Nigeria the Hausa, who are arable farmers, pay the Fulani to bring their cattle to graze off the crop residues and so manure the land. It should also be remembered in this connexion that farmyard manure has its greatest value on the higher and lighter soils.

As much of the cultivated land is on the heavier soil types it is unlikely that the demand for properly made farmyard manure will become acute in central and southern Sukumaland though in the north the sandy soils are more prevalent.

SLAUGHTER

Formerly, it may be supposed, cattle were not even used for bride-price and being few they were only slaughtered on occasions of considerable importance. Later a beast might be killed to entertain a stranger or to provide meat for a ceremonial feast. Now, as the numbers of stock have increased considerably, the slaughter of cattle is much more common, and in many parts has become the normal method of paying for collective or village labour in lieu of beer, which, of course, entails increased work in cultivation.

LAW AND CUSTOM

It is not easy to translate African concepts of the usage of land into English terms which have originated in a totally different environment. 'We are apt to forget that land, even potentially fertile agricultural land, has no absolute value, but only that by which it is endowed by man acting as the agent of a given economic system.'[1] I have now given an outline of rural economy in Sukumaland and Zinza. For the sake of brevity it has been necessary to generalize on subjects which could well fill separate volumes if every local variation were to be included. The most important difficulty which requires explanation here is the use of the word 'right'. Anyone can fish in the sea and it is not until there is competition in a limited area that rights acquire definition. Anyone can use the land and it is not until habitable land becomes limited or a permanent crop appears, that rights acquire a value and gain definition even in the minds of those who exercise them. While much of the uninhabited country which surrounds Sukumaland is not as fertile or favourable as that of the cultivation steppe, it is still largely habitable land. Sukumaland is not an island.

The village headman has the right to allocate land to a newcomer, but it is the custom that he should do so with the advice and assistance of the village elders and often it is the custom that the actual work of allocation should be left in the hands of the

---

[1] M. Perham, *Native Administration in Nigeria*, p. 311.

basumba batale. Law, custom, rights, and usage are closely knit; consequently some of the organization and activities to which I have given definition for the sake of lucidity should, perhaps, more properly appear in the blurred outline of a photograph which is out of focus by European standards.

5

The Administration of Local African Government in Sukumaland Today and Tomorrow

WE have now seen something of the indigenous social structure of Sukumaland, but the organization described is customary and originates in the mists of unrecorded history before European penetration into the Dark Continent.

That this organization is resilient and adaptable is shown by its continued existence under the impact of alien culture and the introduction of a cash economy. The machinery of Native Administration in Sukumaland has remained substantially intact under European rule. The chain of authority still runs from the chief down through the sub-chief and the senior and junior grades of village headmen, as has already been described. The 'Council of State' still has a powerful influence upon the chief and the court elders are still an integral part of his court. To bring the picture up-to-date it is necessary, however, to indicate some of the modifications and adaptations which have taken place as the result of ordered development, to meet the needs of more complex administration.

When the British took over Sukumaland during the First World War, they found the country split into some forty independent chiefdoms many of which were not being administered by chiefs chosen by the people. There followed a period of reorganization. Chiefdoms which had been fused under an alien African ruler, for convenience of administration, regained their independence and selected their own chief. Boundary disputes and claims to chiefdoms were rife and it took the new authorities some years to settle down, and to absorb the atmosphere and the traditions of British Colonial Government. The history of the practical introduction of the conscious policy of Indirect Rule by Sir Donald Cameron is too well known to require recapitulation here. In September 1930 Sir Donald Cameron wrote as follows:

In pondering on the political development of the native peoples in this Territory, especially in connection with the conception in some minds that the best, if not the only, solution must be along the lines of British constitutional development, it is interesting to consider the analogy afforded to us by India. Writing of the situation in India in the *Spectator* in August last a correspondent remarked that 'the truth is that we have to clear our minds of a confusion between democracy and the British Constitution. India wants the former, and we offer a modified and diluted form of the latter.'

In regard to local government he is intensely interesting. 'The point at issue is not really whether there should be democracy, but how democracy can be made effective, and this is where the traditional institutions of India come to our aid. For innumerable centuries before the English came to India the country was divided into small village republics, of which Sir Charles Metcalfe (a member of the Governor's Council and subsequently Lord Metcalfe) wrote in 1830: "Dynasty after dynasty tumbles down; revolution succeeds revolution . . . but the village communities remain the same. The union of the village communities, each forming a separate little state in itself, has, I conceive, contributed more than any other cause to the preservation of the people of India . . . and to the enjoyment of a great portion of freedom and independence." '

The letter in the *Spectator* continues: 'Two of the finest administrators that Britain has ever sent to India have added their praises to the many commendations that have been made of these village republics. Sir Thomas Munro spoke of the "strong attachment of the natives to trial by *panchayat*" (village council), and described the British system which supplanted them as "not only most expensive and vexatious, but totally inefficient". (East India Paper, London, 1820.) Lord Elphinstone found the same facts to be true in an entirely different part of the country. He discovered that people in the Mahratta country were "exempt from some of the evils which exist under our more perfect government", and put this down to the fact that "the native government although it did little to obtain justice for the people, left them the means of procuring it for themselves". (Report of October, 1819.) Elphinstone spoke strongly of the *panchayats* in the same report. Mr. Bernard Houghton, a former member of the Indian Civil Service, has stated that "in some respects, particularly in its village organisations, its civilisation (i.e. India's) is more democratic than ours".'

It is one of the feats of British efficiency that where previous conquerors had left untouched those centres of village liberty and self-government, our 'more perfect government' began their systematic destruction. The historian Dutt, in his 'Economic History of India', deplores the effacement of village self-government 'as one of the

Local African Government

saddest results of British rule in India', while Sir Henry Cotton, who is of the opinion that the people of India possess 'an instinctive capacity for local self-government', gives it as his opinion in *New India* that 'a costly and mechanical centralisation has taken the place of the former system of local self-government and local arbitration'.

There still remains that instinctive capacity for local self-government, however, and even skeleton organisations on which to build. The gravest essential for operative democracy is that representatives should be personally known to their electorates, and this is doubly important among ignorant or illiterate people.[1]

With the experience of India before us, suffice it that the indigenous institutions of Sukumaland were accepted as the organs of local African government through which British Administration would function. The chiefs' courts were recognized; their powers were defined and their cases were recorded and subjected to educative supervision and revision by the District Commissioners.

Government granted to each chiefdom a rebate from the direct native House and Poll Tax at the rate of a quarter of each tax collected. From this revenue the Native Treasuries of the chiefdoms were born. Previously, the chiefs had received tribute in grain from the people and they had used this tribute largely for the good of their people, so that, when Native Treasuries were instituted, tribute was commuted and the treasuries simply represented a change of currency from grain to cash, rather than a completely new principle. As in the case of the courts of justice, it was therefore possible to exert an educative influence over their subsequent conduct and development.

At that time there were many who considered that these steps were premature and that the chiefs and their advisers were not ready to shoulder the responsibility of recognized courts and the administration of local government finance. But there were only two alternatives. Either to ignore the form of local government evolved by the people and drive it underground by reliance on alien African subordinate officials, or to utilize it to the full and guide its subsequent development.

'In politics, in industry, and in education, it is a truism that half the battle consists in knowing what will arouse enthusiasm, what will stimulate energy, what will engender suspicion and what will

[1] Sir Donald Cameron, *My Tanganyika Service*, p. 111.

meet with blind obstinacy or even bellicose opposition.'[1] Clearly no alien organization would have the intimate contact with the people that is enjoyed by the social and political organization which they themselves have evolved. In the event the experiment has, in fact, proved its value, as I shall endeavour to show. The work of supervision and educative influence by the District Commissioners is onerous and sometimes almost heartbreaking, but it has gone on steadily ever since.

The first signs that this work was having its effect in the political sphere came when, in contrast to inter-chiefdom rivalry, disputes, and petty parochial nationalism, the majority of the chiefs in the Shinyanga District formed a federation in 1926, which was later joined by the remaining chiefdoms in the district. In 1927 Maswa District followed suit and the Binza Federation came into being, followed by a district-wide federation in Kwimba and smaller federal units in Mwanza. These federations with their unified treasuries represent a striking advance. Their councils constitute very valuable legislative, advisory, and judicial bodies. Every chief sits upon the council as a peer in his own right; that is to say, there is no paramount chief, although the most influential of them occupies a somewhat nebulous position as *primus inter pares*. The local federations of chiefs are constituted as the highest Native Authorities in each district and the Sukumaland Federation as the supreme Native Authority of the whole area.

It is the practice of the federal councils to meet about three times a year. Many of their deliberations then take place in company with an Administrative Officer and much useful ground is covered. Matters of common interest to all the chiefdoms are discussed, new governmental measures or requirements are explained, projects involving the expenditure of Native Treasury money are planned, and, should it be necessary, new regulations under the Native Authority Ordinance are enacted. The explanation, co-ordination, and opportunity for enlightened discussion to which these meetings give rise are of the utmost value and importance.

In November 1932 the first meeting of all the chiefs of Sukumaland was held in Mwanza. That was the first tentative step towards the federal union of all the chiefdoms of Sukumaland which took

[1] Professor Daryll Forde, 'Social Development in Africa and the Work of the International African Institute.' *Journal Royal Society of Arts*, 1945.

Local African Government

place on the 18 October 1946, twenty years after the first district federation. So much for the process of federation, which has steadily grown up in place of pre-existing distrust and rivalry between many little independent units. But to gain a clear picture some account must now be given of the detailed workings of the local African government of the district federations now operating and of their constituent chiefdoms. To do so it will perhaps be advisable to examine a sample, since such minor differences as exist are mainly due to the personality of the chiefs concerned, to differences in the state of development of their people and the like, and are not differences in intrinsic organization.

Let me then attempt to draw a sketch of the Native Authorities and outline their scope and functions in the spheres of legislation, administration, finance, and justice.

The Legislative and Administrative Functions of the Native Authorities.

The separation of legislative, executive, and judicial functions is beginning to take place. Legislation is becoming more and more the sole prerogative of the federations and there are indications that the Sukumaland Federation will soon become the sole local legislative assembly. Executive functions remain with the chiefs and judicial functions are being delegated more and more to so-called sub-chiefs with their panels of elders. The Sukuma name for this sub-chief is *Ng'wambilija*, which might reasonably be translated as judicial assistant. Their powers are regional but in most chiefdoms there is a chief's deputy whose main function is to deputize for the chief in court work, sitting with the normal panel of elders.

Since the institution of chieftainship was first evolved, the chief, as the final arbiter in his country, has been empowered by the people to issue orders and to enforce them as well as to settle disputes. With the recognition of indigenous African systems of local government these powers have been not only recognized but also extended to meet the requirements of modern administration. Section 8 of the Native Authority Ordinance gives a long list of subjects in regard to which orders may be made. They include:

   a. Intoxicating liquors.
   b. Gambling.
   c. Arms and ammunition.

d. Riots, disturbances, and breaches of the peace.
e. Pollution and obstruction of water-courses, &c.
f. Destruction of trees.
g. Infectious or contagious diseases.
h. Reporting of offenders.
i. Paid labour for essential public works.
j. Migration of natives.
k. Reporting of births and deaths.
l. Movement of livestock.
m. Provision of food for travellers.
n. Burning of grass or bush.
o. Tsetse fly.
p. Adequate supply of food for maintenance of dependants.
q. Native law and custom.
r. 1. Coffee.
   2. Locusts.
   3. Hunting of game.
   4. Poisonous plants, roots, &c.
   5. Cotton.
   6. Erosion.
   7. Essential products, &c.

Other local legislation can be enacted by the Native Authorities under other sections of this Ordinance, principally by rules under Section 15.

The practice of a single chief issuing orders concerning any of these matters for application only within the boundaries of his chiefdom has largely passed away and, for the sake of achieving uniformity throughout the whole area of a district, legislative powers are now normally exercised only by the council of the district federation; though while the district federation will retain power to legislate on matters of local application, it is probable that legislation affecting the whole of Sukumaland will be enacted by the Sukumaland Federation. Legislation and administration are closely interwoven in the practice of the federal councils and perhaps there is no better way of illustrating this point than by mentioning some of the subjects dealt with at a meeting of the Binza Council of Chiefs of the Maswa District.

But before doing so, let me describe a typical district federation council meeting, part of which took place in my office. The proceedings have an air of informality by European standards. There is no official chairman. There is no inflexible agenda.

Propositions are thrown into the arena, some by myself as a result of official correspondence or at the previous request of members of the council; others are originated during the meeting. On my left sits Chief Majebere[1] (though he may sit anywhere) who on account of his age and standing is tacitly recognized as the leader of the Binza Council but without any formal acknowledgement of his status. All are equal and anyone can speak on any subject or sum up the views of the council at the end of a debate. Round the room on benches and chairs sit the other Binza chiefs. Ndaturu of Ntuzu is perhaps the best educated and most intelligent but neither he nor Majebere monopolizes the debates. With Chiefs Majebere and Ndaturu, Chief William Nhumbu of Ng'unghu is a member of the Executive Committee of the Federation. All three own motor-cars and Chief Majebere has a salary of £1,000 per annum. The Executive Committee is simply the three most accessible and mobile chiefs who have been empowered by the council to act on behalf of the federation in matters the urgency of which precludes postponement, pending the next plenary session of the council.

I have never yet seen a proposition put to the vote. I have never yet seen an argument reach an unseemly heat. No one speaks for the sake of speaking. In some way each point is discussed until doubters are convinced and an agreed decision is reached as in the case of a British jury. The debates of the council are conducted in the Kisukuma language which I can only just follow. Decisions are conveyed to me and recorded in Kiswahili. Thus I may throw the ball in from the touch-line and endeavour to follow its progress amongst the players. Their deliberations are remarkably quick; far quicker than those of some European committees and commissions of which I have been secretary. One or two of the chiefs who are now old men only occasionally join in the debates even in Kisukuma and can hardly follow Kiswahili.

The federation of chiefs in Shinyanga is somewhat more advanced than that of Maswa as there are four chiefs who speak English fluently, one of whom, Chief Kidaha of Busiha, is a member of the Legislative Council of Tanganyika. Possibly the federations in the Kwimba and Mwanza Districts may not be quite as advanced as the Binza Federation of Maswa but the differences are

---

[1] Elected permanent president of the Sukumaland Federal Council. See pp. 146–9.

hardly significant and the Kwimba Federation has gained from the fact that its most influential chief, Balele of Nera, spent some time in England. This comparative note will give some indication of the position which the sample drawn from Maswa would occupy in relation to the other federations in Sukumaland.

So, with this sketch of the strength and the weaknesses of an average council of Sukuma chiefs as a background, we can now see something of the work which they undertake at one of their periodic meetings which are held three or four times a year.

Subjects Discussed at the Meeting of the Binza Federation Council of Chiefs, August 1945

1. Tax Rates 1946—increase from Shs. 10/- to Shs. 12/-.
2. Grazing reserves for trade stock on the North Eyasi stock route.
3. Livestock marketing—encouragement of.
4. *Striga helmonthica* (parasitic weed)—legislative and administrative action for its eradication.
5. Tie-ridging—legislative and administrative action; suitability under various soil conditions.
6. Native Court fees—revision.
7. Limitation of suits in the Native Courts.
8. Clarified butter and ghee industry—encouragement and organization of.
9. Gogadi, son of Bagome, ex-chief of Sanga (Meadu)—application to visit Sanga.
10. Native Treasury Estimates of Revenue and Expenditure 1946, including *inter alia*, salary increases, new appointments, antifamine measures, provision for expenses of chiefs on educational visits to other areas, and grain storage.
11. Smallpox epidemic—request to encourage indigenous system of vaccination from mild cases.
12. Construction of Lock-ups at Courts.
13. Rural education policy.
14. Non-co-operation by Chief Jimola of Bugarama[1]—a warning by the Federation Council.

The council also formed a sub-committee of three chiefs to give further consideration with the Senior Veterinary Officer to the

[1] Chief Jimola of Bugarama was subsequently removed from office at the request of his people and this small chiefdom was placed under mandate to the chiefdom of Ng'wagala at the request of the people, pending an increase in population.

problems of village grazing rights in relation to the requirements of trade stock on the North Eyasi stock route.

It is perhaps noteworthy that the minutes of this meeting ran to eighteen pages of foolscap in single spacing and contain numerous extremely sensible and enlightened resolutions including, for example, that all posts in the Native Administration service up to and including that of sub-chief be open to returning members of His Majesty's Forces.

From the point of view of the District Commissioners who have been working for years to get this council to stand on its own feet, and to express its own independent opinions, a most encouraging point to notice was that two suggestions, which I put forward in connexion with the pulling of *striga* and the organization of peripatetic cream separators, were turned down by the council. This was indeed a most encouraging advance. In the past there had been a tendency for chiefs, either individually or in council, to accept any suggestion made by a European officer and to approve it out of deference. This habit, born of innate politeness, had made administration doubly difficult because it had often taken a long time to find out why it had not been possible to put apparently reasonable suggestions into practice in spite of verbal acceptance by the chiefs.

The castigation of Chief Jimola was perhaps a point of outstanding interest, as was the general admixture of legislation and administration throughout. The recommendations of the council which required legislative implementation, such as those concerned with the demarcation of grazing reserves, *striga helmonthica*, the introduction of tie-ridging, native court fees in inheritance cases, and possibly the reorganization of the clarified butter industry, would be drafted as orders and regulations for the subsequent signature of the members of the council, who had to hurry back to their chiefdoms.

Finance. Among the subjects discussed at the Binza Federation Council meeting noted above, we have already seen something of the preliminary consideration given to matters concerned with the native treasury estimates of revenue and expenditure. Such preliminary proposals concerned with alterations in recurrent expenditure and all extraordinary expenditure are prepared by the constituent federations in each district for submission to the Sukumaland Federal Council. When the Sukumaland Federation came into being in October 1946, the treasuries of the district federations were amalgamated, with a single bank account. All resources were pooled. Thus, the district or constituent federation treasuries became accounting branches of the unified Sukumaland Native Treasury, on behalf of which they collect revenue and effect expenditure. Draft estimates for each treasury branch are prepared, as I have indicated, by the local federation and are co-ordinated and adjusted primarily by the Executive Committee of the Sukumaland Federation for the approval of the Sukumaland Federal Council in plenary session, whence the full estimates for the whole Sukumaland Federation Native Treasury are submitted to the Provincial Commissioner for the final approval of Government.

In the present stage of development, the District Commissioner plays a large part in the detailed preparation of branch treasury estimates, while the Provincial Commissioner keeps a tight hand on any tendency to increase recurrent expenditure, and particularly salaries, along lines which would leave too small a margin for necessary development works and for essential local social services. Inevitably the higher direction of finance comes from Administrative Officers for neither the Sukumaland Federal Council nor their civil servants are yet capable of handling unaided the sums of money which are now involved in every annual budget. But this proviso applies only to the higher direction of native treasury finance. All the executive work is done through the African organizations.

The House and Poll Tax is collected by the chiefs and their clerical staffs with all native administration revenue, such as court fees and fines, market dues, beer licences, and the like, and is forwarded to the Branch Native Treasury offices at District Headquarters. The proceeds of the direct tax are then paid in to Government and the Sub-Accountant repays the rebate to the Secretary and Treasurer of the treasury branch who in turn makes out all salary and other vouchers for the local federated native authority, for payment either at the treasury branch or by the chiefs at their court offices. This work is a heavy responsibility but it is well and faithfully discharged. It must be realized that the sums of money thus handled amount in an average Sukuma district to over £12,000 of revenue and over £10,000 of expenditure each year.

Local African Government

A natural result of the Sukumaland Federation is that the Native Treasury manages in common the finance of all the chiefdoms in the combined budget. The advantages of this system are obvious, for it carries with it all those assets which the large financial unit always has over the small one. Whereas the chiefdom of average size cannot afford its own school or dispensary or whatever it may be, it can now be confident of getting its fair share of social services which are spread over Sukumaland as a whole. This is a very important point and one of which the chiefs have shown themselves very conscious. It has been remarked that the ultimate guidance of large matters of finance is in the hands of the European Administration, but that must not be taken to mean that the chiefs play no part in such matters. They play a very large part. All new schemes, from the building of a dam or a school to salary increments for dispensary 'sweepers', are thoroughly examined and a number of sensible observations and suggestions can always be counted upon as forthcoming from the chiefs. The final decisions are always made with their full understanding and consent. There is every reason to hope that before long, with improvements in the civil service, this local African government will have complete control of its own budget, subject only to the confirmatory approval of the Provincial Commissioner in Council.

Justice. The recognized courts of which the cases are recorded and which are subject to educative supervision, begin with those of the sub-chiefs or *bambilija*, although it is well known that a vast number of petty cases are disposed of by arbitration and otherwise before the village headmen and elders. If, in a petty case, the village headman sentences the delinquent to pay a small fine, such as a goat to be eaten by the village community, and the delinquent accepts the sentence, the matter ends there. Similarly the village headman and elders may sentence a man to pay compensation and if he pays without more ado, the case will never be recorded. However, should either of the parties be dissatisfied with the judgement of the village headman and elders, or should the case be of any importance, it will be heard *de novo*, and not as an appeal, by the sub-chief's court. The courts of the sub-chiefs are constituted either as 'B' Courts with powers to impose sentences of one month's imprisonment or a fine of Shs. 50/- or whipping up to six strokes or as Intermediate Courts with powers extending to three months' imprisonment or Shs. 100/- fine or six strokes. The grade of a sub-chief's court depends only on the competence shown by that court in the past and on the degree to which the burden on an overworked chief's court may be alleviated by enhancing the powers of his sub-chiefs' courts. Appeal lies from the 'B' or 'Intermediate' Court to the chiefs' 'A' Court, which is also a court of first instance for the more important cases in the area, with powers of six months' imprisonment, a fine of Shs. 200/- and whipping up to eight strokes. Thence an appeal lies to the court of the local federation, constituted by four or more chiefs sitting together. This court's powers, as a court of first instance, are considerable for it can pass sentence of imprisonment up to one year, as much as a European second-class magistrate may do, fines up to Shs. 400/- and whipping up to eight strokes. From the local federation court appeal now lies to the District Commissioner, thence to the Provincial Commissioner and finally to the Governor. Of course, as I have mentioned, all cases in the Native Courts are also subject to review and revision by the District Commissioner at the end of every month and on tour. It should also be noted that while powers to pass sentence of whipping exist on paper, they are subject to confirmation by the District Commissioner before being carried out and are practically never used. The Sukumaland Federation will have an appeal court, but this court is not yet constituted, as the Sukumaland Federation has first been giving consideration to the local law and custom to be applied, with a view to achieving some measure of uniformity throughout the whole Sukumaland area. This process of co-ordination of the laws to be applied is now complete and the integration of the Sukumaland Federation Appeal Court into the appeal system, if possible without adding an extra rung to the ladder, is now under consideration.

Now we have seen that the chief no longer issues orders or legislates by himself and the legislative functions of the chiefs have been taken over by the councils of the federations. Therefore, in practice, it is normally impossible for a chief to be put in the position of enforcing an order which is solely his own. Moreover, the chief cannot sit in court alone because the constitution of every chief's and sub-chief's court lays down explicitly that no less than three court elders or *banamhala ba ibanza* must be present sitting together with the chief before the judgement of the chief's court can be considered valid. Indeed any idea of a chief making

Local African Government

autocratic judicial decisions without the essential help of the *banamhala* is utterly foreign to all Sukuma custom and tradition. No chief would ever consider making a decision by himself in any court case, nor would it be recognized if he did.

As in the proceedings of the local federation councils, so in the native courts, the procedure has an air of informality. The case for the prosecution or the civil complainant is first stated in the normal way. Witnesses are called and cross-examined by the defence. The case for the defence is then presented and witnesses are heard and cross-examined by the prosecution or complainant. So far the procedure closely resembles that of British courts of justice. The element of informality, however, arises from the fact that not only may the public attend the case or trial, but also the public may join in the proceedings. This opportunity is not abused; young men or children who know nothing of the case do not intervene, but elders, village headmen or others who have knowledge of the case or matters relevant thereto may and do speak up if they feel that the interests of justice will be served by their doing so. In the chiefs' courts the proceedings take place in well-built masonry court houses. Those of the sub-chiefs are usually of a less expensive standard of construction; sometimes indeed they may consist only of the cool shade under the spreading branches of a huge fig-tree. There are no advocates. In general it is considered wrong that anyone should come between a man and his judge. I have never seen a man show any hesitation in speaking freely in his own defence. Possibly, as the arts of reading and writing are little known, the art of public speaking is more strongly and widely developed than amongst some other races. It is certainly considered wrong that anyone should gain material profit from the misfortunes of others, except he be the aggrieved party obtaining compensation as a result of a judicial decision. But should anyone wish to bring a friend to speak for him there is no possible objection to his doing so and this practice may grow.

The chiefs and elders sitting in court have immense patience and even the young and educated chiefs rapidly acquire an intimate knowledge of their people. In general, it may be said that infinite trouble is taken to bring out the relevant points both for the prosecution and the defence and to give unbiased justice to the people.

Chieftainship and Democracy. The hedging and circumscribing of the authority of the chief is rarely as open and obvious as in the provision that he may not sit alone upon the bench; but although his personal power in the past was great and is actually considerable in the present, there is a sanction that ensures that he shall use it well; that is the favour of the people, by which alone he governs. I have already explained that in the days gone by the position of chiefs was far from secure. In those days a failure of the rains would often bring about the deposition of a chief, if not his demise. Now the position of the chief is more secure in that his life is not at the mercy of the weather, but the power of the 'Council of State' is still very considerable and although the people of Sukumaland are, in general, easy going, no chief who becomes autocratic and unjust will remain in his post for long. Chiefs may yet be weak or stupid but there is no place for the bad or vicious chief either in the custom of the past or the practice of the present.

The usual course of events which now precedes the termination of the rule of a bad chief is that vague rumours reach the ears of the District Commissioner that 'all is not well'. A timely warning may save a change of chief but otherwise in all probability a number of citizens will accuse their chief before the 'Council of State' of the chiefdom. The 'Council of State' may admonish him and, if he is a wise man, such an admonishment may bear fruit. If not, things will go from bad to worse until either a specific charge is laid directly before the District Commissioner who, after investigation, will request the Provincial Commissioner to withdraw the recognition of Government and ask the 'Council of State' to appoint a successor, or the 'Council of State' may proceed against the chief before the court of the local federation and, on the recommendation of the federation, the District Commissioner may seek the withdrawal of Government recognition. Recent examples of this process are those of Ndugulile, the Regent of Busanda in Shinyanga District; Chenge, Chief of Itilima; Mushuda, Chief of Dutwa; and Jimola, Chief of Bugarama in the Maswa District, who have been removed during the last six years or so, in accordance with the wishes of their people. Therefore every chief understands clearly that he is the representative and servant of his people and that he will hold office at their pleasure during good behaviour. As his term of office is not limited to a set period of years he has everything to gain if he adheres steadily to impartial justice and to working faithfully for the good of his people. He has everything to lose if he forgets this.

It is reasonable also to hope that the chiefs of the future will be increasingly less weak or stupid than some of their predecessors, for a great deal of care and attention is paid to the education and upbringing of the sons of chiefs. Naturally this is a matter that must finally be left in the hands of the parent, but Government officials strongly encourage, and the chiefs themselves fully appreciate, the best possible education for their sons. Increasingly, these days, the sons of chiefs have read to an advanced standard and certainly in the future it can be expected that there will be, as chiefs, more men of the calibre of the late Chief Balele of Nera in Kwimba, who studied in England at an Agricultural College, and Chief Kidaha, M.L.C., of Busiha, recently elected as chief, who is a young man with a highly educated mind as the legacy of his advanced agricultural training at Makerere College in Uganda and a year at Oxford.

The custom of selecting the new chief from among the sons of the late chief's sisters is disappearing, but the 'Council of State' still maintains a fairly wide group from which to choose, as chiefs with several wives usually have many sons and so attention must be paid to the education of the sons of chiefs and not to that of a single son. As in East Africa generally Sukumaland is free from the restrictive influence of primogeniture with its insistence on the one candidate, whether he be fit or unfit for his important office; the range of choice that is conferred by the ability to select any one of the sons or nephews of a chief is yet another powerful sanction by which the tenure of the office is made to conform to the will of the people. From several candidates there is a fair and reasonable hope that a good man may be available and there is also a powerful inducement for each of several possible candidates to make himself better than his fellows. There are plenty of recent examples of the working of this excellent system by which talent and character are preferred to seniority. In Shinyanga, on the death of Chief Malingira of Busanda, his son Ng'honge was elected in his stead and not the eldest son, Ndugulile, who had shown bad character as regent during his father's illness. Chief Kidaha was preferred to two elder brothers with bad records. In Maswa, Chief Limbe of Itilima has an elder brother, who was not selected as chief by the 'Council of State' of that chiefdom for the single excellent reason that they thought Limbe would make a better chief. There are many such instances.

This freedom of choice for the 'Council of State' carries with it certain obvious dangers. One is that a weak chief may be chosen for the benefit of ambitious *banang'oma* who hope to dominate him and thereby profit themselves. Another is that inability to decide between two strong candidates might lead to the selection of a mediocre third—but this form of compromise is an unfortunate risk concomitant with free election by any system. A third danger is that of deadlock among the *banang'oma* themselves, though in such a case the village headmen are called in to broaden the electorate. Moreover, it must not be forgotten that the decision of the *banang'oma* is conveyed to the people at a vast gathering at which popular approval or disapproval is most clearly and unmistakably voiced. Thus the 'state councillors' know that their choice must not be influenced by personal considerations or they will have to answer to an angry mob. But, in the wavering scales of an election, there is one heavy weight which has not yet been described in this account. That is the wish of the dead chief himself. His will, if it has been expressed before his death, carries tremendous weight with the *banang'oma* and it is very improbable that anyone whom he had nominated as his heir would be disregarded by them. Unbeknown to the European Administration, Chief Makwaia of Busiha thus nominated Kidaha as his heir two years before his own death and it is probably on that account that no trouble was made by the elder sons on the occasion of Kidaha's installation. On the other hand, chiefs are generally reluctant to name their heirs; they fear that they lay themselves open to poisoning by the interested party or that some unpleasant action will be taken by those who are disappointed. A way of avoiding this difficulty is in use in Maswa and promises a fair measure of success: by it, each chief nominates his heir in a confidential letter addressed to the District Commissioner personally. Then, should there eventually be any dispute or deadlock the voice of the deceased chief can still speak with decisive effect. The final approval or veto, of course, still rests with Government, which would withhold recognition of an obviously unsuitable candidate.

General Considerations. Let us hope that the Native Administrations in the future will be judged by two great tests: their reasonable responsiveness to the ascertainable will of the people and their efficiency. It is important that they should not be too responsive. Public opinion is apt to blow hot and cold and good government should not be blown about by it. Here the Sukumaland system has great advantages in that the chiefs with reasonable security of tenure can carry through even unpopular reforms for the good of the country. The most frequent example is the construction of dams. No individual is delighted to turn out for ten days' work as the human animal is lazy, but the successful completion of some of the large dams has evoked remarkable expressions of gratitude from the people. The planting of cotton was at first unpopular; now it is a welcome source of cash income. Cattle sales too, from being a much resented war measure, have already become a customary monthly voluntary market.

It has been shown that the form of local African government practised in Sukumaland is not the autocratic form, which those who are ignorant of African custom sometimes assume it to be, but is in a real way conditioned by the needs and desires of the Sukuma people themselves. Is it also an efficient form of government?

In answering that question it must be borne in mind that the African local government of a peasant community must necessarily be a lightweight structure and not the top-heavy bureaucracy which administers advanced communities. Its paucity of officials and the cheapness dictated by its limited revenue mean that it will not grind as small as the governmental mill in a European industrialized country. That is to be expected and allowances made for it; nor is it a state entirely to be deprecated. Bureaucracy is unfortunately necessary in complicated communities but is to be avoided in simple ones. European standards are not the right measure of African conditions.

With due allowance for its lightweight structure an estimate may be made of the efficiency of native administration in Sukumaland. Perhaps the most important aspect of its work is the judicial. Without fair and honest courts all else fails and the peace and content of a whole area will turn on the certainty of quick and even justice. Every Administrative Officer knows that his best measuring-rod of the 'tone' of an area is the complaints, or the lack of them, which he receives about maladministration or delays in its courts. This is a test which Sukumaland administration passes with flying colours. The proof of the honesty of its justice is the comparative rarity with which decisions are reversed in higher courts and the proof of its speed is the rarity of the occasions on which the Administration has to intervene to secure the hearing of any particular case. It is in very few areas indeed that general conversation with the inhabitants will bring to light complaints about the conduct of the courts, although it is a subject on which any African is ready enough to talk. In general it may certainly be said that justice in the native courts is both quick and fairly administered.

Another valid test of the efficiency of the native administrative machine is its capacity to convey and to enforce its own enactments under the Native Authority Ordinance, and orders and instructions from Government. This we must judge by its capacity to carry out that which is unpopular but necessary, like the many measures in support of the war effort which had to be enforced in recent years. The strain of imposing them would have been utterly impossible for so comparatively light a machine, had it not real authority and support amongst the Sukuma people. There are other examples from peace-time. The uprooting and burning of cotton plants before the next planting season, once its value was understood by the chiefs, was vigorously enforced in the courts over a number of years. It has now become almost customary practice. Similarly, in Shinyanga District, at least, the uprooting of the *striga* weed is on its way to adoption as normal farming practice. These things can be done by the Native Administrations, which have shown an astounding capacity to shoulder new and often unpleasant burdens. Let it not be thought, however, that the people have no voice and cannot resist a measure initiated by the chief, which they do not consider to be just or *pro bono publico*. Besides the weapon of passive resistance, which is so effective against such a light administration, the *basumba batale* have occasionally voiced the will of the people and their voice can never be ignored.

There is one great imponderable factor in any discussion of the efficiency and potentialities of our present system of native administration and it would be foolish to close our eyes to it. That factor is the amount of influence which the presence of the British Government wields upon the day-to-day existence of the indigenous structure. Is it only the awesome weight of the *Serkali* in the background that lends its air of success and popular backing to the Native Authority? If that weight were suddenly lifted from the scales, would the system collapse or would a new freedom more than compensate for the lack of wise guidance? These are questions to which there are, as yet, no answers, but each man has his own reply, which will influence his assessment of the capabilities of the Sukumaland African form of local government. All that is certain is that the authority of Government must and does influence any judgement of the capabilities of native administration. In one important way this influence can plainly be detected. This is an enhancement of the power and importance of those officials whom Government has seen fit to adopt, and a pushing into the background of those indigenous authorities who have not been so recognized. The village headman and the *nsumba ntale* no longer bear to each other quite the same intimate relation as in the past. The one is the salaried official of the Native Authority; the channel by which all administration, European and African, is brought to the ordinary man. The other is the man of the people; the product of the village's own institutions. We must take great care that it does not come to be felt that these two men are upon two different 'sides'. It is probable, however, that the *basumba batale* will gain prestige as the leaders of village co-operative societies as the co-operative movement gains impetus and importance. The *banang'oma* present a similar case. They are still powerful, but it cannot be supposed they are quite so powerful as of old when they only draw the attention of European officers at the selection of a new chief.

Besides efficiency we must also consider adaptability, not only adaptability in relation to the increasingly complex problems of administration, but also adaptability in relation to the structure of the organization itself. With the march of progress, the spread of education and of a cash economy, a young intelligentsia will arise. Can and will the existing structure provide a place for the highly educated African? Must the house we have be burnt and replaced by another, or can a room be built on? Clearly for many years to come the educated African will be absorbed into the Civil Service either of Government or of the Native Administrations. More and more are urgently needed, but that is not the point. The crux of the matter is political and, however well the sons of chiefs are educated, there will come a time when a demand will arise for admission to candidacy for the post of chief and perhaps for a broadening of the franchise. Have we any indications as to how the people will react? We have. As yet they are but ripples on the water, but nevertheless they indicate the direction of the wind.

Lord Hailey has suggested that: '... we should consciously try out any expedient, not only the expedient of the Native Authority system, but any expedient, however novel, which promises to quicken the process of political education'.[1]

But political evolution is showing signs of remarkably rapid progress. I have already mentioned the tendency of the *banang'oma* to select the son of a chief. In doing so they are departing from traditional precedent. Now a further tradition has been broken by the unanimous appointment, with the acclamation of the people, of a complete outsider to the chiefdom, as Regent of Dutwa in Maswa. Previously regencies have been undertaken only by an uncle or other near relative during the minority of a young chief. Now we see an assistant secretary and treasurer to the federation appointed as regent on account of his education and well-proved character.

Clearly there is nothing to preclude further changes widening the choice of candidates for the post of chief. It would not surprise me to hear within a decade that the will of the people had been made known through their elected village leaders and the 'Council of State' and that a chief had been chosen from outside the normal lines of succession, on account of his education and character.

Sir Bernard Bourdillon has pointed out that:

Perhaps the most frequently made criticism of the native authority system is that which alleges that those who administer it tend to treat the native authority as a museum piece which must be carefully preserved in its original form. In practice there may occasionally be some justification for this criticism; in principle there is none. For even in Nigeria, where the native authority usually takes a shape which conforms pretty closely with tradition, it has frequently been laid down, and is clearly understood by all administrative officers, that conformity with tradition is not an end in itself. It is merely the means (and generally the most effective one) of securing the main aim—that of acceptability to the people themselves. Once they become dissatisfied with the traditional form, or realise that it is not altogether suited to modern conditions, a departure from tradition becomes not only permissible, but necessary. Among the newest native authorities in Nigeria, those in Lagos colony, there are several, devised by the people themselves, whose form has but slender foundations in local tradition, and elsewhere, among the older-established native authorities, there have of

[1] The Lord Hailey, G.C.S.I., G.C.M.G., G.C.I.E., 'Native Administration in Africa', *International Affairs*, July 1947.

recent years been many departures from tradition. The only essential thing about any innovation is that it must be either suggested by, or be unquestionably approved by, the people themselves. Native authorities must be dynamic in form and not static; they must be living organisms and not fossils.[1]

The term 'chief' has come to be associated in some people's minds with 'the noble savage'. A picture is conjured up of a befuddled old gentleman sitting on a stool and wearing long robes and strange ornaments. It is often suggested that in continuing to use them we are perpetuating an anachronism; preserving a museum in the guise of government. Nothing could be farther from the truth. There are some chiefs who appear befuddled old gentlemen to European eyes but often under an uncouth exterior they have great qualities of leadership, great sympathy and understanding for their people, and great wisdom. Even so the exterior is rapidly changing. The new generation of chiefs in Sukumaland is leading its people in both education and culture. The process of election is capable of change and will certainly undergo progressive modification in accordance with the needs and wishes of the people.

Encouraged to develop along indigenous lines, I have no doubt that African local government will steadily maintain and expand the position of advisors and councillors to include important citizens. This process is already visible in many parts of Tanganyika, where important traders, medical men, and other citizens of acknowledged standing are becoming more closely integrated with the machine of local government without regard to their educational qualifications. I feel it is of the utmost importance that evolution should not be coerced and that outside pressure based on ignorant assumptions should not be allowed to stampede us into interference with one of the most excellent and most democratic systems of government to be found anywhere today. Experience indicates only too clearly that a high level of academic attainments is no criterion whatever of good citizenship and no qualification to become a legislator. The most highly educated people in Great Britain are not necessarily to be found congregated in the Houses of Parliament, rather they may be sought in the Universities. It would be the gravest possible error to attempt to influence and mould the existing structure into an oligarchy of intelligentsia.

[1] Sir Bernard Bourdillon, K.C.M.G., 'The Future of Native Authorities', *Africa*, vol. xv, No. 3, July 1945.

The great town of Ibadan is in many ways one of the most progressive [in Nigeria] and its native authority enjoys a very considerable measure of responsibility in civil affairs. But its people manifested unforeseen dissatisfaction with the constitution of an Advisory Board recently set up for the express purpose of keeping the Native Authority in touch with public opinion. Although established with a laudable desire to secure the advice and help of the younger and more politically-minded elements of the community, it clearly out-ran the sentiments not only of the chiefs but also of the main body of the people. On further investigation and consultation with the various organisations in the town, it was found that something more nearly related to the traditional system of grouping and control would alone satisfy the people as a whole, and that attempts to ignore the influence of the chiefs would prove an obstacle to progress and even a danger to peace. This is a sharp reminder of the knowledge, patience and constant endeavour required to reconcile the demands of progress with loyalty to vigorous traditional institutions.[1]

The chiefs of Sukumaland are very much alive to the desirability of broadening the basis of popular representation and the Binza Federation of the Maswa District put forward proposals for the election by the *basumba batale* of representatives to accompany the Binza chiefs to the plenary sessions of the Sukumaland Federal Council. These proposals are still in the exploratory stage but the recognition by the chiefs of the desirability of such a form of popular representation leads one to ponder upon the possibility of the eventual evolution of even a two chamber system with the chiefs in the upper house.

I have already shown that, in selecting a new chief, the 'Council of State' act on behalf of the people. The village headmen may and often do help them in their choice which is subject to ratification by the people themselves at the huge inaugural gathering. This process also may change. There is nothing reactionary in the attitude of the Sukuma and no hidebound adherence to custom and tradition if an innovation appears to offer clear advantages.

The growth of a political institution is not likely to be spectacular in the absence of revolution and only close contact with the day-to-day administration can give an insight into the very real progress made during the last twenty years. The very fact of the existence of the Sukumaland Federation is not an isolated advance. It is the culmination of a steady process of mutual trust and

[1] Professor Daryll Forde, 'Social Development in Africa and the Work of the International African Institute', *J.R.S.A.*, 1945.

Local African Government

co-operative effort amongst the chiefdoms concerned and is, in itself, only a milestone on the road to further progress. Henry Morton Stanley passed through Sukumaland in 1875 and slept the night at Malya (now the headquarters of the Sukumaland Federation) on 22 February. That is only seventy-three years ago. A comparison of his description of the country and its people at that date with the resolutions of the Sukumaland Federal Council at its first meeting (extracts of both are included at pp. 146–9) provide a comparison giving a clear indication of the immense progress made. At no stage in the evolution of local government in Europe is there any comparable advance and I feel sure that, while advice and discussion in the normal course of educative supervision provided by the district administration should continue to assist evolution, we should guard against the effects of ill-considered external pressure.

Some of us have wondered whether the creation of the great Sukumaland Federation, which was suggested by the chiefs and elders of Sukumaland themselves, would tend to entrench the power of the chiefs and make it more difficult for the people to obtain the removal of a bad chief. Such experience as we have leads me to believe that this is not the case. Let me give concrete instances. When the misrule of Chief Chenge of Itilima came to a head, the 'Council of State' of Itilima brought their complaints against him before the Binza Federation which, after investigation, recommended his deposition. When the removal of Chief Mushuda of Dutwa was under consideration, the Executive Committee of the Binza Federation informed me that he had already been warned by the Federation and recommended the immediate withdrawal of recognition by Government, on the grounds that he was incorrigible and that a bad chief would bring the whole Native Administration into disrepute. Moreover, the Federation supported the appointment of its Assistant Secretary and Treasurer as Regent of Dutwa on grounds of suitability without a moment's hesitation about the breach of precedent. Consequently there is good reason for confidence that the existence of the Sukumaland Federation will do nothing to stifle the will of the people or to oppose the inevitable process of change and adaptation.

Lord Hailey has noted that: 'In the majority of the African colonies, we are working towards the creation of African States, with African Governments, under forms determined by local conditions, in which European control or guidance will diminish until it reaches a vanishing point.'[1] In any event the formation and consolidation of a larger unit of local government can only be advantageous and it in no way binds the future to the past in respect of the method of selection or election of the representatives of its constituent units who will form its council.

Have we then a form of government that is fit to last? It is suggested that this form of government has shown itself efficient; has risen during the war to demands far greater than those for which it might have been supposed to be ready, and may be believed to possess a resilience and an adaptability which will survive the impact of civilization. If it be asked whether it is democratic, it is suggested that it is a form of government quick to respond to public opinion and reliant on the people's favour. Granted this paramount consideration, it must also be admitted that a government of administrators, who are experienced because their lives are spent in the art of government, and whose interest it is to be good administrators if they are not to be forced to leave the stage, is not a bad system of government. Democracy has many forms; representative government as practised in Great Britain is one; it may not be audacious to suggest that Sukumaland has another.[2]

[1] The Lord Hailey, G.C.S.I., G.C.M.G., G.C.I.E., 'Native Administration in Africa', *International Affairs*, July 1947.
[2] Extracts relating to the constitution of the Sukumaland Federation from the minutes of the first plenary session of the Sukumaland Federal Council, Oct. 1946, pp. 145–9.

6

Sukumaland Problems

INTRODUCTORY NOTE

As I have mentioned in the preface, the first edition of this study contained a discussion of the problems of Sukumaland followed by recommendations. These recommendations, which were worked out in collaboration with Mr. J. G. M. King, Agricultural Officer, included *inter alia*, provision for the creation of an interdepartmental team of specialist officers and for funds with which to undertake the rehabilitation of Sukumaland. Those recommendations were accepted by Government; the team of experts is in being; funds in excess of £500,000 have been provided and therefore any recapitulation of those detailed recommendations would be superfluous, more particularly as the work of rehabilitation is now the responsibility of the Sukumaland team. Therefore, in place of the original concluding chapters, it is now only necessary to discuss various aspects of the main problems in so far as they influence, or are influenced by, the land tenure, land use, social structure, and customs of the people, thus bringing into focus the facts which have been set out in previous chapters.

It will be appreciated that this study is limited to the existing tenure and use of land and possible lines of agronomic development. I have excluded discussion of large-scale irrigation schemes, which might be practicable for such parts as the Manonga valley. Such projects are outside the scope of this study but irrigation is yet another means of extending the brief planting season and may ultimately be required.

POPULATION, LAND, AND PRODUCTION

The basic problem in Sukumaland, as in so many other relatively densely populated rural areas, is essentially one of population in relation to production. If the human and stock populations of Sukumaland were decreasing, then proportionately more land per head would become available and increase of production per head and per acre could be contemplated with equanimity as more land could still be rested as required. In effect, a rising standard of living could be confidently predicted for such a decreasing population.

But is not the exact opposite in fact happening? Is not every increase of production, brought about by improved methods of husbandry, improved strains of crops and the like, largely offset by loss of fertility resulting from increased population requiring additional land largely at the expense of fallow, so that no technical advance has yet produced an appreciable rise in the standard of living?

During the last century, prior to the beginning of European influence, the numbers of men and stock were kept in check by disease, famines, and inter-tribal wars. Arable agriculture, in the absence of cash crops, was confined to relatively limited areas. The system of shifting cultivation including a bush fallow, often as long as thirty years, coupled with the absence of efficient metal tillage implements, limited production but prevented major damage to the land. With the introduction of European security and science, however, the pre-existing balance has been upset. Medical and veterinary services have reduced mortality amongst human beings and stock; protection from war and famine has had similar results.

Now let us look at such indications as we have of population trends. From early German records it appears that the mainland population of the Mwanza, Maswa, and Kwimba Districts to the east of Smith Sound was approximately 400,000 in 1913 with well under 1,000,000 cattle. The human population of approximately the same area was some 600,000 in 1943: an addition of 50 per cent. in thirty years. Such figures as are available indicate that the cattle population has increased by about 75 per cent. since 1913 and the increase is becoming more rapid. Admittedly, statistics produced by the lightweight structure of early colonial administrations cannot be considered accurate. Nevertheless, all observers with any considerable experience of this area are agreed that the numbers of both human beings and domestic animals are in fact increasing rapidly and it is immaterial to this discussion of the problem whether the human population will double itself in forty, fifty, or sixty years.

While there is, then, no doubt of rapid population increase, what of production? As I have mentioned, the average annual cash income of an adult male taxpayer has risen from about Shs. 30/- in 1938 to more than double that figure today. Prices both of

Population, Land, and Production

imported goods and of produce have also risen sharply, so that the rise in average cash incomes is partly due to a fall in the value of the shilling. There is little evidence of any considerable net increase of production per head or per acre. Overall increases of production in Sukumaland are due rather to the increase of population and to increased cattle sales. In short, such rise in the standard of living as has taken place is at the expense of the land.

Assuming that the population is increasing at such a rate as to double itself in fifty years, to maintain the existing standard of living with the existing methods of husbandry the occupied area must be doubled in the same period. But as it is desired to raise the standard of living, the occupied area must be more than doubled in fifty years and/or the means of production must be improved by the introduction of farm mechanization and by better husbandry, thereby obtaining more per man and more per acre while at the same time maintaining soil fertility. In fact the provision of increased habitable area and improved means of production is a race against population increase.

The objective of Government is not only to maintain but also to raise the standard of living. Experience has shown that, in relation to a conservative peasant community and a very brief planting season, improvements in the means of production alone are not yet likely to provide an adequate margin over population increase. Government's fundamental land policy is therefore

(a) to improve methods and means of production as a matter of the greatest urgency,
(b) to open up new habitable land as quickly as possible, and
(c) to control the use of all lands, under the Natural Resources Ordinance (not only newly opened areas).

Thus, as Dr. Worthington points out in relation to Uganda

... the fundamental problem divides itself into two parts, first how to increase the output per head of African, and second how to remove the handicaps which render large areas unused or unusable, and to ascertain how these areas could be developed in the best interests of the inhabitants.... Since the standard of living cannot rise unless the income of the individual family rises ... the prime object should be a concentration on productive effort *to ensure that production increases rapidly, at a rate much higher than population.*[1]

[1] Dr. E. B. Worthington, *A Development Plan for Uganda*, Government Press, Entebbe, 1946.

That, then, is the outline of the basic problem in the briefest possible compass and I will now examine some of the numerous interrelated factors which go to make up the rural economy of this predominantly annual crop area.

LAND POLICY AND LAND TENURE

The German Government, when it first assumed sovereignty in Tanganyika, recognized all existing rights to land, individual or tribal, but took to itself all sovereign rights and all land to which no title could then be shown. The British Government stepped into the shoes of the Germans. Recognition of pre-existing titles was maintained, including titles granted by the Germans. The only real change was that the peculiarly English conception of freehold was introduced in place of the German conception of absolute ownership. The result was that the Crown became the ultimate owner of all land and, at the same time, the direct owner of all land to which no title would have been recognized by the German Government. So far as tribal land is concerned, there is therefore an academic distinction between land to which the British Government recognized a pre-existing tribal title and lands which the Crown, as direct owner, has subsequently permitted tribes to occupy.

African Land Rights. Below the level of this ultimate ownership of the Crown, traditional African land-holding custom will adjust itself to modern conditions and will be influenced by judicial decisions. This process of adjustment will hardly be affected by the existence of the superior ownership of the Crown. Experience indicates that where such ultimate ownership is seldom actively exercised, private rights may develop and may even take a highly crystallized form, *inter se*, notwithstanding the absence of written records of title.

It is, then, with these African customary land rights that we are primarily concerned. They are being indirectly affected by Government action; administrative officers in their everyday work are continually guiding decisions which have a cumulative effect on land tenure development. It is therefore necessary to consider the type of rural economy which it is desired to foster so that this influence may be based on a previously determined land policy.

Land Policy and Production. Clearly the main object of land policy must be to conserve and develop land resources as one of the

Land Policy and Land Tenure

primary means of raising the standard of living of the rural population. Within the purview of a comprehensive land policy lie such major requirements as the preservation of a salutary balance between such types of land use as forest, arable agriculture, and grazing, and the optimum form of utilization for each.

Besides these considerations there are yet more fundamental issues. Is the most economic unit of tropical production the individual peasant and his family in a system embodying the main features of a proprietary régime, or the organized village group of cultivators maintaining direct community control over the distribution of land, or some form of plantation system utilizing a measure of foreign capital and supervisory organization? If some form of plantation economy is considered preferable, should it be based on full plantation practice with the African as a paid labourer to begin with, or on a dual partnership between capital and a group of cultivators, or on a tripartite partnership such as that of the Gezira in the Sudan where cultivator, capital, and Government join in a large development project?

Until recently in Tanganyika there was no half-way house between the foreign plantation and African peasant agriculture which, however, lacked means of capitalization. Now experiments have begun with a dual partnership, Government supplying both the skilled organization and development funds.

Land Policy and Social Organization. In pondering issues such as these, the social aspects are no less important than the economic. The effects of land policy cannot be confined to the objective of increased efficiency in production. Inevitably they will affect the social organization so that policy should be conditioned to the promotion of only such efficiency of production as is compatible with the ordered progress of the community. Within the term social organization I include the political organization which is inextricably bound up with social structure. Were the land tenure of Sukumaland to evolve into a fully developed landlord system (which is a possible result of individual ownership) or into plantations employing large numbers of agricultural labourers, the resulting social and political structure would undoubtedly differ fundamentally from the structure which one could anticipate as a result of evolution along existing lines.

Policy, then, should take account of social and political structure. We are committed to a policy expressed by the Land Ordinance to pay due respect to the existing customary rights of the Africans which are to be 'assured, protected and preserved'. These customary rights were evolved to meet the conditions of a closed subsistence economy and are necessarily being modified to meet the new conditions which the impact of a wider economy has created.

Individualization. In tropical African conditions the development of more definite individual proprietary land rights is due to a variety of causes, the most important of which are:

(*a*) the introduction of permanent crops,
(*b*) pressure of population in restricted areas such as islands or mountains, and, to a lesser extent,
(*c*) economic development encouraging agricultural specialization particularly in the neighbourhood of urban centres.

Although bananas are grown along the Lake Victoria littoral and some of the major river systems, in general it may be said that conditions leading towards individualization are not marked in Sukumaland. Nevertheless, they are not entirely absent and it is therefore desirable to discuss briefly the advantages and disadvantages of individualization which is undoubtedly both a natural and a powerful movement engendered by the spread of education and a cash economy. The essence of proprietary systems is an individual right in land, which is not usually limited by conditions of effective occupation and which the right-holder is free to encumber or alienate. There can be no doubt of the value of the growth of a sense of individual right in the land, as an incentive to its improvement. Experience has, however, shown that individualization, although accompanied by certain definite advantages, may lead to developments prejudicial to both the social and economic life of the community. The danger actually arises only when the individual can transfer or encumber land at his pleasure. Such a development would mean that a community had lost its ultimate control over land, and the whole basis of the social and political structure of Sukumaland might well be undermined by the progressive acquisition of larger holdings by individuals resulting eventually in the appearance of a landless labourer class followed by rack renting, insecurity of tenure, agricultural debt, absentee landlordism, and all the familiar attendant evils.[1] As we have seen

[1] Cf. M. L. Darling, *The Punjab Peasant in Prosperity and Debt.*

Land Policy and Land Tenure

on a small scale in relation to personal grazing reserves, individualization might lead to the acquisition, by individuals or groups, of holdings in excess of the areas which they could beneficially occupy and also in certain parts fragmentation could produce holdings too small to support an adequate standard of living and too small for efficient farming.

Of all these evils, perhaps the most serious but, at the same time, the least imminent in Sukumaland conditions, is agricultural indebtedness, the far reaching effects of which can be seen in such countries as India, Egypt, and in some areas of the Colonial Empire including parts of Africa.

In the middle of the nineteenth century, when Maine's *Ancient Law* was written, it was axiomatic that individualization of land holding was the goal towards which civilization was moving. The same view could not pass unchallenged today. There is, indeed, no reason to suppose that the social and land organization evolved in Africa is inferior, in its own environment, to its European counterpart. The absence of litigation concerning land in such densely populated parts of Sukumaland as Busmao and Bukumbi, where village tenure exists (and shifting cultivation including a bush fallow has long since disappeared), compares favourably with the difficulties experienced in areas where individualization has begun.

Legislation, to mitigate the damage caused by individualization and agricultural indebtedness, may attempt to restrict the right of transferring or encumbering land or may limit the right of transfer to certain classes of people or may subject transfers to official sanction in order to try to control the size of land holdings and particularly to obviate fragmentation. It may also regulate the relations of landlords and tenants. Such legislation is, however, likely to be opposed by vested interests and its implementation might well require a costly and complex organization out of proportion to the means of any local African government which can yet be envisaged here. In industrialized countries the results of individualization have been mitigated by the absorption of landless labourers into industry. In African conditions, however, the adequate development of such a palliative cannot be anticipated within measurable time. Moreover, the formal creation of individual title might not only be premature in existing economic conditions, but might also impugn the validity of customary tenures, and there are areas where the formal creation of individual title would be likely to arouse African fears that their land was to be used as a basis for taxation. The seriousness of this difficulty is indicated by experience in India.

Sukuma Land Tenure Development. Thus the problem in Sukumaland is how to enable the community to retain at least such minimum powers over land as are essential to obviate the deleterious consequences which could attend the growth of exclusive individual rights, while permitting such a measure of individual development under adequate community control as may be essential to an ordered economic advance.

With this end in view, let us then examine the existing Sukumaland system of land tenure to assess its suitability for development and to consider what modifications may be required to provide scope for economic advance. Sukuma land tenure can be summarized as a system based on the village group of peasants. In essence it consists of individual land rights limited to the period of effective occupation, restricted as regards rights of transfer, controlled in relation to succession, and collectively forming the village unit of occupancy. Subject to the overriding needs of the community, it does not involve insecurity for the cultivator. It therefore presents no difficulties in the way of concentrating, though not of accumulating holdings. Those few who have taken to the plough provide examples of the ease with which a compact holding may be obtained. At present fragmentation cannot occur, though the multiplicity of soil types and the custom of lending land may give to field distribution the erroneous appearance of fragmentation.

Experience in Sukumaland shows that exclusive individual control of pasture land causes endless trouble. It is now generally accepted that some form of rotational grazing is highly desirable for the maintenance of fertility in grass-land, but rotation on individual pastures could only be organized by staked grazing or by the construction of fences or hurdles. Supervision would be more difficult, and litigation is a normal corollary of individual grass-land management, more especially in areas where stock have to trespass in search of water. Thus, there are very considerable advantages in the system of village control. As I have mentioned, arable land, in this annual crop area, is half-year land, so that village pasture control covers the whole village during half the year and perhaps three-quarters of the area for the whole year, and so enables arrangements to be made for rotational use, resting, deferred grazing and the like in the best interests of all the arable, fallow, and pasture lands of the unit.

Existing village land tenure not only avoids the dangers which flow from the unrestricted rights of encumbering or transferring land, but is also susceptible to modification to meet the needs of changing economic conditions. It does not prevent the eventual development of a proprietary régime, whereas individual ownership, once established, can only be controlled or modified at the risk of serious social and economic dislocation. Monetary rents, which may follow the adoption of individual ownership and the spread of a cash economy, show little elasticity in periods of falling prices. A comparison of the history of the world economic depression here and in India, where, in the United Provinces, for example, rents had to be drastically reduced by State intervention, indicates that there are many advantages in the Sukumaland system which permits the peasant to benefit from high prices while remaining relatively little injured by a falling market.

Finally, as Lord Hailey has said, it must be noted that the advantages held to be inherent in individualization are not necessarily to be obtained only by vesting rights in the individual. There are some types of land occupation, such as those which occur in sparsely populated areas, growing annual crops, which may make the family group the most suitable economic unit in cultivation. In such areas as Sukumaland, however, the village group, being the smallest permanent geographical and social unit in relation to land, and containing an indigenous co-operative organization, is clearly the optimum stock on which to graft improvements.

Sir George Campbell's summing up on this point in relation to the Punjab is equally applicable here.

... by the indigenous system ... the Government is enabled at once to deal with the body of the cultivators, and to acknowledge and enlarge their rights, to the satisfaction of the people and the advantage of the Administration. It can do this without incurring the much more serious evils and drawbacks which have always been found to attend the attempt of a great foreign government to deal separately with each petty holder.[1]

A relatively static agriculture is necessary to the preservation of soil fertility, and security of tenure is necessary to a balanced

[1] Sir George Campbell, K.C.S.I., M.P., 'The Tenure of Land in India'.

husbandry, but it would be a grave mistake to suppose that individual ownership is a *sine qua non* without which security of tenure cannot exist. In fact, the Sukumaland system can give greater security, and therefore more incentive to improvement, than is often associated with a landlord and tenant régime.

Here, then, we have a most valuable indigenous African system of land tenure which can stand comparison with any to be found elsewhere. It provides the individual with adequate security and, at the same time, avoids all those evils which derive from the absence of community control. What then is required to enable this indigenous system to meet the foreseeable needs of rural development?

One of the strongest arguments in favour of individual alienable title is that, in the ordinary way, capital is raised against the security of a saleable title. Individual borrowing, however, is neither the only nor necessarily the best means of capitalizing agriculture and indeed capitalization in some form by the community on co-operative lines or by Government or by the Native Administration, appears a more probable line of development and will be discussed further.[1]

It has been suggested that the most important matter not yet covered by indigenous practice is the provision of compensation for unexhausted improvements. Any efforts to restrict individual rights to a purely usufructory tenure would be doomed to ultimate failure in an area where there is some pressure on land resources, where some permanent crops are grown, and where education and propaganda are directed towards the construction of improved and more permanent houses. In the circumstances of Sukumaland I should emphasize that the only 'improvements' with which we are yet concerned are semi-permanent houses and permanent crops such as bananas and fruit or fuel trees. Thus, unless some arrangement can be made for the payment of compensation on behalf of the community for such improvements as may have been effected by the occupier, he will either make no improvements or will eventually be driven to obtain such compensation by direct sales. As I have pointed out such sales of improvements by individuals would, in the first instance, separate the proprietary rights in these improvements from the usufructory rights in the land itself. In theory, the village community could admit sales of the proprietary

[1] pp. 127–30.

Land Policy and Land Tenure

rights in improvements and retain direct control of land allocation; but in practice it would be difficult if not impossible to deny the use of the garden to the buyer of the house. Thus, direct sales of improvements would undoubtedly form a challenge to the community's control of land allocation.

The crux of the matter is the immense value of the existing system whereby the community through the village headman, working in collaboration with the representative of the people, retains complete control of land allocation. Thus, improvements of land use such as contour hedges, strip cropping, village woods, and the like can be instituted as and when required with infinitely less difficulty than would be the case were land to be held on individual alienable title.

When an individual takes up a farm, the thought of moving does not occur to him and the compensation for such improvements as he may make is the increase in the products of the land which he will enjoy. But a few illicit sales of improved houses in the neighbourhood of alien settlements have taken place. To replace the need for these sales it would clearly be an inestimable advantage to retain the interim period between the outgoing and the incoming individual occupiers, during which time the land and its improvements are directly in the possession of the community, when the land can be reallocated for other uses or the opportunity taken to increase or diminish the size of holdings. But to retain this opportunity the local organization, perhaps as agent of the Native Treasury or a union of primary co-operative societies, must be prepared to pay compensation to the outgoing occupier for the improvements which he is leaving behind him and which are either his property or the product of his work.

At present the village organization has no means or arrangements for the payment of compensation for improvements which can only be abandoned or the subject of illicit sales. The problem is therefore to find means of encouraging development by providing for compensation without losing the invaluable asset of land allocation control. It has therefore been suggested that Sukuma land tenure is now at the cross-roads. If the village, acting on behalf of an organization covering the whole area, can arrange payments for improvements, the existing type of land tenure should be enabled to evolve on lines adequate to provide for the needs of development. If no such provision can be made, then, bearing in mind the necessarily lightweight structure of the Native Administration, individual sales of house property, trees, and other permanent improvements will inevitably become more numerous and will cumulatively lead to the establishment of customary exclusive individual rights in the land itself. These are the cross-roads but there are no signposts for the people, as neither they nor the Native Administrations themselves have any knowledge of the alternatives before them or of the means available to them of maintaining and expanding their own existing system in order to avoid the pitfalls of exclusive individualization which I have already outlined.

Should it prove possible to organize a 'village chest' as agent for the Native Treasury or a union of such primary co-operative units, perhaps related to the village grain stores which exist in some areas, this would form theoretically the best solution, as thereby all property could continue to revert to the community and all compensation could be paid by the community with no direct vendor/purchaser relationship. Where numerous sales, transfers, and mutations on inheritance are taking place in any area, the appearance of the parties to obtain sanction for a prearranged sale gives little or no opportunity to the community to control the size of holdings or the form of land use. In practice, the tendency would be to accord approval almost automatically until such time as either unduly large land holdings or extreme fragmentation became serious. To maintain adequate control it is therefore essential for the community actually to enter into possession of the land between the outgoing and incoming occupiers. At this stage it is possible either to subdivide a large holding or to amalgamate smaller holdings in accordance with the desiderata of the land and its beneficial use in relation to the rural economy and the standard of living of the area concerned.

There are, nevertheless, obvious objections to the payment of compensation by the community which, however, are mainly mechanical. In the first place, the organization would certainly need to be at the village level in order to provide an intimate knowledge of values and of movements. Clerical staff and accounting arrangements would be required. Secondly, funds would be needed not only to meet the initial cost, as payments would precede sales, but also to meet an almost certain recurrent loss which seems an inevitable consequence of community control. Thirdly, the danger of corruption is inescapable. These organizational difficulties are

Land Policy and Land Tenure

very real and may indeed prove insuperable. If so, the next best solution would perhaps lie in the community retaining a right of pre-emption; but a right of pre-emption in the circumstances of Sukumaland would be unlikely to have a greater effect in practice than arrangements for the approval of prearranged sales. Moreover, it would require virtually the same organization and it would not be likely to be exercised before maldistribution of land became serious.

While, as a result of this study, I am very deeply impressed with the immense value of the existing land tenure, particularly from the point of view of assuring beneficial land utilization, yet the problems attendant upon any attempt to graft on to it provision for compensation for unexhausted improvements may well prove insoluble and, in default of far-sighted and determined leadership, an increasing measure of individualization appears inevitable.[1]

LAND UTILIZATION

In order to examine the implications of the basic problem of population, land, and production, it is necessary to consider land utilization in relation to the social structure and customs of the people.

What forms should land occupation take? Is agronomic specialization desirable, that is to say, should arable agriculture, forests, and animal husbandry tend to occupy different areas, thus leading to specialized agricultural communities, large forests, and pastoralists operating an African ranching industry? Alternatively, should endeavours be made to keep cattle and crops together, to encourage mixed farming with village woods rather than regional forests? On the answers to questions such as these will depend the social and economic picture of tomorrow. The maintenance of soil fertility is the *sine qua non* of land use, because, if the planned use of all lands were to succeed in maintaining and improving soil fertility, then most of the more serious rural problems would be solved.

A dense rural population, *per se*, is not an evil, provided that the land is used in such a way that soil fertility is not diminished and

---

[1] Since writing this I have learned of the introduction of 'Planned Group Farming' into the Nyanza Province of Kenya and, as this system may well provide a means of retaining the best of what we have while gaining the best of what we know, a note on it is included in the appendix, p. 210.

that the standard of living consequent upon the level of production of an agricultural community can be raised and ultimately maintained. Thus 'over-population' and 'over-stocking' are not really separate problems and are in fact misnomers for malutilization of land, because, were the dense population to employ a balanced husbandry with manuring, fallowing, and anti-soil-erosion methods of cultivation and thus maintain soil fertility, no damage and no problem would result. It follows, therefore, that the maintenance of soil fertility is a basic problem of which the remainder are but facets.

Much has been written on the various component subjects of over-population, over-stocking, and soil erosion, but were they to be dealt with separately the results might well fail to combine to bring about a fundamental improvement in land utilization. For example, if the problem of 'over-stocking' were to be met by measures resulting in a considerable decrease in the stock population of Sukumaland, any such reduction might well deprive the country of adequate supplies of farmyard manure, as there are none too many cattle in Sukumaland for this purpose at present.

'Over-stocking' can be more accurately termed regional 'maldistribution' and some redistribution of stock is undoubtedly necessary, but were vast new areas to be provided, unlimited by considerations of the general requirements of a balanced husbandry, it is possible that an unduly large percentage of the cattle would be removed from the neighbourhood of the arable land. Properly organized resting periods under grass fallow were generally accepted as perhaps the most important means of restoring and maintaining fertility and soil crumb-structure, but more recent scientific investigation in Sukumaland has established that here the use of farmyard manure is an even more valuable means of increasing the supply of plant nutrients, so that there is much to be said for a balanced system of mixed farming as a means of achieving the maximum productive capacity.

It is axiomatic that in the conditions of a rural economy such as those which obtain in Sukumaland, some pressure of population is one of the primary factors inducing the adoption of improved and more intensive methods of agriculture. Thus it is even conceivable, though admittedly improbable, that the reclamation of unused lands might proceed unduly rapidly and induce a reduction of population pressure below the level at which improved

Land Utilization

methods are economic while retaining sufficient pressure to continue the process of soil fertility destruction.

It follows that any suitable solution must contain co-ordinated measures for the general improvement of the whole corpus of rural economy, to avoid the dangers inherent in any differential treatment of what is clearly the indivisible problem of land utilization.

Land Occupation

The optimum form of land occupation for any particular part of Sukumaland will depend primarily on soils and topography. For example, there can be no better use for the rocky granite outcrops than as forest reserves under regenerating bush cover, since these 'granitic inselbergs' are useless for arable agriculture and could only be grazed or rather browsed by goats. But, if so denuded of their natural vegetal cover, the run-off from them would accelerate erosion on the lower slopes. That, however, is an extreme and obvious case. Most of Sukumaland is generally suitable in varying degrees for man and stock or could be made so, primarily by the construction of additional watering points.

But the technical advances in methods of husbandry are being largely offset by reductions in resting periods due to the increased land requirements of an expanding population, so that in undulating country which is susceptible to erosion and contains dense populations and numerous cattle, the damage which is being done to soil fertility is beyond question. In these areas the density is too great to permit the practice of bush fallowing which is common in areas of relatively sparse population. As long resting periods under regenerating vegetation restore soil fertility, it is in these relatively densely populated areas that the problem, not only of improving the condition of the people but even of maintaining their present standards, is becoming critical. In Sukumaland the degree of fertility losses in both arable and pasture lands is directly related to the local topography, water distribution, and the incidence of human and animal populations. In the case of arable land, deterioration is aggravated by bad husbandry. This is illustrated by the fact that the Ukiriguru Experimental Station achieves, even with the hand-hoe, a production three or four times greater than that of neighbouring peasant farms. Also, the physical damage to the soil by cattle while feeding on weeds and crop residues during the dry season paves the way (in the absence of tie-ridging) for the first rains to accelerate erosion and to complete the list of destructive agencies. Moreover, it is in the most favourable areas, with the heaviest populations, where an increase in cultivated land has taken place to provide for economic crops, that losses of soil fertility are most serious and the level of production is falling in land which the decrease of fallow has deprived of adequate resting periods. But the semi-parasitic weed *striga helmonthica* has some influence in the reverse direction in that, by reducing yields of sorghums, it induces the people to abandon land at an earlier stage than they would otherwise consider necessary.

The deterioration of grass-land is due to over-grazing, excessive trampling, with consequent sheet erosion where pasture management is still unsatisfactory. Further, even where improved methods of management exist, the maldistribution of water leads to cattle tracks which are sometimes as much as 300 yards wide and up to fifteen miles long and cause both sheet and donga erosion. The term 'over-grazing' is often used to denote the physical effects of heavy stocking on the soil itself rather than on the pasture grasses. It must be borne in mind, however, that the Busiha system of rotational grazing,[1] where it exists, is well suited to local circumstances. It is undoubtedly capable of maintaining the grass-land in good condition by keeping down unpalatable weeds and regenerating bush, and the resulting short grass pasture is unsuitable for ticks and is therefore inimical to east coast fever, heartwater, and other tick-borne diseases of stock. Experience has shown that pastures which are sufficiently grazed to European standards tend to become coarse and unpalatable and that relatively heavy stocking, in default of hay-making, is a satisfactory method of maintaining a good herbage.[2] The Busiha system is therefore a very valuable stock on to which to graft improvements in grass-land management.

But the salient fact remains that the densely populated parts of Sukumaland are carrying a greater population than the present system of husbandry can support without detriment to the land, and in consequence land degradation results.

Improved Husbandry

As we have seen, the balance which obtained before European penetration has been upset. Land is being damaged as a result of

[1] pp. 76-77.
[2] See footnote concerning heavy stocking as a method of rough grazing reclamation in England, p. 78.

Land Utilization

the continuation of an anachronistic system of husbandry. The increasing population requires more land, mainly at the expense of resting periods. What, then, are the prospects of restoring the balance by improving the methods and means of husbandry and what are the prospects of gaining time by the expansion of the habitable land for the redistribution of population in order to reduce pressure in the critical areas?

For many years the need for medical and veterinary work has been recognized and these services have been making steady progress. It has been much less easy to appreciate that every advance in the sphere of these services has aggravated the ultimate problem by enabling more rapid population increases to take place. The time has now come, however, when an agricultural revolution is essential, for all observers are agreed that the existing system of husbandry cannot maintain much longer even the present standard of livelihood of the people.

Methods. Here, it is no longer necessary to discuss in detail all the pros and cons of the various methods of improving husbandry which have been advocated from time to time.[1] Besides numerous improvements of relatively minor importance the three main innovations required to raise the standard of husbandry are tie-ridging (known as basin listing in the U.S.A.), manuring, and improved grass-land management.

From the point of view of the introduction of tie-ridging into general practice on the higher and lighter soils, land tenure is of little importance though even here community land control would be a help. Manuring also is little dependent on land holding custom and the primary problems connected with it are making and transport, which are discussed in connexion with farm mechanization.[2] The custom of borrowing animals makes it possible for anyone desirous of obtaining manure to acquire the means of so doing; for, while the animal and its progeny, dead or alive, are the property of the owner, the by-products such as milk and manure (at present used for fuel in some parts) are the perquisite of the herdsman or borrower. As has been seen, the adoption of manuring will not cause owners to recall their animals which are out on loan, as considerations of herding remain unaltered and disease often makes it advisable to avoid keeping the whole herd in one place.

Now the introduction of proved methods of better husbandry,

[1] p. 142.   [2] pp. 130-1.

such as contour grass strips, contour hedges, and rotational grazing, would be much more easily effected and supervised if they could be laid out over considerable areas, and this would be facilitated if the existing system of community control of land allocation could be maintained. Therefore, the urgent need for the introduction of such methods is an additional argument in favour of dealing only with the village group rather than with the individual.

Where necessity presses, the progressive farmer leads the way, as Arthur Young did in England, but in this country it is desirable to introduce reform prior to the development of conditions which would constitute necessity in African eyes. Thus if improved methods are to make adequate progress they must come to the village group through constituted authority and the leaders of society. As we have seen, the village is the smallest permanent geographical and social unit of which the head exercises the delegated powers of the chief in relation to land. The village community is self-contained and, in effect, an embryonic co-operative body with a well-developed system of collective labour and collective bargaining. Therefore it is through this specific channel of traditional authority that the approach lies to the development of the rural economy of Sukumaland.

Means

The Hand-hoe. Only in exceptional circumstances, such as in conjunction with permanent crops or irrigation, when the time factor is not so pressing, could the hand-hoe support more than a subsistence economy. In Sukumaland conditions of soil and rainfall, its days as practically the only implement of cultivation are surely numbered. Here the arable acreage is restricted, not only by the limited strength of human beings but also, for all crops with a long growing period, by the very limited duration of the best planting season which is coincident with the short rains during about six weeks in November and December. To obtain the maximum yield, cotton should be planted in November. To obtain the maximum food supply, hard sorghums should also be planted at or before the beginning of the short rains. Food must have priority and, therefore, most of the cotton crop is not planted until much too late. Only a very small percentage of Sukumaland soil types can be dry-cultivated with a hand-hoe before the onset of the rains. Most cultivable areas must await the softening effect of the first few

Land Utilization

showers. The heavy lands are like concrete when dry and like glue when wet, so that the period during which they can be hoed is extremely brief.

Time is crucial, and where the people have to grow every mouthful of food, build and repair their own houses and stockyards, make their own hoe-handles, cooking pots, winnowing baskets, food stores, mortars, and indeed everything they use, with the exception of a few cotton clothes and the iron heads of their hoes, they have a very small margin of time available for increased production.

We have found from experience that increased attention paid to 'cash' crops inevitably reacts to some extent on the food harvest, so that a *démarche* becomes necessary, as food must come first. The standard of living can only be raised if the percentage of the available time, surplus to requirements for subsistence, can be increased, and this balance can then be devoted to production for export or exchange. Assuming that 100 time units are available to the African, say 90 are now used for subsistence. How can we achieve a substantial reduction of this percentage required for subsistence, leaving say 40 or 50 units available with which to raise the standard of living?

The revolutionary rise in the nation's income in Great Britain followed the Industrial Revolution. The high standard of living in the United States of America is closely related to the high degree of mechanization which increases production per worker to a higher level than that which obtains in Great Britain or Germany. Therefore, from experience elsewhere in the world it would appear that if we are to inaugurate any major improvement we must look for some revolutionary innovation which can increase the production per head of the population without upsetting existing social structure and so bringing chaos in its wake.

The following summary of the position, written by Sir John Hathorn Hall with reference to Uganda, is equally applicable here:

> . . . if not to-day then to-morrow, larger individual holdings will become necessary both to allow for the conservation of soil fertility by rotational resting under grass (. . . to restore the crumb structure of the soil) and to permit of an increased cash return to the cultivator; and I have mentioned that this will not be practicable unless human labour can be supplemented by the use of mechanical implements. These implements (ploughs, rotary hoes and the like) are at present beyond the means of the peasant cultivator, and even on an enlarged holding would

be idle much of the year and therefore uneconomical. This suggests communal ownership, and that in turn suggests co-operative societies for primary producers. ... These co-operative societies, which in turn would be linked to co-operative unions which would take care of the local storage and marketing of agricultural produce, could obtain, maintain and lend to their members the agricultural plant and equipment without which larger holdings would not be a practical proposition.[1]

Implemental Tillage. With the growing demands of a cash economy it is inevitable that implemental tillage must make progress. Ox-drawn ploughs are already on sale to individuals, but the spread of their use has been delayed by the fact that the Sukuma are not good at handling and training cattle and there is some prejudice against the use of oxen for work. Let us then examine the impact of the use of the plough on society.

In the hands of individuals it has many dangers:

1. As a larger area can be cultivated, the increase tends to be at the expense of fallow or pasture, thus diminishing the resting period in arable land or intensifying the problems of regional maldistribution of stock.

2. Experience in Northern Rhodesia has shown that the introduction of ploughs prior to the establishment of customary contour cultivation can cause serious fertility loss by accelerating erosion.

3. The man-power that is sufficient for ploughing an increased area is insufficient for weeding or harvesting and therefore paid labour must be used or other implements purchased. In the absence of a landless labourer class, those who use ploughs and paid labour tend to become richer and those who work for them spend correspondingly less time in their own fields. This process is substantially the same as that already taking place on a small scale as a result of collective work by the dance societies.[2]

While the differentiation of a hitherto undifferentiated society may well be inevitable with the advent of a cash economy, any sudden and unnatural acceleration likely to produce dislocation is clearly undesirable. Native Treasury or Government advances to individuals were condemned by Mr. Harrison[3] as a serious impediment to progress. They not only create a load of debt, which experience in the Union of South Africa and Nigeria indicates to

[1] H.E. the Governor of Uganda in the Foreword to *A Development Plan for Uganda*, Government Press, Entebbe, 1946.   [2] p. 42.
[3] E. Harrison, C.M.G., formerly Director of Agriculture, Tanganyika.

The water-holes at Ng'wajijenge in Busule

Maldistribution of water leads to cattle-tracks

The late Chief Makwaia and one of his surface-water catchment tanks

Panicum and *cynodon* pasture in rich flat land

Land Utilization

be irrecoverable without inflicting serious hardship in periods of depressed produce prices, but also in such circumstances the erroneous impression of an endless source of supply is inevitable. It has been suggested that provision must be made to finance graduate pupil farmers so that oxen and implements can be purchased. As will have been seen from the foregoing chapters, the number of men who do not own cattle and could not borrow the animals required is not great in Sukumaland. The collective purchase of implements on the lines of the collective purchase of cream separators in Busmao, would naturally obviate any necessity for advances to individuals, together with all the concomitant disadvantages of debt and dislocation of society.

In some parts of Sukumaland such as the Nyanza Federation the area actually under cultivation has already been extended to the limit and therefore any innovation likely to cause a further increase, particularly on the higher and lighter lands, will require most careful study with a view to the institution of adequate safeguards, at least until the universal use of manure and anti-soil-erosion cultivation methods are firmly established practices.

The 'go-slow' policy adopted in Nigeria and Nyasaland with regard to the introduction of ox-drawn ploughs has much to recommend it and the Sukumaland Native Authority, being alive to these dangers, has introduced local legislation for the control of ploughing. Should the use of the ox-drawn plough by individuals become general the supervision of perhaps 100,000 units to obviate soil damage would be an enormous task. But the use of ox-drawn ploughs by individuals does not alone appear likely to improve the means of production sufficiently rapidly to outpace the increase of population.

Mechanical Cultivation. Tie-ridging, which is the most important method of moisture conservation and erosion control, may need to be done mechanically if a really high standard of cultivation is to be established. Moreover, the first signs of a demand for mechanical cultivation, using tractors, has made its appearance. If this demand grows and is met, what effects could we anticipate in relation to land tenure and social structure? For the sake of discussion we may take it that the actual purchase of tractors and tractor-drawn cultivation implements by individuals is improbable on any appreciable scale within measurable time. We may therefore assume that arrangements will be required to provide mechanical implements for hire to individuals or groups. Obviously the easier approach would be to hire tractors and implements to individuals. Should such a practice develop, it will inevitably have the disadvantages already mentioned in connexion with individualization and ox-drawn implements. What, then, is the alternative?

As we have seen, in most villages in Sukumaland a co-operative organization of the working age group exists. In a considerable number of villages, particularly in the south of Sukumaland, this village co-operative, besides working for members, cultivates a village field. The proceeds of this field are used for social insurance—securing a food supply for the old, the sick, and the unfortunate, such as those who happen to have their houses and food reserves burnt—while the balance is shared by the villagers.

It should be possible to arrange for the mechanical cultivation of these village fields and for their extension to cover a very considerable percentage of the main grain crops of the people. Thus, one could envisage perhaps 1,000 village fields throughout Sukumaland mechanically cultivated on contract for the village societies and mostly situated in the flatter and heavier valley lands. Though admittedly more difficult to organize initially, such an arrangement would have the following advantages:

1. Many of these grain fields could be dry-cultivated at almost any time during the dry season after the preceding harvest and after the grazing or removal of crop residues. This would mean that the vast majority of the hard sorghum crops could be in at the best possible time and ready to germinate with the planting rains.

2. Individuals, with their main staple already planted, would be in a position to start planting cotton immediately at the beginning of the rains without fear of jeopardizing their food supply by so doing. With cotton planted early, up to double the crop should be obtainable without increasing acreage and the way would thus be cleared for planting groundnuts at the optimum time in December and January.

3. Supervision of perhaps a thousand large village fields would be relatively simple as, although the area involved would be about the same, individually owned ox-drawn plough cultivation would normally be sited on lighter soils and would therefore be less concentrated and would entail approximately a hundred times the number of units on more easily erodable lands.

4. Existing village organization would require no modification

Land Utilization

to undertake, after cultivation, harvesting, storage, and distribution amongst individual householders. It would merely require expansion to cover, not one relatively small field, but one large field approximately equal in area to the total pre-existing grain fields of the village unit.

To take advantage of years of good rainfall and as an insurance against bad years, the existing village grain stores could also be extended *pari passu* with such other territorial and provincial measures for grain storage as are being taken. The village stores would thus assure the local food supplies. It is clearly advantageous to have local storage under the control of the producers' own elected representatives in order to minimize transport.

5. The use of implements either owned or hired by the village would eventually make a larger variety available than any one peasant could himself afford and would also assure that full use is made of each. In both Europe and America it is becoming increasingly unusual for any one farmer to own all the plant which mechanized farming requires.

6. The soil map of south central Sukumaland[1] shows the very large percentage of the whole area which consists of the heavier soil types which are difficult to cultivate with the hand-hoe or with ox-drawn ploughs but which could take their place in the arable-pasture rotation if cultivated with relatively heavy tractor-drawn implements.

Of these advantages perhaps the most important is that of making the best possible use of the brief planting season. Increased cotton yields alone due to timely husbandry should more than meet the increased cost of mechanical cultivation, while the earlier planting of subsidiary crops such as groundnuts should contribute to raising the standard of living.

It is not within the scope of this study to discuss all the technical details involved in progress towards the capitalization and mechanization of agriculture. It must suffice to draw attention to the advantages which would accrue were it found possible to graft development on to the existing stock of the village community organization. The existing village co-operative has, as yet, little contact with Government and is consequently shy. Elsewhere I have mentioned the dangers to the social structure which might arise as a result of Government contact being confined to the hierarchy

[1] Facing p. 175.

of the chief and his representative, the village headman.[1] Here then, by the introduction of planned group farming, perhaps using the village as the group, is an opportunity of integrating the people and their elected village representatives with the inevitable march of economic progress. With the simpler alternative of using the individual rather than the group, the consequent probability of a breakdown in the existing excellent system of land tenure would be inescapable.

Transport and Manure. On the farm and within the village, transport is still by head porterage. A small fraction of inter-village grain transport is done by pack donkey. Pack freight is high as, recently, the hire of five donkeys for one day's work cost one heifer. Away from the roads there is, as yet, no wheel in the agronomy of Sukumaland. Nigerian experience illustrates that manuring is a prerequisite to the introduction of other essential features of a balanced practice of mixed farming and is the basis of all good husbandry.

The advantages of manuring particularly on the higher and lighter soils can be summarized as follows:

1. Manuring increases the yield per acre not only of crops but also of stover and so augments the dry season feed for stock.

2. Increased yields would reduce the necessity for clearing bushland and much poor land could be rested, thus producing something of the same effect as a redistribution of population.

3. Land in good heart will yield larger crops even in years of short rainfall, thus reducing the risk of famine.

Although the huge increases[2] in production from good manuring are well known, head porterage of manure infringes too greatly on the time available to be worth-while in the eyes of the African, except in the most densely populated pockets on the most impoverished soils. Ukara Island in Lake Victoria, and also southwest Sukumaland, where manuring was practised during the period of pre-European congestion, show that dire necessity will cause the people to manure their land. But it is necessary to find a way to introduce manuring before the soil has reached this impoverished state. To do this in areas where conditions have not yet compelled

[1] p. 101.
[2] Applications of from three to five tons of manure per acre have given yield increases of up to 300 per cent. on some of the lighter soils—Mwanhala Native Administration Farm, Northern Nzega, 1937-8. Moreover the residual effects are considerable for more than four years.

the African to take action on his own initiative by head porterage, it is necessary to find a labour-saving method which he will adopt. In any case propaganda during the last ten years has not yet succeeded in securing the general introduction of manuring by head transport and efforts to use pack oxen have also failed for various reasons.

Therefore it seems that any general use of manure must await the introduction of the wheel, perhaps in the form of the wheelbarrow which would facilitate the transport of stover to the stockyards and manure to the fields.

In 1944 the Native Authority of Bukumbi Chiefdom made an ox-cart and oxen available, free of charge, for carting manure. It was used in conjunction with the village associations and was successful in so far as the stockyards in several villages were emptied of manure. Cost and maintenance were the major difficulties. Steel wheelbarrows look more promising as the Sukuma like using them and, being single track, they can be used on existing footpaths.

In any event, if the wheel can be introduced into general use in order to expedite transport and if, as a result, manuring can be adopted at an earlier stage, the wheel can contribute substantially to the production of more per man and more per acre, which in turn gains time in the race against population increase and could help materially towards raising the standard of living.

It is even arguable that it would pay the community to subsidize the introduction of wheelbarrows for the first few years in order to get their use recognized and established as customary practice.

RESETTLEMENT

Redistribution. The expansion of the occupied area has been going on steadily ever since the early days of European penetration. The increasing population has been spreading not only into adequately watered bush areas and along the major river systems but also into land which had been occupied long ago and which had reverted to a long term bush fallow. The conscious effort to accelerate redistribution by facilitating the movement across Smith Sound and by the provision of water supplies in hitherto waterless areas, began in about 1934 and, from 1941, the construction of numerous surface-water catchment works by the Native Authority in the Maswa District made some 500 square miles of country available for settlement. The maps of water supplies and both human and cattle populations[1] indicate that this process of redistribution during the past thirteen years has succeeded in relieving population pressure in several of the more congested areas where longer resting periods under fallow are now possible.

It is often argued, however, that such redistribution of population can only be a temporary palliative if the population increases as it is undoubtedly doing. It has even been suggested that no new lands should be made available as they will only be ruined. There is a germ of truth in this suggestion because, without successful complementary action to improve husbandry throughout, redistribution into new areas would simply represent unlocking the store cupboard. The justification for the use of reserves of land must lie in the ability to replace them with reserves of fertility born of improved husbandry in all the lands of the area.

Meanwhile, there is a second point; Sukumaland is not an island but an integral part of Tanganyika where the general position can be summarized by the following approximate figures:

	Acres	Acres
Total land area of Tanganyika		219,500,000
Less forest reserves, urban and mining areas and other land not suitable for agriculture		97,000,000
Total cultivable area		122,500,000
Area at present under cultivation (under crop)	6,500,000	
Additional area used primarily for grazing	43,000,000	49,500,000
Cultivable land in reserve		73,000,000

Some of this reserve land is tsetse infested and much of it is deficient in water supplies, but it is capable of reclamation as and when required, either on a large scale, as is being done under development schemes by wholesale bush clearing and the construction of dams, &c., or by minor local expansion. In Sukumaland both methods are facilitated by the indigenous organization and customary practice already described.[2] With this vast territorial reserve it should therefore be a considerable time before rural population density reaches an optimum throughout the whole country, the habitable areas of which can be greatly extended by the almost unlimited multiplication of watering points. Thus, if

[1] Facing pp. 149, 9, 63.　　　　　[2] pp. 29–31.

Resettlement

redistribution is sufficiently rapid to reduce population pressure to a point at which land can be adequately rested, either under trees or grass, and if fertility reserves are maintained in the occupied areas by improved methods of husbandry and land use, then redistribution will indeed be more than a palliative.

Cattle and Water. As I have mentioned, the possession of stock resembles invested capital at a high rate of interest rather than a currency, and it would be hard to find a better investment in the circumstances of Sukumaland. This valuable capital asset, which makes a vital difference in times of food shortage, should play an integral part in a balanced rural economy, for which purpose the number of cattle will be none too great when redistribution has been carried out.

To achieve a balanced husbandry the cattle population and the arable land need to be situated, as far as possible, in the same neighbourhood in order to make the keeping of cattle a useful adjunct to plant husbandry with full use of manure for mixed farming. To secure an advance on present methods, which in many parts tend to permit stock to destroy the land upon which they live, a system of rotational grazing is also necessary if soil fertility in grass-land and fallow is to be maintained, and erosion avoided.

The Busiha village *ngitiri* system of pasture reservation and rotation has been described[1] and this method of management, which assures the protection of standing grass throughout the year, is slowly spreading. As we have seen, the personal *ngitiri* of central Sukumaland has many disadvantages,[2] the most serious of which is that large areas of grazing can be locked up by *bahabi* (who have no stock), whereas the Busiha system makes full use of both arable land and pasture by means of an organization controlled in the interests of the community by the village headmen.

In many parts of Sukumaland stock as at present distributed are too numerous to allow a purely internal village system, however effective, to provide a solution, and consequently rotational grazing schemes have been considered with the object of providing a period of absence from the village pastures by the utilization of the great plains. The existing custom of lending animals to friends, relations, or professional herdsmen who live on the edges of the *mbugas*, produces this result, but the effects are limited by the restrictions of season and area imposed by the maldistribution of water supplies.

[1] pp. 76–77.   [2] pp. 75–76.

If soil fertility is one of the basic assets of the country, water is the catalyst without which the land cannot be used.

While the *mbuga* systems have hitherto been considered as a single type of country, it is now desirable to indicate a subdivision necessary to the consideration of their use. For the most part the upper reaches and the lateral slopes, including the fan slopes, contain *ibambasi, ibushi,* and *itogolo* soil types as well as *mbuga,* and they are not subject to prolonged inundation. Here permanent agriculture with a variety of crops is possible. In the lower reaches, however, the relatively small central areas of pure *mbuga* soil are subject to periods of flooding, though the *mabaga* islands of raised land which frequently occur belong rather to the upper group. It is in this latter type of lowland flat that seasonal grazing by stock is perhaps the optimum use to which the land can be put, as arable agriculture is restricted on the wetter *mbuga* soils.[1]

Were the construction of tanks, dams, and *hafirs* to be confined to these lower areas, there is no doubt that seasonal grazing would be extended and larger numbers of animals would be lent to spend a portion of the year away from the village pastures. While this would provide a resting period for the highland village grazings, it would accentuate the division of plant and animal husbandry. It is therefore clear that in the first instance water supplies might well be provided on the upper slopes or marginal *mbugas* in the first category mentioned. These watering points would then first facilitate seasonal grazing and, as the numbers of watering points increased, settlement would follow.[2]

Not only would the pressure of stock within the highlands of the cultivation steppe be diminished by lending to those who settle in these areas, but also the arable land would penetrate with settlement into country hitherto confined to seasonal use by cattle. Thus the steady advance by permanent settlement will naturally produce a corresponding reduction in seasonal movements of stock, until the redistribution of population to the marginal *mbuga* slopes is complete. The objective of a balanced mixed farming practice could thus be reached, not by withdrawing the cattle from seasonal grazings to the arable areas, but by extending plant husbandry and

[1] See Sukumaland Soils, pp. 174–91.
[2] As the late Mr. Milne in his Soil Reconnaissance Report has mentioned: 'The soil is moving downhill ... thither inevitably the cultivator must follow. ... The productive lands of the future in Sukumaland will have to be the *mbugas* and their sandy and "hardpan" fringes.'

Resettlement

with it surplus stock to utilize the vast rich lowlands, which, owing to lack of water, are now only available for sporadic grazing.

The old saying that 'breeding goes in at the mouth' is particularly true of Sukumaland and improvements in food supply are a necessary prerequisite to the increased production of meat and milk. Thus, from this point of view also, improved utilization of available land is of the first importance.

In relation to soil fertility conservation, cattle are perhaps more important than human beings, and therefore their redistribution is relatively more urgent. During this process there will be a period of respite in which agricultural and economic education can open every avenue for the use of stock increases, so that by the time redistribution is far advanced, consumption may naturally balance reproduction.

Internal Redistribution. Ways and means of improving the agronomy of Sukumaland have been discussed. There remains the problem of their introduction. Perhaps the first need is for space and time. In areas where practically all the land is already under cultivation and pastures are grazed to capacity, redistribution is required in order to reduce density and so provide space to enable land to be rested and improved systems of rotational grazing to be effected. Time is needed at lower densities in order to allow the improved practices to become customary before further population increases take effect.

Within the general perimeter of the inhabited area of Sukumaland[1] there are parts where, although the soil is reasonably good, human habitation is impossible and cattle can only graze during limited periods on account of the absence of water supplies. These waterless areas are surrounded by densely populated lands and so can be regarded as suitable for what I will term 'internal redistribution'. In these parts the provision of surface-water catchment works would enable the land to be used and a redistribution of population and stock could follow. As the Sukuma do not readily move house over long distances, redistribution in the neighbourhood is of more immediate importance to the preservation of soil fertility than external redistribution to areas outside the perimeter of the cultivation steppe which are farther from the centres of pressure. Besides redistribution to such uninhabited areas where

[1] See vegetation, population, and water supplies maps, facing pp. 5, 9, 149.

the provision of water is immediately followed by new villages, there are many existing villages which have little water of their own and depend largely or entirely on the supplies of their neighbours. In these a redistribution of stock would be effected and tramping to water would be reduced were existing supplies to be improved or new sources provided. The possibilities of improvements in land utilization by the provision of water throughout the country are therefore considerable.

There are numerous springs and seepage areas whence excess water runs to waste during the rains, where an increase in the number of small tanks, such as those which exist already, would retain water during the whole of the dry season. Larger surface-water catchment works at suitable points throughout the cultivation steppe and sub-surface dams to retain water along the whole length of the sandy river-beds could not only improve stock distribution but might also provide some water for irrigation of rice, vegetables, and other crops by means of *shadufs* during the interval between the two rainy seasons. Quite a small quantity of water used in this way at the right time might well make all the difference between a fair harvest and a crop failure. It has been estimated that if the best possible use were made of water within ten miles of Shinyanga alone, the rice crop from the whole district could be quadrupled, and irrigation, even if only as a supplement to a fickle rainfall, is yet another means of improving production and gaining more per man and more per acre.

Thus as regards resettlement there is much to be said for initiating improvements in land utilization both within and adjacent to the areas at present inhabited.

External Redistribution. While internal redistribution is giving a more uniform density over the whole inhabited area, an expansion outside the perimeter of the cultivation steppe relieves pressure where densely populated parts are situated near the bush edge. In connexion with this external expansion the following points need consideration.

The complete depopulation of sleeping sickness areas to form concentrations in large villages instead of scattered homesteads has usually proved successful. For example, the evacuation of the islands of Rubondo and Maisome by the German Administration on account of this disease was completely effective. On the other hand, an attempt to reduce the congested population of Ukara

Resettlement

Island, also in Lake Victoria, by the transfer of part of the population to the Majita peninsula was a failure (partly owing to the soil being too heavy for the wooden hoe of the Bakara). While other instances could be quoted of failure to start migrations from overcrowded areas into clearings to which no natural movement existed, the above will suffice to illustrate that there are difficulties in dealing with questions of density reduction as opposed to complete depopulation. Moreover, as the French have found on the Niger irrigations, it is one thing to reclaim land with glowing prospects of its *mise en valeur* but it is quite another thing to find the population requisite and willing to fulfil such hopes if there is no neighbouring centre of dense population from which to attract settlers. These facts point to the need to assist existing movements or to the complete closure and depopulation of worn out and eroded areas.

Thus it is a matter for consideration whether reduction of population densities can be effected by stimulating and assisting existing movements or whether it must be effected by compulsion. If the latter, whether redistribution can best be achieved by compelling selected individuals or classes (e.g. bachelors) to move, or by complete depopulation of the more seriously damaged parts which would then be reserved as blocks for a period under bush or grass fallow.

Although the problems raised by the existence of the tsetse fly in the bush surrounding the inhabited area do not fall within the purview of this study, I should perhaps mention that they are very much in the forefront of the work now being undertaken by the Sukumaland Development team. Broadly speaking, however, it may be said that the tsetse fly makes the reclamation of bush country more difficult than it would otherwise be and thereby acts as a brake on the expansion of the occupied area. As we have seen, this is by no means entirely a bad thing, as a certain measure of population pressure is necessary to induce the adoption of improved methods of husbandry. When reclamation becomes essential it can be achieved despite the tsetse fly, either by large-scale clearing (as in the groundnut areas and elsewhere) or by more limited advances on to new watering points situated near the perimeter of the cultivation steppe. Thus, the primary tsetse problem in relation to land is how to organize reclamation by methods less expensive in both cash and man-power than those already known.

Methods of Effecting Redistribution. In considering the problems of redistribution we meet the alternatives of persuasion and compulsion. Before proceeding to consider whether persuasion and inducement are likely to be adequate and, if not, to whom compulsion should be applied, it is perhaps desirable to discuss the circumstances in which inducement can legitimately pass into compulsion.

It has long been a principle of English Common Law that, whatever the tenure of land involved, no one is entitled to damage his neighbour's land. He is, however, free to destroy his own in so far as he is permitted to do so by the State. But the State has unfettered powers of legislation and State control of the use of land is becoming more and more common. The fact that land is one of the most important fundamental assets of the community is now fully recognized and legislation exists in most civilized countries to prevent damage which would reflect on the economic life of posterity. Thus compulsion in relation to land occupation is justified in so far as it is designed to preserve the people's heritage—their land, though whether it can be more successfully applied than inducement is another matter.

Let us then consider the alternatives. We have learnt from experience that the provision of new water supplies in hitherto waterless areas will attract surplus population from centres of pressure within reasonable range. These areas of pressure can at the same time be closed to immigration. This simple method produced the results which can be seen on the population maps, pp. 9 and 132. These effects were both marked and rapid but depended entirely on the provision of adequate numbers of new watering points in areas selected by the people themselves.

In the event of this method of inducement failing, then and only then would consideration of compulsion become necessary. Assuming for the sake of discussion that in certain parts compulsion is established as a necessity, it is one thing to legislate but quite a different matter to enforce such legislation. It is many years now since the pulling of *striga* became compulsory but it is not yet universal practice. That is only one example. Many of the improved methods of husbandry already mentioned have been the subject of propaganda and regulations for a long time. Progress is very slow, so slow indeed that there are many who believe that resort to compulsion, possibly even as much as is applied in Great Britain,

Resettlement

will be inevitable if the race against population increase is not to be disastrously lost.

Where the enforcement of legislation is not supported by popular appreciation of the need for it, law-making for application to individuals is apt to be 'action' confined to the paper on which it is written. As an eminent veterinarian once said of Sukumaland, 'with limited staff, laws cannot be enforced and so are better not made. Numerous subordinate staff only make for corruption and bad Government.'

How then might compulsion be successfully applied? Let us assume that an area is occupied at a density which precludes the adoption of improved methods of husbandry and at which soil damage is taking place. Any attempt to reduce the density by the removal of individuals or classes is obviously a most invidious process and, if enforced by subordinate staff, is clearly likely to lead to corruption. Who should move and who should stay? It follows that both from the point of view of administration and from the point of view of fairness and facility of enforcement, the damaged and eroded part of the area should be closed completely. It would probably be adequate in most circumstances to close it to stock, which are the greatest cause of soil damage. The area would thus become an *ngitiri*, a reserve for resting, which is a well-known indigenous customary arrangement and which would therefore occasion neither surprise nor resentment. If it were closed to cattle only in the first instance, cattle-owners could either lend their stock to friends elsewhere or move with them to newly opened areas. In all probability the stock-owners (often the majority of the villagers) would move with their animals; thus a reduction of both animal and human populations would have been effected without the invidious selection of individuals.

This, however, is very drastic treatment suitable only for seriously damaged land, in that it prescribes practically a complete rest and has the disadvantage that cattle and so manure are removed.

All this points to dealing with the land and not with the people. If a block of land is worn and tired and requires rest, that block of land should be rested. This is a simple thing to explain and everyone on it is affected alike.

Under the Natural Resources Ordinance, before such a block can be closed, an adequate alternative habitable area must be prepared. The people cannot be compelled to reside in such a new area but, if other adequately populated villages in the neighbourhood are closed to immigration under African customary law,[1] the resettlement of those who leave the damaged area will tend to be canalized in the right direction. Moreover, experience in Somaliland shows that it is possible to control and close very large areas with a very limited staff. One man can supervise about one hundred square miles, though in Sukumaland individual blocks requiring rest will seldom, if ever, need to be that size.

So much for the inducement to or control of redistribution. What of subsequent density control both in the old areas and in the new? In the old areas the resting blocks, when recovered, could be exchanged for other blocks and, if their total area is adequate, a rotational use of land and overall density control would result.

In the new areas, besides the possibility of exchanging reserved woodland blocks, perhaps the simplest method of density control lies in the limitation of the number and capacity of new watering points. Taking into consideration the average carrying capacity of the country, evaporation, and the water requirements of men and beasts, surface-water catchment works of some ten million gallons capacity at five-mile intervals are considered likely to limit the human and stock populations to densities which the land can support without detriment, while providing water at adequately frequent intervals to reduce cattle tracks very considerably.

As in the case of organizing redistribution it is clearly desirable that the method of density control should be both indirect and within the power of the local government. Block reservations of land and limitations of water supplies seem to bid fair to achieve these ends, while avoiding the dangers and costs of the invidious selection of individuals to 'move along'.

Further, in the application of legislation to control improved methods of husbandry, experience in Uganda indicates that there should be no distinction between old and new lands, as such legislation applied solely to new lands retards redistribution.

Land Resting. Now a block of tired, worn, but not yet exhausted land can be reserved and treated in several ways. It can just be left alone under whatever weed, grass, tree, and shrub growth will make its appearance. That is the well-known traditional 'bush

---

[1] Native Authority Ordinance, § 8 (*j*), and § 15 has been so used by the Sukumaland Federal Council.

Resettlement

fallow'. Alternatively, it can be planted with trees or with grass—village woods or grass leys. Naturally the simplest treatment is the bush fallow which may contain certain indigenous trees much valued by the Africans for the provision of necessities such as hoe-handles. But a bush fallow may be uneconomic in comparison with afforestation and slow to restore soil fertility in comparison with other methods.

In considering the treatment under which resting land is to be renovated perhaps the most cogent argument in favour of afforestation is the prevailing shortage of fuel in the cultivation steppe of Sukumaland. At present the stalks of sorghums and dried cow-dung are used for fuel. Fuel plantations would therefore free large volumes of the very materials required to make good farmyard manure and consequently a large afforestation programme is an important part of the Sukumaland Development plan. In connexion with such fuel plantations, the considerations concerning individualization are identical with those related to grass-land management. As large belts of forest obstruct communications in so densely populated an area, there are clearly strong arguments in favour of village woods which, incidentally, being surrounded by arable and pasture lands are less likely to become infested by tsetse fly than are larger areas of forest.

Perhaps the most serious obstacle to reafforestation is the fact that vast flocks of small weavers and other graminivorous birds, which usually breed in the uninhabited country to the east of Sukumaland, invade cultivated lands just before harvest and use trees for perching and roosting. The Sukuma, therefore, very reasonably fear to have trees near their crops. I have often seen whole fields of millet reduced to empty husks by such flocks of birds.

Thus to replace plant nutrients removed by crops, we need well-made manure; to release the materials to make good farmyard manure we need fuel plantations, and to escape the dangers inseparable from the provision of perches, we may need to turn out in force and go birds' nesting in the bush many miles away—a long chain but a clear one, which illustrates the tenuous links of cause and effect which are seldom so immediately obvious.

Another similar consideration in relation to fuel plantations is that while coppiced woodland will harbour porcupine and other vermin which destroy crops, pollarding leaves a more open habit and, by providing better visibility, discourages vermin. Thus, the relationship of trees to vermin, though apparently unimportant at first sight, might well make all the difference between the acceptance of tree planting by the people and silent obstruction.

But besides the advantage of gaining manure, not only do the trees themselves break up sub-surface soil pans but also the leaf fall provides a considerable quantity of minerals absorbed by the roots from great depths. Moreover, Vageler's view that 'on a cautious estimate, the yearly production of fresh organic matter in a tropical forest amounts to over one hundred tons per acre' is of the greatest interest and importance, provided that the termites alone do not reap this rich harvest.

CONCLUSIONS

This study of the people of Sukumaland and their country is in itself but a summary of some of the more important facts which I learned during many years there. Our knowledge of the rural economy of the African peasant in the wide range of environment in which he lives is still in the early stages, so that the solutions to the difficult problems which face us will depend largely on the attitude in which they are approached. In order to obtain the active co-operation of the people there is much to be said for the positive approach to the intricate problems of Sukumaland. Negative laws, rules, and regulations to *prevent* soil erosion and to *stop* soil fertility degradation and the like, may compel a grudging measure of compliance; but a positive effort to *promote* better land use has a far greater long-range prospect of enlisting active popular support and so of ultimate success. In the art of man management 'let's do this' is always preferable to 'don't do that'—in the long run.

Let no one believe that the complexities of the rural economy of so large a country can be compressed into a few brief generalizations. But, bearing such limitations in mind, I think we can draw the following general conclusions:

1. The ultimate objective is to ensure that production per man and per acre increases much more rapidly than population.

2. The *sine qua non* of ameliorative measures is the maintenance of soil fertility.

3. (a) To achieve greater production per acre requires the adoption into customary practice of improved methods of husbandry such as tie-ridging, manuring, rotational grazing, contour cultivation, strip and rest cropping.

Conclusions

    (*b*) To achieve greater production per man requires the adoption of labour-saving devices such as mechanical cultivation and the wheel.
4. To facilitate the introduction of these improvements:
    (*a*) Redistribution of population by a more even spacing of water supplies is needed in order to provide both time and space for the adoption of better farming.
    (*b*) The existing political organization, social structure, and land tenure afford a sound foundation on which to build.
    (*c*) In relation to the rotational use of land and the resting of worn areas, there would be advantages in dealing primarily with the land rather than with the people.
    (*d*) Great advantages in relation to improving husbandry are likely to accrue from dealing with the village group rather than with the individual.

The existing village organization would, however, need to assume new responsibilities to meet the needs of a wider economy and to effect an increase of production more rapid than the increase of population. These responsibilities would include:
    (i) Provision for the payment of compensation for unexhausted improvements.
    (ii) The collective hire or purchase of mechanical equipment and farm implements.
    (iii) Given the retention by the community of powers of land allocation, the village organization would also be concerned with the implementation of many of the improved methods of husbandry.

Now, is it possible for the existing village organization to cope with such responsibilities, some if not all of which are new? I would suggest that the answer is—Yes, but only as a result of patient educative work. Grafting is a matter of growth. Any attempt to rush the assumption of such responsibilities by the shy and simple co-operative groups which exist today would surely be doomed to failure. As in so many other spheres of administration, development policy needs to deal with one thing at a time, to avoid dissipation of effort, and so to obtain acceptance.

However, mercifully, it is not necessary to decide which improvements are less urgent and to postpone their inception indefinitely. Each village or group of villages has its own particular characteristics and consequently in each case one improvement will be most urgent.[1] Provided that no village association is asked to begin more than one thing at a time all the necessary improvements could be started simultaneously in various parts of Sukumaland. Then, as many villages copy their neighbours (as they did with the Busiha *ngitiri* system), it should not be necessary to persuade each and every village association to assume all the responsibilities requisite to progress.

In my original terms of reference I was instructed 'to bear in mind the necessity for grafting new ideas as to organised resettlement, land tenure and agriculture on to existing customs'. Those words were written thirteen years ago. Time and experience have only served to convince me of their wisdom. Innovations, however desirable, introduced without the good will and co-operation of the people may have an apparent ephemeral success, but it is quite another matter with so slight a Civil Service to influence the daily lives of the people to the extent of obtaining the adoption of improved ways and means into accepted permanent customary practice.

We are indeed fortunate in finding an indigenous system of land tenure which can give that security of occupation which is undoubtedly a prerequisite to progress. In conjunction with this there are numerous advantages in being able to deal with the village and thereby avoid the difficulties and dangers of having no unit larger than the individual. Moreover, the organization of society including the village associations could open the door to progress while, at the same time, avoiding intractable problems of debt and the like. Clearly it would be the greatest mistake to attempt to alter the existing structure which, being malleable, can be steadily developed and modified by time and necessity to conform to the requirements of changing economic conditions.

No European officer can know all the components of the environment of every village of even one district. Thus, while experience is invaluable, much must necessarily depend on the closest co-operation with the Native Authorities and village elders whose detailed empiric knowledge is of undoubted value in relation to the application of specific measures to particular areas. That the Sukumaland Development team and the Sukumaland Federation

[1] e.g. in areas where manure is used for fuel, village tree-plantations may well be the first necessity.

Conclusions

of chiefs are sharing a joint headquarters at Malya should, therefore, augur well for obtaining the maximum co-operation. I believe that planned group farming, using the village or the *kibanda* as the group, could be adapted to the circumstances of Sukumaland and so build tomorrow on the firm foundations of yesterday and today.[1]

[1] See p. 210.

Appendix

NATIVE ADMINISTRATION

Extract from Through the Dark Continent, *by H. M. Stanley,
Vol. i, page 140*

22nd February 1875

Our next camp was Marya[1], fifteen miles north by east Mag. from Mondo, and 4,800 feet above the sea. We were still in view of the beautiful rolling plain, with its rock-crested hills, and herds of cattle, and snug villages, but the people, though Wasukuma, were the noisiest and most impudent of any we had yet met. One of the chiefs insisted on opening the door of the tent while I was resting after the long march. I heard the tent-boys remonstrate with him, but did not interfere until the chief forcibly opened the door, when the bull-dogs 'Bull' and 'Jack', who were also enjoying a well-earned repose, sprang at him suddenly and pinned his hands. The terror of the chief was indescribable, as he appeared to believe that the white man in the tent had been transformed into two ferocious dogs, so little was he prepared for such a reception. I quickly released him from his position, and won his gratitude and aid in restoring the mob of natives to a more moderate temper.

A march of seventeen miles north by west across a waterless jungle brought us on the 24th to South Usmau.

Extracts relating to the Constitution of the Sukumaland Federation from the Minutes of the First Plenary Session of the Sukumaland Federal Council, October 1946

1. It was agreed that all the fifty-one chiefdoms of Sukumaland should form a federation without prejudice to existing federations which must continue.

2. It was agreed that the laws and customs of the non-Sukuma tribes of the Zinza and Ng'ambo federations should be respected and that native laws and customs should be reviewed by the federation and adopted for general application on their merits without regard to their areas of origin.

3. It was agreed that Chief Majebere, K.M., C.M., of Ng'wagala Chiefdom, Maswa District, should become the permanent leader of the federation, subject to the following provisos:—

(*a*) that this appointment of leader or chairman should not increase his power in any way *vis-à-vis* the other members of the federation,

---

[1] *l*'s and *r*'s are interchangeable in Kisukuma.

Native Administration

(*b*) that he would remain a chief, a full member of the federation in his own right like all the others, but *primus inter pares*,

(*c*) that the Sukumaland Federal Council could rescind this appointment at its pleasure and select another leader should they find it desirable to do so.

4. It was decided that an executive committee of fourteen members should be formed, empowered to act on behalf of the federation.

5. It was agreed that each year four members of the executive committee should be replaced so that in due course all the chiefs of Sukumaland would have experience on the committee.

6. It was agreed that appointments to the executive committee should be made annually at a plenary session of the Sukumaland Federal Council and not by the constituent federations.

7. It was agreed that plenary sessions should be held twice a year.

8. It was agreed that the executive committee should meet at four-monthly intervals, giving three meetings a year, two of which would be arranged immediately before the plenary sessions in order to avoid unnecessary travelling.

9. It was agreed that a Federal Appeal Court would be required.

10. It was decided that the appeal court should not begin to function until the laws to be applied had been agreed upon.

11. It was decided that, in order to expedite the formation of the Federal Appeal Court, considerations of the laws of Sukumaland should be undertaken at the next meeting of the executive committee.

12. Following agreement on the laws of Sukumaland, it was decided that the Federal Appeal Court should then hear appeals from the courts of the constituent federations. The Sukumaland chiefs added a rider to the effect that the venue of appeal from the Sukumaland Federal Appeal Court would lie to a Government Officer, either back to the District Commissioner of the district of origin or to the Deputy Provincial Commissioner or the Provincial Commissioner and that the decision on the venue after the Federal Appeal Court must lie with Government.

13. It was agreed that appeals to the Sukumaland Federal Appeal Court should, in the first instance, be heard by the executive committee.

14. It was agreed that the Sukumaland Federal Court would only require appellate jurisdiction to begin with.

The Sukumaland Federal Council recognised that a unified treasury would be vital and it was clear that the Sukumaland chiefs considered the formation of a unified treasury as an essential prerequisite to an effective federal organisation. The following organisation of the Sukumaland Treasury was approved by the council:—

(*a*) The existing seven bank accounts should be amalgamated under the title of the Sukumaland Native Treasury.

(*b*) No. 2 Accounts should remain as No. 2 Accounts of the Sukumaland Native Treasury.

(*c*) Existing treasuries should continue to function as branches of the Sukumaland Native Treasury.

(*d*) Branches would sign cheques on the amalgamated Sukumaland Native Treasury account within the limits authorised by their approved estimates.

(*e*) In order to keep track of the position of the Sukamaland Native Treasury, a monthly return of cheques drawn and deposits made by each branch would be required for checking against the bank pass book.

(*f*) Possibly, a monthly abstract of revenue and expenditure would be required to enable a Sukumaland Native Treasury vote book to be kept.

(*g*) In the first instance the Provincial Office might undertake the checking of returns of cheques and deposits against the bank pass book. As soon as possible, however, a competent African clerk should be employed to undertake this work at Malya.

(*h*) Each constituent federation should prepare and submit its own estimates to the Sukumaland Federal Council.

(*i*) Such estimates will be considered and approved (perhaps after amendment) by the Federation.

(*j*) Approved estimates constitute authority for expenditure of Sukumaland Federation funds.

(*k*) The Mwanza branch of the Sukumaland Native Treasury will assume responsibility for the operation of accounts now operated by the Provincial Office. Estimates for these purposes including the Medical School, etc., will be included in the Mwanza branch estimates.

(*l*) For the time being responsibility for revenue and expenditure at the Sukumaland Federation Headquarters of Malya will be assumed by the Sukumaland Native Treasury, Binza Branch. Actual receipts and payments made at Malya will therefore continue to be operated on imprest from the Binza Branch, as at present.[1]

(*m*) Monthly abstracts of revenue and expenditure would supply adequate information on which to prepare the final financial statement for the Sukumaland Native Treasury.

(*n*) It was noted that just as District Commissioners have to assist with Native Treasury accounts at present, so the Administrative Officer at Malya and perhaps later the Accountant would have to afford the same educational supervision and assistance to the African charged with keeping the accounts of the Sukumaland Treasury from the returns rendered by its various branches.

[1] The unified Sukumaland Native Treasury on these lines came into being on 1 Jan. 1947 and the Malya headquarters branch of the Sukumaland Treasury was separated from the Binza branch during that year.

(o) It was recognised as axiomatic that the Mwanza Islands would have to be separated from the Mwanza Native Treasury and run as a separate unit.

The outstanding advantages of amalgamation on these lines were thus:—

1. The Sukumaland Federation retained the power to raise its own revenue for the Sukumaland Native Treasury through its branches and constituent federations. This power to raise revenue was recognised as a *sine qua non* of survival.

2. The pooling of resources precluded hypothecation of revenue within constituent areas. The resources of Sukumaland would become available for the benefit of Sukumaland as a whole.

3. The retention of existing treasury organisations as branches of the Sukumaland Native Treasury retains local control and local interest in the revenue and expenditure of Sukumaland. Moreover, undue centralisation of executive financial functions is avoided though ultimate control will rest with the Federal Council.

4. The difficulty of drawing a dividing line between the powers, functions and duties of a Federal Treasury and those of local treasuries is obviated.

5. The invidious question of subventions to a Federal Treasury is also obviated.

SUKUMALAND SURFACE-WATER CATCHMENT WORKS

In response to numerous requests I include the following notes on the making and mending of hand-made surface-water catchment works by amateurs in Sukumaland. As a result of observations here during the last seventeen years I feel convinced that the days of amateur dam and tank construction by all and sundry should be numbered. Even a small pair of tanks holding half a million gallons represent a lot of arduous toil on the part of the people who build them. If they are inadequately sited or designed, particularly if they are too shallow, the people suffer grave disappointment. Redistribution may and indeed will be retarded. With the growing strength of the Water Development Department in Tanganyika, it is therefore to be hoped that amateur siting and design will rapidly disappear, and even now professional advice should always be available even if the supervision of the construction of smaller works may fall to local officers. A permanent dam foreman will learn much from his mistakes. Amateurs seldom have that advantage as they seldom remain on the job long enough to see their mistakes and failures, which are undoubtedly at least as valuable as, if not more valuable than, successes from the point of view of experience. So, for what it is worth, here are

150 *Sukumaland Surface-water Catchment Works*

some notes on what I have learned largely from mistakes and failures following a study of minor 'administrative surface-water catchment works in Basutoland, the Transkei and Ciskei, other parts of the Union of South Africa, West Africa and the Sudan, as well as of the earlier tan[1] and dams of Sukumaland'.

As my experience of actual making and mending is confined mainly to the Maswa District of the Lake Province, these notes are written with that area in mind.

1. POLICY

The policy of tank, *hafir*, and dam construction in Maswa has been one of self-help. The chiefs and elders of the Binza Federation decide where water is most urgently needed and then the people of all chiefdoms co-operate in construction. The object has been to open up waterless bush areas for human habitation and stock in order to rest the hitherto more densely populated areas of Sukumaland both within the Maswa District and in the neighbouring districts of Shinyanga and Kwimba.

The maps of human and cattle population (pp. 9 and 63) give general pictures of the distribution, density, and movements of the people and their stock during the last thirteen years. In some cases, however, movements out and back within that period are naturally cloaked. Read in conjunction with the map of water supplies (p. 149) the success of the Binza Federation in relieving population pressure can be seen. The construction of some twenty dams, *hafirs*, and tanks between 1941 and 1947 has contributed largely towards the remarkable reduction in human population density shown in Kigoku (37),[1] Ng'wagala (32), and Ntuzu (27) with a corresponding increase in Itilima (29) and with smaller increases in Kanadi (28), other parts of Ntuzu (27), and Sengerema (30). A similar redistribution was achieved in relation to domestic animal population. Excess stock were drawn from Kigoku (37), Ng'wagala (32), and from Ng'wadubi (40) and Buchunga (44) (both in the Shinyanga District) towards the newly watered areas in North Ng'wagala (32), Ng'unghu (31), Itilima (29), and North Sanga (33). It is perhaps worth noting here, that this redistribution was effected simply by the provision of new water supplies, some organized bush clearing, and by the prohibition of immigration into overcrowded areas.

2. ORGANIZATION

The branch Native Treasury Estimates normally contain provision for a number of surface-water catchment works. During the preparation of the branch estimates, which are of course subject to amendment and

[1] Numbers in brackets are chiefdom index numbers on the relevant maps.

Organization

confirmation by the Sukumaland Federation, the chiefs of the constituent federations, after consultation with the elders and village representatives of their chiefdoms, have a fair idea of the number and location of the waterworks required during the following year but, as population movements take place towards the end of the dry season, priorities may change. Therefore, final arrangements are left until the following February or March when, at a full meeting of the constituent federation, with the approved estimates before them, the chiefs go over the year's programme in detail, define the exact location of each work required, assess the number of men required to build it and arrange for mutual help between chiefdoms for such works as are beyond the capacity of the individual chiefdom in which the work is situated. Thus, at this meeting, a list of development works including water catchment works, bush clearing, &c., is prepared showing the names of the villages in which the works are to be undertaken, the number of men required per ten-day *safari*, the number of *safaris*, the number of cattle required to feed the people, the exact cost, and the number of men and *safaris* to be contributed by other chiefdoms of the constituent federation. Besides the normal advantages of co-operation, this help from other chiefdoms has the great advantage of letting men from overcrowded areas see the new land which is being opened up. Co-operation is therefore organized with this point in mind and sometimes those who have helped to build a dam are some of the first to move to it from the overpopulated areas.

Annual village road work should begin on or about 15 May. Tracks of access to all surface-water catchment works on the final list are completed before the middle of June to enable an officer to inspect by car. At each site 4-foot peeled pegs are provided in considerable quantities so that on this first survey *safari* it is only necessary for the officer to take levelling instruments, measuring tape, and heavy hammers (6 or 8 lb. sledge). (Where no telescopic level exists, serious mistakes can easily be made by eye. A Government officer when siting a tank in the Shinyanga District neglected to ask the local inhabitants which way the water flowed. He put the spoil heaps upstream and so prevented any surface water getting into the tank! A small drain had to be dug to bring the water round the end of the wing banks and into the tank.) Chiefs or sub-chiefs with advance parties of the men who will do the work are also due on site at the time of this preliminary survey and layout *safari*. In areas where high grass would make survey during June exceedingly difficult, it is, of course, advisable to carry out the preliminary survey the previous year at the end of the dry season and, as wooden pegs are not sufficiently permanent, demarcation lines have to be trenched or marked with planted aloes (*magaka*). If test holes are required to find out what subsoils underlie the site, these should also be dug at the end of the previous dry season.

It should perhaps be explained that the reason why it is necessary to have everything well organized and to lay out all surface-water catchment works as soon as possible after the end of the rains, is because these works are normally situated at some considerable distance from permanent water supplies. For a month or so after the end of the rains, water for the labour can be obtained from pools and depressions in the *mbugas*. Moreover, the ground is still soft and relatively easily worked. Later on it becomes exceedingly hard. If work is ill organized and begins late, it may be necessary to arrange costly motor transport to bring water for the working parties. Alternatively, large numbers of man-days are wasted fetching water for themselves and their friends.

3. DEFINITIONS

In these notes, the following names of various types of surface-water catchment works are used with the following meanings:

Dam. Water retained by an earth bank running more or less straight across a valley.

Hafir. Water retained in one or more excavations in the ground *and* by the bank of spoil from the excavations which is normally U- or V-shaped with the wing banks at right angles to the contours.

Tank. Water retained in an excavation in the ground. The spoil bank may also be U- or V-shaped but normally gives little assistance towards the retention of water above ground level. With tanks the position of the spoil banks is dictated primarily by the need to cut down spoil transport to a minimum.

The distinction drawn here between *hafirs* and tanks follows the local use of these words, though in the Sudan, the home of the *hafir*, the bank does not always assist with water retention. However, here the difference is simply one of gradient. Tanks belong to flat country and the dividing line has been taken at a fall of 1:100. A water point is required at a certain place. If there is no gradient there steeper than 1:100 then the answer will be a tank as it is generally not worth-while to build a very long bank in order to impound a depth of only one two-hundredth of its length, though in India some immensely long banks have been built for a much smaller fraction. Thus each case must be considered on its merits and it is possible that circumstances might exist where it would be worth-while to build a bank on a slope of 1:300, but it would have to be 600 yards long for a dam to impound a maximum of 3 feet of water over the sumps or pits and cancel out the dry season evaporation only. Is it worth the tremendous task of spoil transport?

Spacing

4. SPACING

The ultimate objective, to provide for the optimum redistribution of population and stock in Sukumaland, is to have a permanent water

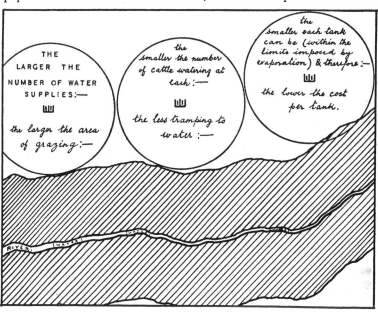

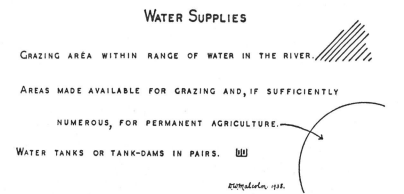

supply every five miles. When this is achieved, cattle will never have more than $2\frac{1}{2}$ miles to walk to water. This will cut down tramping, grass destruction, and erosion. At present there are parts of Sukumaland where some people live as far as 9 to 12 miles from permanent water and some cattle have to tramp as much as 15 miles to water every third day in the dry season.

5. CAPACITY

At the beginning of the conscious effort to organize population redistribution in 1941, dams had to be large to meet the needs of large numbers of cattle. Progressively they can now become smaller. The optimum capacity, when the ultimate objective of a permanent supply every five miles comes nearer, is about 10 million to 15 million gallons depending on the conformation of the country, catchment area, spillway, &c. In this rather flat country, it is often necessary to build a dam with a greater capacity in gallons than is actually required for use, in order to achieve the necessary depth requirements. A good example of a most suitable little dam is the one at Shishiyu sited by the chief and the District Commissioner, confirmed and constructed by the Department of Water Development. A capacity of around 10,000,000 gallons will limit the number of stock based on it to a reasonable density. Similarly a small water supply will also limit human population density within the area it serves. It should be noted that the Sukuma do not as a rule use tanks or small *hafirs* for watering their cattle.

6. CATCHMENT AREA

A very large catchment area makes surplus water disposal difficult and spillway capacity must therefore be large and costly. On the other hand a small catchment area is dangerous in a year of poor rainfall and may well result in the dam failing to fill and so drying out completely before the next rains.

7. DEPTH

The minimum useful depth of any surface-water supply is about 14 or 15 feet. Evaporation in Sukumaland is some 8 to 9 inches per month of the dry season so that an early cessation of the rains followed by a late start without heavy downpours might result in a total loss by evaporation of up to some 7 feet (though such a heavy loss would be exceptional). In 1947 between the last heavy rain in June and the first heavy rain early in December, the level of the Malya dam (440,000,000 gallons) went down 39 inches, which includes use by cattle and people as well as losses from evaporation. The 1947 season was, however, very favourable. With tanks and the smaller supplies silting is more serious and it has been found advisable to adhere to the depth figure of 14 to 15 feet assuming not more than half the volume to be available for normal annual use.

8. MAINTENANCE

A. *General.* As the routine inspection and maintenance in good working order of all existing surface-water catchment works is more important even than new construction, these notes precede notes on layout and new works. A tank dug to 15 feet may silt to a point at which evaporation ends its useful life. Dam banks constructed by hand labour settle unevenly every year over a number of years and therefore require subsidence refilling and relevelling frequently. This important maintenance work is only too often neglected by amateurs owing to pressure of other business. If a dam is built and fills, people build near it and rely on it. If it fails and is not promptly repaired, they lose faith and the word goes round from mouth to mouth that it is unwise to rely on these man-made supplies. Redistribution of population would then suffer as it has done in the past where shallow supplies gave out before the end of the dry season. People are forced back into the overcrowded areas. Thus, it is not advisable to go on building new tanks until existing pairs of tanks have all been dug to the full depth of 15 feet. While it is theoretically possible to drink from one tank until it is empty and then clean it out and deepen it whilst drinking from the other until the end of the dry season, yet, in practice, this method depends on good village organization and prompt information being brought in when one tank is so emptied. I feel convinced that it will be a long time before this method can be employed effectively and, in the meanwhile, means of pumping water from one sump to the next are therefore essential. Hand-operated Dando pumps will probably prove most suitable as they are simple and capable of pumping mud and slush.

B. *Leaks.* With hand-made dams and *hafirs* it is practically impossible to achieve adequate consolidation. The first earth from the sump excavations tends to come out in large lumps. The men avoid walking on knobby lumps and so consolidation comes only with time and settlement. Rain has little effect. With *mbuga* soil, hardpan soils, and the whitish detritus of granite known as *ndoba*, which is often found underlying *mbuga* in Sukumaland, an impervious layer is quickly formed and, after the first year's rain, if this layer, which seldom exceeds 2 inches in thickness, is opened, the original soil will be found as dry and dusty as when the bank was first built. Now, in spite of this habit of self-sealing, the larger lumps at the base of the bank often leave small gaps through which the water finds a way. Ant-bears and even mice have been known to lend a hand. Naturally, spoil from pervious strata should never be included at one place in any bank which will retain water, though it can be utilized by careful intermixture with the heavy clays. The smallest trickle from the downstream base of the bank is a danger signal. It may stop itself by subsidence but more probably the

SURFACE WATER CATCHMENT WORKS, SUKUMALAND

Plan No. 1.

STOPPING A LEAK

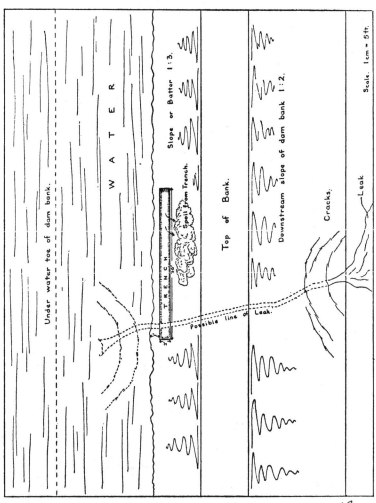

Maintenance

trickle will increase and if unstopped will end in a breach. It is a fascinating sight to watch. It is, of course, useless to attempt to stop such a leak from the downstream side of the bank. Given early information of the start of the trouble, prompt—immediate—action can save a breach and many man-days' work. The simplest method which is sometimes successful is to tip impervious soil into the water along the upstream face of the bank opposite the leak. Men, standing in the water, feel for the depression, which will exist at the beginning of the leak, and trample the earth into it. If this method is not immediately successful dig a trench in the dam bank about a foot from the water and parallel to it. The trench should be about 2 feet wide and perhaps 30 feet long so as to cut through the leak even if the leak is not coming through at right angles. The trench may have to be widened if the dam bank is high and the trench is, therefore, likely to be deep. Care must be taken to see that the sides of the trench do not fall in on the men working in it, though I have never yet had to shore the sides. Cracks on the upstream side of the bank may help to indicate the direction of the leak. The trench should go down to ground level which can be recognized by the dry grass (if any was left). If the trench does not cut across the leak, it must be extended at either end until it does. Then refill and damp and tramp. If the leak has been a bad one, it may also be necessary to follow it right through the bank (after refilling the trench), but in small leaks in small banks the puddled trench is often enough in conjunction with annual subsidence replacement and relevelling, which is a most important recurrent work. See Plan No. 1, p. 156.

C. *Breaches*. No breach is irreparable and they seldom remove much of the bank. I have seen three major breaches to ground level in dams of 10,000,000, 200,000,000, and 180,000,000 gallons capacity. None exceeded 50 feet in width and in filling them the water which remained in the excavated sumps not only supplied the working parties but also was used to damp the earth which was stamped and rammed in the gap. The patch was thus made stronger and better consolidated than the original bank. In mending a breach the sides should first be cut away to a slope of about 1:2 and keyed in. No uninterrupted transverse planes through the bank should be left. See Plan No. 2, p. 158.

D. *Sealing Dam Basins*. In some parts of Sukumaland pervious strata are found within the first 15 feet below otherwise suitable sites. During a visit to the Sudan I inspected a *hafir* during construction which was situated on extremely pervious sandy soil. In reply to my astonished inquiry, I was told that it was not expected to hold water during the first few dry seasons but that puddling by cattle combined with the influx of silt and fine particles of manure would seal it effectively. There is very pervious *ibushi* soil and limestone under the Ng'wandu dam. I took

158 *Sukumaland Surface-water Catchment Works*

a chance, based on experience in the Sudan and, although this dam did not hold water well during the first few dry seasons, it is now nearly

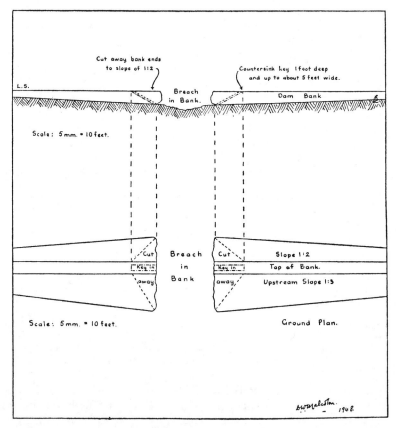

completely sealed as a result of the use of cattle. The *ndoba* subsoil, a detritus of granite, which I have mentioned, is gritty and looks porous but is not. Of all the tanks and dams that I have had dealings with in Sukumaland, the only seriously pervious strata I have encountered are either old sandy river-beds or concretionary limestone deposits. Of

SURFACE WATER CATCHMENT WORKS, SUKUMALAND

Plan No. 3.

DAM SITES

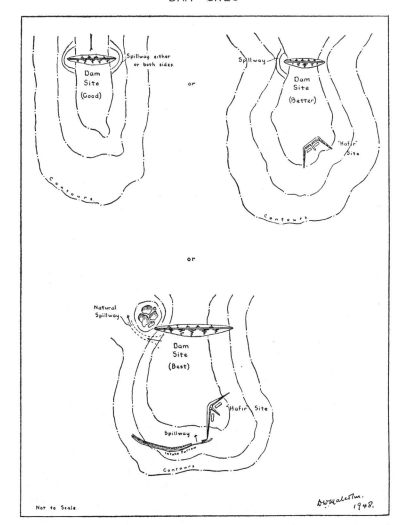

these the sandy river-beds are much the more dangerous. Normally murram or laterite seals itself quickly.

9. NEW WORKS

A. *Dams*

1. *Siting.* Some of the chiefs are getting very good at site selection. Both the Dutwa dam at Ng'alita and the Sanga instalment dam at Kisesa were selected without any European help. The steepest sided valley should be chosen with an adequate catchment area of at least 2 square miles if possible. Catchment areas in excess of 6 square miles produce a volume of water coming in after a heavy rain at the beginning of the season which can be so large that the spillway necessary for safety becomes very wide and expensive. Whenever possible the contours on each side of the valley should be parallel or converge. See Plan No. 3, p. 159. There are places where even better dam sites exist with a rocky outcrop on one side providing a good natural spillway. Examples are seen at the Sola dam, Shishiyu, and Ng'wamapalala. Such a site is shown in Plan No. 3, p. 159.

2. *Layout.* The simplest and quickest method of pegging a dam is as follows. This is *not* the method used by qualified engineers from which quantities can be taken but it is quick and efficient. It has been used successfully on all the hand-made dams in Maswa. The Nhomango dam was levelled and pegged in an hour and a half.

First look for the place in the valley where the water has begun to cut a *sluit*. Lower down, where there is a stream-bed, there is a danger of sand in an old stream-bed to one side or below the existing bed. Such an old bed would cause a leak and breach. Higher up there might well be too little catchment area. Next look for a natural spillway site and take the difference in level between it and the lowest point of the valley (not in the *sluit*.)

Now drive a line of pegs about 3 feet high across the line of the *sluit* and then up the slopes of the valley at right angles to the contours. If the difference between the spillway level and the bottom of the valley is, say 6 ft. 6 in., the eventual consolidated height of the bank at the centre may be 10 feet. This first line of pegs will be the position of the crest of the bank on the downstream side. Draw a cross-section of the bank, berm, and sump excavations and use the proposed height of the bank to determine the other measurements, as in Plan No. 4, p. 161. At the lowest point of the valley put a tape on the line of pegs and unroll it upstream at right angles to the pegs. Drive pegs at 10 feet for the upstream crest of the bank, 30 feet for the upstream toe of the bank, 15 feet for the berm, and 60 feet for the upstream edge of the excavations,

Cattle, sheep, and goats congregating at mid-day for water in the plains of central Sukumaland

The construction of the 200,000,000 gallon Ng'wamapalala Dam opened up some thirty square miles of hitherto waterless and tsetse-infested bush

The excavation is at right angles to the bank, thus increasing the transport of soil

The people are not carrying on the shortest haul, though consolidation on top should be relatively good

New Works 161

if they are to be the same width as the bank. Next drive in a peg 20 feet downstream from the original line of pegs for the downstream toe of

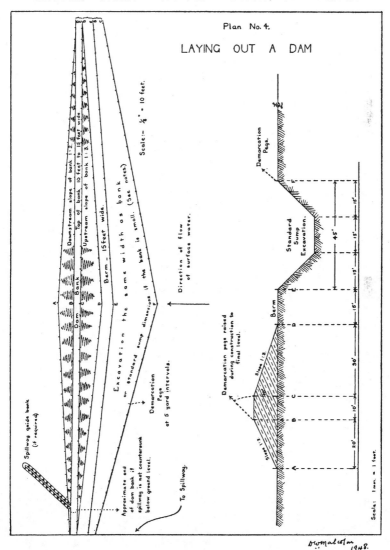

SURFACE WATER CATCHMENT WORKS, SUKUMALAND.

Plan No. 4.
LAYING OUT A DAM

the bank. These measurements give a slope of 1:2 on the downstream side and a slope of 1:3 on the upstream side of the bank, which in this case will be 10 feet high at the centre of the valley. These slopes are standard for all earth banks retaining water.

Next, at each end of the original line of pegs, set off again upstream at right angles to the line and drive a peg at 10 feet (the width of the crest of the bank). Both front and back slopes diminish to nothing at the ends unless the spillway is not countersunk and goes round the end of the bank as at Nhomango, when the bank will be shorter and will end at the height of the freeboard allowed, e.g. 3 ft. 6 in. in the case quoted above. Drive another peg at 15 feet for the berm and one at 10 feet for the upstream edge of the excavations. Now join up the pegs at the ends with those in the centre with lines of pegs as shown in Plan No. 4, p. 161. The pegs defining the bank and excavations must be fairly close together as otherwise ragged lines tend to occur during construction. Pegs at 5-yard intervals have been found satisfactory. The excavations mentioned, although they may be the same width as the dam bank, should be treated as sumps of about 150 feet in length each, with gaps of perhaps 10 feet between them, so that should the bank breach, water will be retained in these sumps thus mitigating the seriousness of the loss of water.

3. *Instalment System.* It is often found that it is either not possible or not desirable to complete a dam or large *hafir* in one season. Clearly it is better to undertake too little, get down to full depth and finish early, than to embark on too ambitious a programme and be caught by the first rains with a number of shallow scrapes which promptly fill with water and have to be pumped out before deepening the following year. An effective instalment system has therefore been evolved. See Plan 5, p. 163.

The dams at Ng'wamapalala and Nhomango are good examples of the ultimate success of this method which consists of digging a sump each year and putting the excavated earth downstream in the shape in which the ultimate dam or *hafir* bank will be required. Each year spoil from a new sump excavation must be keyed into the previous year's bank so as to avoid a cleavage line between the spoil compacted by a rainy season and settlement, and the new loose spoil. A cleavage line will probably lead to a leak and a break.

The pegging of a dam to be constructed on the instalment system can be done exactly the same way as described above, but the resulting lines of pegs showing the shape of the bank and sumps are then divided up into sections to be built in annual instalments, and the sections to be done in subsequent years should be marked with trenches and aloes (*magaka*). See Plan No. 5, p. 163.

4. *Spillways.* The most important part of a dam of adequate depth is the spillway. A figure of 32 feet wide by 2 ft. 6 in. deep or some 80 sq. ft. spillway section per square mile of the catchment area is sound for

New Works

Sukumaland. A lot depends on the type of catchment area which, if it contains much rock or hardpan soil, will have a higher run-off than from

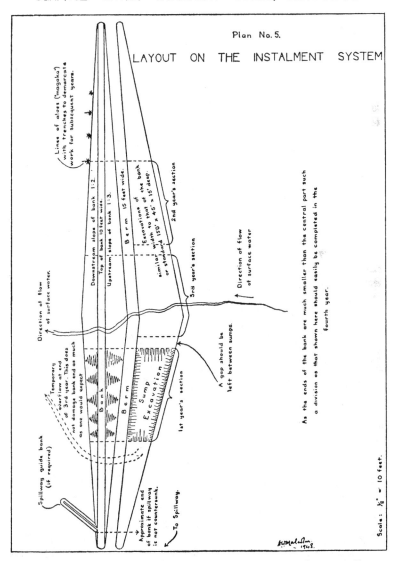

more porous soils. It is worth noting that at Malya the run-off was measured at 67 per cent. in December 1945 when the first heavy rain

164 *Sukumaland Surface-water Catchment Works*

fell before new grass had come up. Later in the season, when the grass and crops have grown, the run-off falls progressively to almost nothing except in very heavy storms. Within the limits imposed by cost, it is, of

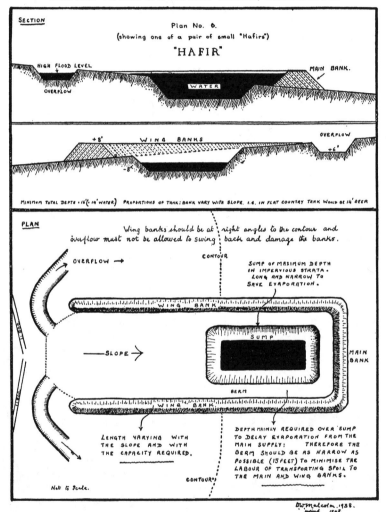

SURFACE WATER CATCHMENT WORKS, SUKUMALAND

course, impossible to have too large a spillway (or wasteway as it is sometimes called). It should always be remembered that it has been stated that some 39 per cent. of earth-dam failures in America have been due to overtopping owing to inadequate spillways. The original Malya dam was breached for this reason. A high percentage of failures from other causes were due to 'sloppy' puddle cores, but we do not use them here as, in the normal dam site, there is no water with which to puddle and in the smaller dams and *hafirs* on *mbuga* or hardpan soil with sparse grass cover little or no preparation of the ground is necessary before building the bank. For slightly larger dams it is perhaps advisable to remove such grass as there may be to get a good bond, but this was not done for any hand-built dam in Maswa, three of which have capacities around 200,000,000 gallons. None of the leaks and breaches I have seen were due to leaving the earth surface under the bank undisturbed. All were due to lack of consolidation or an inadequate spillway. If a valley has one side steeper than the other, a dam spillway would normally be sited on the side with the gentler slope where less excavation would be required.

B. *Hafirs*

The siting of *hafirs* where there are slopes exceeding 1:100 is similar to the siting of dams in that they are often at the head of a broad valley where the contours form an arc, though they can also be sited on one side of a valley. In either case catchment drains may well be needed if the distance to the watershed is not great. Typical *hafirs* and *hafir* sites are shown on Plans Nos. 3, 6, and 7, pp. 159, 164, and 166. It is advisable to allow for two excavations per *hafir* with a dividing bank to facilitate cleaning and deepening. The excavations should run parallel with the greatest length of bank to reduce spoil transport to a minimum.

C. *Tanks*

The siting of tanks on plains where no suitable valley exists for a *hafir* or dam is fairly simple. Choose *mbuga* soil nearly at the bottom of any long slope where the people say that water moves. As with *hafirs* the greatest length of the sumps should be parallel to the greatest length of bank to reduce spoil transport to a minimum. Catchment drains may be needed to fill the tanks which should never be at quite the lowest point in the plain where the greatest volume of water passes, owing to silting and scouring. Allowance should always be made for building tanks in pairs so that one of the pair can be used first and then cleaned out while the other remains in use up to the beginning of the rains. Such tanks, where the banks do nothing to assist the water retention, are illustrated in Plan No. 8, p. 167. They are seldom required in Sukumaland though such flat areas do exist in the Huruhuru *mbuga* system and in parts of Buhungukira.

D. *Size of Excavations*

As a result of much experiment and experience it seems that the

166 Sukumaland Surface-water Catchment Works

optimum size of sump excavation to dig for dams, *hafirs*, and tanks is one measuring 150 feet long, 45 feet wide, and 15 feet deep. On the long

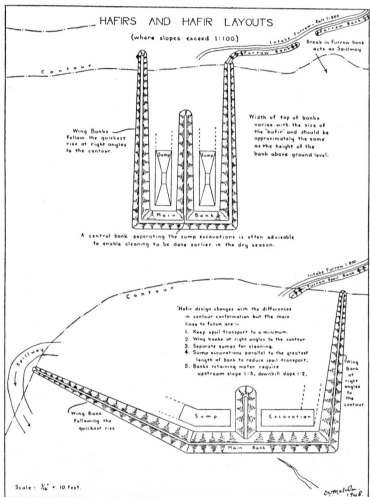

sides of the sump the slope is about 1:1, while on the short sides a slope of 1:4 provides safe access to the water for the women. This size and shape has become almost standard design and gives a capacity of

New Works 167

about a quarter of a million gallons. Thus a pair give a tank water point of half a million gallons. In practice with hand labour all slopes tend to

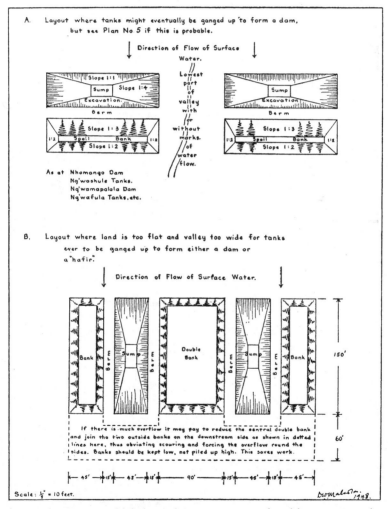

be much steeper, which is no harm except on the side nearest to the bank owing to the danger of subsidence reducing the berm. Possibly,

168 *Sukumaland Surface-water Catchment Works*

if such water points become numerous, the peasants will begin to use them to water their stock.

SURFACE WATER CATCHMENT WORKS, SUKUMALAND

Plan No. 9.

INTAKE FURROWS

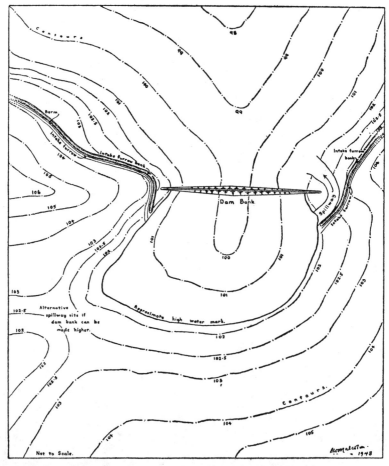

E. *Intake Furrows*

Catchment drains or intake furrows can also be used to advantage to increase the catchment area supplying a dam if the best site happens to be rather too high up the valley and too near the watershed. A good example can be seen at Nyalikungu in front of the District Office where the total length of the intake furrows is about two miles. These drains

SURFACE WATER CATCHMENT WORKS, SUKUMALAND

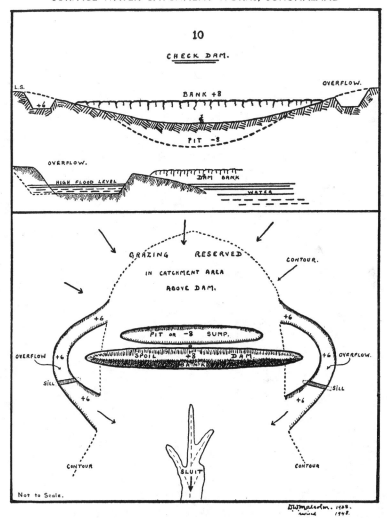

must be cleaned and repaired each year in November if they are to serve their purpose, as they are constantly subject to damage by cattle crossing them and they also tend to become choked with grass. Possible layouts of such intake channels are shown on Plan No. 9, p. 168. In the

170 *Sukumaland Surface-water Catchment Works*

intake furrows at Nyalikungu the fall is 1:600, but from experience it has been found that 1:800 is better. That is 1½ in. fall in every 100 feet,

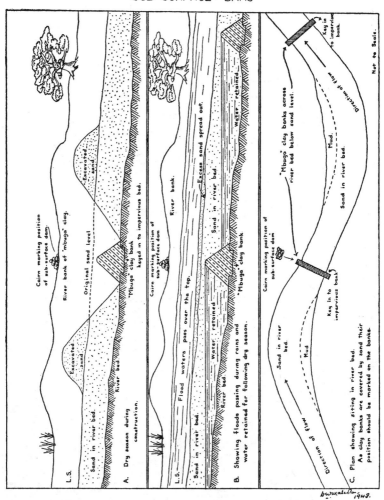

SURFACE WATER CATCHMENT WORKS, SUKUMALAND

Plan No. 11.

SUB-SURFACE DAMS

which is easy to remember and to set on the levelling staff. Adequate dimensions for the furrows are about 6 feet wide and 1 foot deep. Deeper digging usually gets into hard stuff in parts and costs too much.

New Works

Smaller width gives too little flow. Naturally the correct size depends upon the area from which the run-off is collected, but this rule of thumb works well as the furrows can always be widened later if they prove inadequate. An advantage of intake furrows is that they can be intentionally cut when the dam, *hafir*, or tank is full, thus reducing silting to the minimum and also reducing spillway wear.

F. *Check Dams*

Check dams are simply diminutive dams across erosion gullies such as the one shown in Plan No. 10, p. 169. They were completely successful in stopping serious gully erosion at Lubaga Farm, Shinyanga District, though their efficacy there was undoubtedly enhanced by the adoption of tie-ridging which considerably reduced the run-off, which was collected by contour banks and discharged into the gulley.

G. *Sub-surface Dams*

These have not yet been used in Sukumaland. As may be seen from the map of water supplies (facing p. 150) the river-beds do not hold water all along their length in pools or in sand and it is believed that water supplies in the river-beds could well be improved by the construction of sub-surface dams of *mbuga* clay to recover the underflow (See Plan No. 11, p. 170).[1]

10. CONSTRUCTION

A. *Tools.* It has been found from experience that for hand-made surface-water catchment works the only tools that should be issued are picks. Between twenty-five and fifty picks are required per 300 men. The actual number of picks is dictated by the hardness of the soil encountered. A pick maintenance organization is very useful. Experience has shown that shovels are a waste of time and earthpans are a waste of money and are too heavy. Once the soil is broken up the quickest and most efficient method is to fill earth baskets by hand and carry direct across the 15-foot berm on to the bank. The Sukuma name for these earth baskets is *maganana*. This name is important because, if it is not specified, the people tend to bring *madoto* which are smaller than an ordinary sun helmet! *Maganana* are much lighter than earthpans and are preferred by the people, who bring their own. Mattocks are useful only in layers of soft soil, which are seldom found.

B. *Earth Transport.* Working parties are very much inclined to carry earth diagonally thus greatly increasing the task. If a strict watch is kept to prevent this tendency and if every man carries only direct to the nearest part of the bank, much time is saved.

[1] See also *A Practical Handbook of Water Supply*, by F. Dixey, pp. 482 et seq.

C. *Working Party Strength.* As a general rule there is not room for more than 300 men to work on one sump excavation at a time and one sump takes about 3 ten-day *safaris* of 300 men = 9,000 man-days. This figure is small but it must be remembered that the people are building their own water supplies in their own way in their own time.

D. *Mechanical Assistance.* The greatest need is to help the people so that their annual production of new water supplies can be increased. Experience indicates that the best way to do so will be to help with digging and consolidation. There seems no possible doubt that some means must be found to obtain adequate consolidation of dam and *hafir* banks. Driving cattle across and across the bank is no doubt one of the better methods but this is difficult to organize and, if it is done during the hours of work, everyone stops to watch the fun! The weight of the men is not sufficient to give adequate consolidation except in the rare cases where it is possible to use water during construction. Naturally this is practically never possible in the first year and is seldom desirable in subsequent years as the water is always so urgently needed for drinking. On sites which have easily worked soils the use of oxen and dam-scoops can be economical. I have seen dam-scoops used with one yoke of oxen and one driver each in the Sudan near Northern Abyssinia. In Sukumaland, however, many of the sites for surface-water catchment works are on much harder soils and subsoils. On the Masinde Canal it was necessary to use up to eight yoke of oxen to a single furrow plough. Dam-scoops cannot transport spoil direct from the excavations to the bank but have to go round to get on to the bank by easier gradients. Thus it is not, by any means, every site on which their use would prove economical, quick or satisfactory though the consolidating effect of trampling by cattle is an important point in their favour.

Experiments were begun in 1947 with mechanical ripping and rolling leaving the short direct transport of the spoil to the people. It is felt that it would be a mistake to do the whole job for them by machinery, not only on account of the very high comparative cash cost but also because the existing practice of self-help has much to recommend it. But if they can be saved the heavy pick work and if the banks can be consolidated by sheep's foot rollers to obviate the serious danger of leaks and breaches in unconsolidated banks, much more progress with redistribution of population and stock will be possible.

E. *Grass Planting.* At the beginning of the rains following construction, grass should be planted on the banks. *Cynodon plectrostachyum* (*Lugobe*) is the best and planting material is readily available in nearly all valleys. It is advisable to employ one caretaker per water point, at least for the first few years, to look after the grass, remove weeds, refill minor subsidences, and to report leaks, &c.

11. LEAKS AND BREACHES IN SURFACE-WATER CATCHMENT WORKS

Names	Approx. capacity in gallons	Leaks	Breaches	Reasons
Sola Dam	220,000,000	2	..	1. Lack of consolidation at junction between work of 2 villages. 2. Lack of consolidation and mice. (Both saved from breaching by trenching.)
Malya Dam (original)	10,000,000	..	1	Inadequate spillways and lack of subsidence refilling and relevelling.
Ng'wamapalala Dam (built by instalments)	200,000,000	..	1	Lack of consolidation and inadequately keyed junction between spoil bank annual sections.
Nhomango Dam (built by instalments)	180,000,000	..	1	Lack of consolidation. Backwash of spillway was minor contributory cause.
Nyalikungu Dam (lower)	10,000,000	1	1	Leak due to ant-bear hole through bank. (Saved by trenching.) Breach (partial). Lack of consolidation causing subsidence and overtopping.
Masinde Dam	3,000,000	3	..	All due to inadequate consolidation. (Saved by trenching.)
Nyalikungu *Hafir*	350,000	1	..	Inadequate consolidation. Saved by adding soil to bank under water.

These are the only leaks and breaches known out of about fifty hand-made surface-water catchment works in Sukumaland. Naturally leaks and breaches are more prevalent in the larger works.

SUKUMALAND SOILS

with Notes on Crops, Cultivation, Flora, and Water

(Being a revision, primarily to clarify Kisukuma nomenclature, and comprising an abridged co-ordination of the work of Messrs. Burtt, King, Milne, Grantham, Williams, and Malcolm.)

THE following list of Sukumaland soils has been arranged in groups, beginning with the lighter soils of the hills and proceeding downwards to the heavier valley lands. They are not necessarily in the order in which they are to be found in any particular catena.[1] The Sukuma terminology for the red fossil or laterized soils is not standardized for the whole area and, as will be seen, dialect variations are responsible for the fact that what is known as *kikungu* in the south is usually called *nduha* in the north. Besides variations in dialect, it must also be remembered that each soil has only a limited geographical distribution. Consequently a man who has been brought up in an area containing only *nduha* will sometimes call all red soils by that name. As plants are the medicine chest of the African doctor, he distinguishes a very large number. Many plants are used not only as medicines but as relishes and pot-herbs, hence the large numbers distinguished and named. Comparatively few of the grasses are named, possibly because they are more difficult to distinguish and are not used as medicines or herbs; but with soils the Sukuma only needs to differentiate from the point of view of suitability for his various crops, and unless soil variations directly influence the crops which can be grown, he will seldom make a clear distinction[2] unless the earth is of use for special purposes such as making pots, plastering houses, or the like. Therefore, in the following notes, the Sukuma name is used primarily of the soil to which it is most commonly applied in the areas where that soil is best represented.

The whole classification of Sukumaland soils and their vegetation and cropping properties depends on the fundamental idea of a catena; that is to say, the natural arrangement of soils from the top to the bottom of the slope, the sequence of gradations usually being repeated in the reverse order on the opposite rise.

A generalized soil map of central and south Sukumaland, prepared in collaboration with Dr. G. J. Williams, is included,[3] which gives an indication of the proportions in which the main soil types occur in that area. A map of this nature covering the whole of the Sukumaland Federation would clearly be of great value from the point of view of

---
[1] See provisional table of catena, pp. 175-6.
[2] See below under *mbuga* types, pp. 183-6.
[3] Facing p. 175.

The Hills and Rocks

assigning priorities to the opening up of bush areas for habitation by the provision of new water supplies where the better soil types exist.

1. THE HILLS AND ROCKS

(A) *Luguru*, pl. *Nguru*. A hill with granite boulders.
(B) *Kiganga*, pl. *Shiganga*. A granite boulder.
(C) *Iwe lya bujeje*, pl. *Mawe ga bujeje*. A granite boulder which has begun to decompose on the surface.
(D) *Ing'ong'ho* or *Isoso*. Any hill without large boulders (includes dolorite, banded ironstone, &c.).
(E) *Mang'ong'ho gape*. A limestone deposit (*Gape* = white, pl.).
(F) *Iwe lya gembe*, pl. *Mawe ga gembe*. Dolorite (*Gembe* means 'ebony').
(G) *Mashororo*. Round stones that can be thrown, often granite rubble.
(H) *Mashishiwe* or *Masikiwe* (in Salawe). Sharp decomposing granite or murram.
(I) *Mbale*. Banded ironstone. Stone from which iron is smelted.
(J) *Butundo*. Pig iron.

Provisional Table of Catena

1. Catena on Granite

```
Luguru————————(granite outcrop)————————Luguru
  Isanga                                  Isanga
   ....[1]                                 ....
       Luseni                        Luseni
          Itogoro[2]——(sometimes)——Ibambasi
          (or Nhogolo)
                      Mbuga
                      Mseni
```

2. Catena on Sand-producing Metamorphic Rocks

```
Ing'ong'ho—————————(hill without large boulders)—————————Ing'ong'ho
  ....                                                      ....
         Itogoro————(and rarely)————Ibambasi
         (or Nhogolo)
                      Mbuga
```

3. Catena on Loam-producing Metamorphic Rocks

```
Mbale———————————(banded ironstone)———————————Mbale
 ....                                          ....
      Ibushi                          Ibushi
                    Mbuga
```

[1] At these points the appropriate fossil soils, *kikungu* or *ikurusi*, are frequently found interposed in catena.

[2] *Itogoro, Natogoro* primarily meaning open space, i.e. relatively treeless.

Sukumaland Soils

4. CATENA ON LACUSTRINE MARL

Mang'ong'ho gape————————(lime)————————Mang'ong'ho gape
Ibushi   Ibushi
  Ibambasi—————(if sand present)—————Ibambasi
                           Mbuga

5. CATENA ON SANDY TERTIARY ACCUMULATIONS[1]

Isanga   Isanga
  Ibambasi   Ibambasi
                           Mbuga

6. CATENA SHOWING CHANGE OPPOSITE

Kikungu (Shinyanga)   Ibushi
  2. Itogolo   Ibambasi 4.
                           Mongo   ya masagali
                           (River)

There are, of course, other permutations and combinations, but these illustrations will suffice to show something of the general run of soil catena in Sukumaland.

2. THE SANDY SOILS

A. *Isanga* (or *Lusanga*)

This is a coarse-grained[2] sandy to gravelly soil of a light reddish colour derived from granite with sporadic laterite, which is a red, ferruginous rock forming a surface or sub-surface covering in some areas. It is noteworthy that in Kizinza the word *isanga* denotes the marshy sandy 'potato' soils on the lake shore and this meaning is found as far south as Msalala and Salawe, where, however, the term *isanga* is also used with its general Sukuma meaning.[3]

Crops. This is the most favourable soil for bambarra groundnuts. It also grows sweet potatoes, millets, some cassava, and groundnuts, and it is used for other food crops such as maize and sorghums for which, however, it is considered to be less well suited.

Trees and shrubs	*Grasses*
Acacia usambarensis	Cynodon plectrostachyum
Acacia rovumae	Cenchrus ciliare
Acacia spirocarpa	Themeda triandra
Lannea Stuhlmannii	
Acacia Senegal	
Combretum Schimperi	
Acacia stenocarpa (rare)	

[1] Catena 1 to 5 are based on Dr. Williams' list, arranged with the assistance of Dr. Grantham.   [2] King, Malcolm, Grantham, Williams.
[3] Dr. D. R. Grantham.

Heavy tractors at work raising the level of the Malya Dam bank

Potatoes must be hoed beautifully clean. Note the rows of hoed weeds prior to burial under the ridges

'... both sorghums and maize give heavy yields ...' (p. 184) This large crop of maize was grown in an *mbuga ya milala*

Sagia speaking at a meeting of Nyashimba villagers during the preliminary investigations for this study

The Sandy Soils

Acacia drepanolobium (clumps)
Grewia fallax (island thickets)
Royena Fischeri
Anisotes dumosus

In the west there are pure stands of *Brachystegia* and *miombo* on this soil.

B. *Isanga ya kinele* (or *shinele*)

This is the *isanga* soil with flowing water from springs or seepage areas.

Crops. As a result of the water it is sometimes used for rice though more often potatoes are grown, and a little maize may be interplanted if the cultivation ridges are high enough. The potatoes must be lifted before the soil dries out and sets. Damp *isanga* can set very hard on drying, and for this reason Burtt included this soil in the hardpan group, but it is not a true hardpan from the agricultural point of view. It is *useless* for sorghums and all other crops.

C. *Isanga ya luselela* (primarily Kinyamwezi); *Isanga ya ikelege* or *Ilago lya ikelege*

These are practically synonymous. A damp sandy patch in which nothing grows well, but the last-named variety, where *ilago* indicates flooding, may be used for the cultivation of rice.

Crops. Besides rice, potatoes interplanted with a little maize on high ridges may be grown at the end of the rains, if there is not too much water. It is *useless* for all other crops.

D. *Luseni* (pl. *Maseni*)

This is a fine[1] sandy gritty soil almost indistinguishable from *isanga*; it is usually pale coloured and is derived directly from granite.[2]

Crops. This is the most suitable soil for cassava and potatoes. It also grows the other crops suitable to *isanga*. It will not grow sorghums or millets well, and groundnuts are usually poor.

Cultivation. On the *isanga* group cultivation is usually *mandi* or ridges, and these are ordinarily higher than on the heavier soils.

Trees and shrubs

Tamarindus indica
Adansonia digitata
Afzelia quanzensis (Nkola)

Thespesia Garkeana
Acacia spirocarpa
Acacia Benthami

[1] Grantham, Williams, King, Malcolm.   [2] Dr. D. R. Grantham.

3. THE RED FOSSIL (LATERIZED) SOILS

A. *Kikungu*

This is the southern Sukumaland name for the transported red and somewhat sandy laterized soil that can be formed either from granite or from sand-producing metamorphic rocks or sandy superficial deposits. It is often of mixed origin and may overlie any rock, lime, or 'cement'.[1] North of $3\frac{1}{2}°$ South latitude this soil, which is the most prevalent red (*yaza*) type, is called *nduha*, though this name is often used to cover all red soils in the north and east.[2] *Ikungu* is the northern Sukuma word for 'bush', which, of course, may happen to be situated on this soil. The southern Sukuma word may occasionally be used in the north, either by southerners who have moved there or by men who have visited the south and learned the word. It is clear, however, that the primary usage both of *kikungu* in the south and *nduha* in the north refers to the same red sandy soil and, as the latter is often used to cover a wider range, *kikungu* would appear to be the more precise term.

Crops. This is the most favourable soil for groundnuts. It also grows cotton, bambarra groundnuts, cowpeas, cassava, tobacco, sorghums, maize, millets, and sesame.[3]

Trees and shrubs	Grasses
Combretum Zeyheri	Hyparrhenia rufa (large pure stands)
Ostrioderris Stuhlmannii	Panicum maximum (large pure stands)
Commiphora ugogensis (thickets)	
Abrus Schimperi	
Adansonia digitata (few)	
Heeria insignis	
Dichrostachys glomerata	

(With alluvial thickets described by Burtt.)

B. *Ikurusi*

This is the general Sukuma name for the rich red to orange loam produced only from metamorphic rocks[4] (though in the south it is occasionally loosely applied to the *kikungu* soils). This soil is not as common as *kikungu* in Sukumaland and is comparatively rare in the chiefly granitic country north of the Shinyanga District. This may account for its frequent inclusion in the term *nduha* which, as we have seen, often covers all red soils in the northern dialects of Salawe, Buhungukira, Nera, Busmao, and much of Maswa.[5] The word *nduha*

[1] Dr. G. Williams, Dr. D. R. Grantham.
[2] Cf. Burtt and King's list.
[3] For the order of suitability of the various soils for each crop, see pp. 190-1.
[4] Cf. Hartley on Maswa, quoted by Milne, para 132.
[5] Hartley, Burtt, and King.

has, however, been borrowed by some of the *badakama* (people of the south),[1] by whom it is used primarily as a synonym for *ikurusi*.[2] But as it has only a limited currency in the south in this sense[3] the name *ikurusi* would appear to be the more precise term.

It is possible that the use of the locality name *ikungu* for bush land, and the soil name *nduha* in its widest sense for the red *ikurusi* soils which are less frequently inhabited, may account for some of the difficulties of nomenclature which have been experienced in the study of the red soils of Sukumaland.

Ikiri or *lukili* is an Msalala name applied there to a pale-coloured powdery form of *nduha* (or *ikurusi*). It is a derivative of the more acid metamorphic rocks, conglomerates, and sedimentaries, and is hardly distinguishable from *luseni*.[4]

Crops. These bright red loams derived from the rocks of the Upper Basement Complex tend to be shallow and are not so good for cultivation as the *kikungu* and are less extensively used, though this may be partly attributable to the absence of water supplies in the metamorphic areas. The red sorghum *busiga wa bukula* and some *wilu* varieties, however, grow fairly well in good rains. This soil is *useless* for potatoes except in years of particularly heavy rain.

Cultivation. It is noteworthy that, while the *kikungu* soils after long and continuous cultivation will produce an *isanga* soil, the *ikurusi* will not do so and remains a relatively heavy loam, though much colour is lost with constant use.[5] Besides the factor of colour, the *ikurusi* loam can be easily distinguished from *kikungu* by its sticky consistency when wet, which causes it to clog on a hoe like *ibushi*. Unlike *mbuga*, however, it does not take long to dry out sufficiently to make cultivation possible. *Kikungu*, on the other hand, is workable even during rain.

Trees and shrubs	Grasses
Acacia hebecladoides	Schima nervosum
Acacia pallens	Heteropogon contortus
Acacia Goertzii	
Acacia stenocarpa	
Combretum ternifolium	

(Also *Brachystegia* and *miombo* proper in the west.)

4. IBUSHI

The use of this name is somewhat variable. It is sometimes applied

---

[1] A considerable number visited the north on railway construction.

[2] Dr. Grantham found that the word *nduha* is often used in this sense in Salawe where there are few true *kikungu* soils.

[3] Of 200 people in southern Sukuma who were asked 'what is *nduha*?' only twenty-two knew the word.   [4] Dr. D. R. Grantham, geologist.

[5] Cf. The small patches of weathered *ikurusi* at Ng'wandogosa near Nkolandoto, Shinyanga.

to a calcareous chocolate loam and sometimes to friable *mbuga*—like soils which show lime nodules. These are also referred to in some parts as *mbuga ya lunongu* (the ostrich flats).[1] There is also a rare distinction between the main class of *ibushi* soil and a more sandy variety known as *ibushi lyapi*, which is a black friable soil, on which groundnuts will grow, often marked by *Acacia Fischeri*. Ordinarily *ibushi* is not as dark as *mbuga* and is not ill-drained, though it will often show small cracks. It usually overlies and is directly derived from beds of detrital material sufficiently rich in lime to yield travertine limestone on erosion.[2] *Ibushi* is mainly found in depressions between the higher-lying blocks of the plateau, but the depressions are not *mbugas*, though they may include *mbuga* areas. They are dissected and drained by rivers of moderate grade and the *ibushi* occupies the interfluves.[3]

Crops. This is one of the most valuable soils in Sukumaland. It is the most favourable soil for cotton. It will also grow good crops of sorghums, millets, groundnuts, maize, grams, tobacco, sesame, and pigeon pea. If heavy, it is *useless* for cassava, and potatoes and bambarra groundnuts on *ibushi* are poor. It is, however, fairly easily overworked and pulverized, thus becoming susceptible to aeolian erosion.

Cultivation. *Ibushi* soils are generally cultivated flat (*sesa*), but when *mandi* ridges are used they are lower than those on the *isanga* soils. Very beneficial effects have been shown from using tie-ridges on *ibushi* soil at Lubaga. This soil cannot be hoed during or directly after rain as it clogs on the hoe like *ikurusi*. It dries out moderately quickly and can therefore be cultivated soon after rain.

Trees and shrubs

    Acacia spirocarpa—Acacia tortillis
    Acacia Fischeri
    Acacia usambarensis

Other species[4] are:
    Acacia Senegal
    Acacia Benthami
    Acacia hebecladoides
    Acacia drepanolobium
    Balanites Aegyptiaca
    Commiphora Schimperi
    Fagara Merkeri
    Dichrostachys glomerata ⎫
    Ormocarpum trichocarpum⎭ generally in pure thickets

---

[1] There is a large *mbuga ya lunongu* near Ngofila. See also the large *ibushi* area round Ng'wamashele marked on the soil map, p. 175.

[2] Dr. D. R. Grantham and G. Milne.

[3] G. Milne. For a fuller description see his reconnaissance report, para. 133 (unpublished).

[4] From C. J. W. Pitt, Assistant Conservator of Forests.

Cordia spp.
Boscia sp.
Boscia caloneura
Dalbergia melanoxylon (rare)
Grewia similis
Albizzia Harveyi
Terminalia Stuhlmannii (v. rare)
Acacia mellifera (rare)
Capparis tomentosa
Delonix elata (only on 'cliffs')

5. THE HARDPAN GROUP

Itogolo (or *Nhogolo*)

This term means 'open space' in Kisukuma and is only secondarily a soil name. It is applied to the foot-slopes merging into marginal *mbuga* where the soil is not a true hardpan or where the hardpan or 'cemented' area has been broken up by continuous cultivation. Thus when formed from granite it is a sandy clay loam which is capable of pan formation and is very soft when wet. It sets to form a thin hard crust when dry. When formed from rocks of the Upper Basement Complex it is a friable grey loam or *quasi-mbuga*. The lowest members of this type may show cracks in the dry season. *Itogolo* is to be found below *kikungu*, *luseni*, and *ikurusi* and often has a reddish surface tinge. In some parts it may occupy up to a third of the open space below the tree line before true *mbuga* is reached.[1]

Crops. Together with *matongo* it is said to be the most favourable soil for cowpeas. It also grows sorghums, cotton, grams, and sesame. It is *useless* for potatoes, while groundnuts, bambarra groundnuts, and cassava are poor.

Cultivation. This soil type occupies considerable areas and when *mandi* or ridge cultivation is used the banks are usually low.

Trees and shrubs
(Hardpan thicket flora)

Combretum parvifolium	*Acacia rovumae*
Commiphora Schimperi	*Balanites tomentosa*
Lannea humilis	*Commiphora sarandensis*
Anisotes dumosus	*Boscia Fischeri*
Commiphora subsessilifolia	*Dalbergia ochracea*
Commiphora Stuhlmannii	*Teclea glomerata*
Fockia Schinzii	*Dichrostachys glomerata*
Combretum purpureiflorum	*Fagara Merkeri*
Capparis sp.	*Maerua Angolensis*
Albizzia Harveyi	*Mimusops densiflora*
Albizzia amara	*Ziziphus mucronata*
Acacia pallens	*Cadaba adenotricha*

NOTE. The following are the true hardpan or 'cemented' soils, and

[1] Dr. D. R. Grantham.

as they are distinguished by the Sukuma entirely by the prevalent vegetation, only the index plant is given for each.

Ibambasi (pl. Mabambasi)

The following *mabambasi* hardpan soils are always characterized (in the dry weather) by a scantily covered hard grey surface with many bare patches and slight sand wash. The top few inches are close packed, but may be of medium texture and moderately friable. In the wet season they are saturated and have an almost buttery consistency. Below there is a well-marked horizon of bone-dry dark grey mottled clay of varying degrees of hardness.[1]

A. *Ibambasi ya masagala*

Masagala are *Anisotes dumosus*. This is the youngest of the true grey soils which show a definite hardpan horizon.

Crops. This soil will grow a fair crop of sorghum in the first year. After two or three years' cultivation it is possible to grow maize, cowpeas, and grams, but it remains less favourable for cotton and millets. All *mabambasi* soils are *useless* for bambarra groundnuts, groundnuts, potatoes, and cassava.

B. *Ibambasi ya malula (gapi)*

Malula are gall acacias. *A. drepanolobium* or *A. formicarum* or *A. malacocephala* are the plant indicators and are dominant. This soil is a little harder than *Ibambasi ya masagala*, but it will grow the same crops, though a slightly longer period may be required under sorghums before the others can be interplanted.

C. *Ibambasi ya mahushi*

Mahushi are *Acacia Fischeri*. The occurrence of these trees on hardpan at any great density is not common, as *mahushi* prefer *ibushi*, or *kigulu* on dark soil. If it is present in sufficient quantities the same crops can be grown as those mentioned above, as the *A. Fischeri* is said to break up the pan to some extent.

D. *Ibambasi ya mkomangwa = Commiphora campestris*[2]

This soil is useless for all crops and is practically never cultivated as it is too hard.

E. *Ibambasi ya mitinje = Lannea humilis*

This is the most fully developed and the hardest of the *ibambasi* group and, as with *ibambasi ya mkomangwa*, it is practically never cultivated.

[1] Burtt and Milne.
[2] Cf. vegetation map, facing p. 5, with population map, facing p. 9.

6. THE *MBUGA* SOILS

Here it must be noted that there is little difference between the various *mbuga* soils from the point of view of cultivation, and therefore the Sukuma classification is more general and shows fewer subdivisions than with other types. In describing a particular locality the Sukuma will often qualify the generic soil name *mbuga* by the name of the prevalent tree, *mbuga ya malula* and so forth. They make little or no distinction between the *mbuga* soils marked by most trees from the point of view of vegetation, arable agriculture being related primarily to position *vis-à-vis* water. There would be no advantage in recording a soil-flora classification such as that which indicates the stages in hardpan formation. The *malula gape* or white acacias (*A. seyal* and *A. seyal* var. *fistula*), however, indicate the damper areas in the lateral plains which are nevertheless subject to inundation. The following list begins with the marginal *mbugas* and moves towards the central river.

A. *Mbuga ya nseseko* (the word is derived from *kusesa*)[1]

Where the seasonal rivers have followed for the most part of their course a well-defined river-channel and then suddenly enter the flat *mbuga* plains, the water spreads out in a fan or delta over a broad sheet of country. During this flooding process, the fine clays are deposited with some sand. In areas where the flood-water has lain for some time, the soil is almost black and cracks deeply in the dry season. The soil in the drier areas is of a grey hardpan-like formation that does not crack.

Crops. The soil of the *nseseko* produces very heavy yields of sorghums, and potatoes interplanted with maize grow well on ridges. Rice may be planted in the flood. It is not used for other crops.

Trees and shrubs	*Grasses*
Acacia Kirkii (all over)	Hygrophila spinosa (in pools)
Acacia Stuhlmannii (in damper parts)	
Drier parts:	
Maerua erassifolia	
Commiphora subsessilifolia	
Acacia drepanolobium	
Salvadora Persica	
Acacia mellifera	
Commiphora stolonifera	
Sansevieria robusta (on occasional termitaria)	

B. *Mbuga ya milala*

Ilala means crack, and thus the term can cover all *mbugas* where cracking is considerable. This is one of the largest types of *mbuga* and varies in colour from a grey similar to that of *mabambasi* to a black.

[1] p. 203.

Like the *mbuga ya bubuni* it is also sometimes called *mbuga ya bololo* or *bubumbila*,[1] which are the names for mud of various consistencies. As I have mentioned, the parts which remain saturated for a longer period than the rest are usually marked with *Acacia seyal* var. *fistula*. These *mbugas* may also be called *mbuga ya malula* (gall acacias) where cracking is not very marked.

Cultivation. Cultivation should be begun during the dry season. Brush harrowing by broadcasting the seed and then dragging a thorn-tree over the field is not sufficient until this soil has been used for some years.

Crops. This is the next best farming *mbuga* to *mbuga ya nseseko*, and both sorghums and maize give heavy yields, but maize can only be planted on the higher parts as it will not stand flooding. The sorghums are dry-sown at the time of cultivation and germinate with the short rains which do not produce much flooding. Then, when the big rains come, the young plants are tall enough to keep their heads above the water, which for short periods may be knee-deep in parts. This soil will also grow cotton and millets in the same areas as the maize, but it is *useless* for potatoes, cowpeas, grams, rice (except in depressions), groundnuts, cassava, and bambarra groundnuts.

Trees and shrubs

Acacia seyal var. *fistula*
Acacia malacocephala
Acacia seyal

C. *Mbuga ya matinde* (or *majinje*)—Tussocks

These are the real seasonal swamps in the lower-lying areas and depressions in the *mbuga* flats. The large tussocks or lumps are called *magaganika, matinde,* or *manonho*.

Crops. Rice is the only crop which can be grown on account of the depth of the seasonal flooding. Its cultivation is, however, often limited because of the large lump formations which necessitate heavy dry-season hoeing.

Grasses and herbs

Setaria Holstii (makes the tussocks)	*Hibiscus canabinus*
Digitaria regularis	*Aspilia* and *Wedelia* spp.
Themeda triandra	

D. *Mbuga ya bubuni* or *Mbuga ya iwawa*

These two names are synonymous and are sometimes supplemented with a third, *mbuga ya bololo*, but *bololo* is only a name for wet mud. This type of open light-grey *mbuga* flat is not common, vegetation is

---

[1] p. 189.

The Mbuga Soils

scanty and the fine powdery ash-like sodium dust is as typical as the peculiarly viscous mud which it forms during the rains. In Sukumaland this type is confined to about two large *mbugas* near the Manonga river[1] and other smaller areas in the south-east.

Cultivation. This type of *mbuga* has to be cultivated during the dry season as it becomes impossibly heavy after even a little rain. Brush harrowing with thorn scrub is sufficient.

Crops. When large it is said to be useless for all crops, but if small it will grow poor crops of maize and sorghums in a year of good rainfall. It is useless in any case for bambarra groundnuts, groundnuts, rice, cotton, cowpeas, grams, cassava, tobacco, sesame, &c.

Flora. Acacia formicarum.

E. *Ilago* (pl. *Malago*)

Is the name given to areas near to the river-banks (*ngegu*) which are subject to inundation and on which alluvial soils are deposited by seasonal flooding. Where the depth of the flood-water does not preclude their use, these rich alluvial soils are extensively cultivated. In parts of Nera and Maswa, where they are porous and of considerable depth, they are sub-irrigated during the dry season from the river-bed water-table. Occasionally, in the narrower valleys, *malago* at the base of the foot-slopes are watered by springs or seepage areas. An *ilago lya ikelege* is similar but situated on *isanga* soil higher on the hillside. Thus the name *ilago* refers primarily to a flooded or irrigated area which may or may not dry out after the end of the rains, according to the source of water supply.

Crops. Though relatively small in area the *malago* are potentially of considerable agricultural and economic importance. The inundated or flood-basin type is used mainly for rice. The damp areas below springs or seepage areas, and those *malago* which are sub-irrigated from the river-bed water-table, are usually planted with sweet potatoes often interplanted with maize on high *mandi* ridges. When the soil is not too damp or subject to severe flooding, these areas can support a market-garden agriculture which, in addition to sugar-cane and bananas, may include many minor varieties such as chillies, onions, and vegetables, as well as date-palms and fruit-trees. Some *malago* discharge an important function in Sukumaland agriculture, as those which remain damp in the dry season can be planted up at the end of the rains as nurseries for the supply of sweet potato vines and for catch-crops of quick maturing sorghums.

---

[1] One is near the junction of the Tungu and Manonga rivers beyond Mihama at Ng'wandinho, and the other is near Ng'wamashele.

1. Riverine forest: *mbuga ya mwilago* (means 'in the *ilago*').

Trees and shrubs

Ficus sycamorus	*Markhamia acuminata*
Tamarindus indica	*Commiphora Stuhlmannii*
Adansonia digitata	*Commiphora boviniana*
Piptadenia Hildebrandtii	*Grewia pachycalyx*
Mimusops densiflora	*Triaspis speciosa*
Albizzia sericocephala	*Acalypha ornata*
Albizzia brachycalyx	*Acacia pennata*
Kigelia Aethiopica	*Phyllanthus*. spp.

2. Riverine grassland:

Trees and shrubs	Grasses and herbs
Acacia albida	*Panicum maximum*
Acacia campylacantha	*Sorghum arundinaceum*
Acacia nefasia	*Hyparrhenia Ruprechtii*
Acacia spirocarpa	*Hyparrhenia cymbaria*
Kigelia Aethiopica	*Rottboellia exaltata*
Lonchocarpus capassa	*Leonotis nepetifolia*
Ficus sycamorus	*Astrochlaena* spp.
Acacia usambarensis (rare)	*Hyacyamoides* spp.
	Hibiscus canabinus
	Abutilon indicum
	Bidens Hildebrandtii
	Aspilia aspera

F. *Mbuga ya ndago*

This is a small strip of alluvial *mbuga* within the old river-banks (*ngegu*) and is characterized by the *ndago* reeds which are used to make sleeping mats, and of which the roots are a laxative medicine for children.

Crops. Clearly where the rivers come down in considerable volume it is not possible to cultivate within the bed, but when this strip is in a safe position sugar-cane is sometimes planted.

Note on Mbuga *Soils.* It has been suggested in explanation of the great fertility of many *mbugas* that the inundated areas may be auto-rejuvenating from depth by the solution of salts, and that the marginal and central flats receive annual depositions of fertile silt from the higher soils. This latter process certainly occurs on the *mbuga ya nseseko* which receives 'delta deposits', and in the *malago* on which riverine alluvium settles.

7. MINOR SOIL TYPES

A. *Termitaria*

Kibandagulu

This is the low or flat termite mound made by the *nswa gwa kaserere*,

Minor Soil Types

which is a small species of white ant. It can intrude in almost any soil, is usually calcareous and is of such frequent occurrence and so widely spread by erosion that it may be classified as a soil type.

Crops. These patches grow the same crops as the soils in which they are situated, but produce larger yields. They are specially sought after for the cultivation of tobacco and onions. *Kibandagulu* is useless for rice and, except in particularly wet seasons, for potatoes.

Flora. The vegetation associations of the termitaria are grouped under one head by Burtt and will be enumerated under *kigulu*.

Kigulu

This is a higher termite mound which is consequently much more noticeable than the *kibandagulu* which may be almost flat on the ground. The *kigulu* (pl. *shigulu*) is made by the *nswa gwa matine*. The soil from these mounds, which are very common in some parts, is also spread over considerable areas by erosion. As Burtt points out, the termitaria are so numerous in some localities that they occupy a position of considerable importance in soil economy. As they are often calcareous even amongst acid soils, they may form a valuable source of lime fertilizers. It is said that apart from shape, the soil derived from a *kigulu* is distinguishable from that of the *kibandagulu* in having a higher clay content and in being more colloidal.

Crops. The same crops are grown as on the surrounding soils, but like *kibandagulu* larger yields are produced. *Kigulu* is useless for rice and potatoes.

Trees and shrubs

Commiphora Schimperi	*Fagara Merkeri*
Lannea humilis	*Maerua Angolensis*
Cassia goratensis	*Commiphora Stuhlmanii*
Albizzia Harveyi	*Euphorbia bilocularis*
Grewia bicolor	*Zizyphus mucronata*
Grewia praecox	*Tamarindus indica* (occasional)
Markhamia acuminata	*Adansonia digitata* (occasional)
Anisotes dumosus	

Note. Both *kigulu* and *kibandagulu* are the circular patches of lighter coloured soils which, from the air, often give the erroneous impression of abandoned house sites.

B. *Itongo* (pl. *Matongo*)

This is not a true soil name but has several meanings[1] in various parts of Sukumaland. In southern Sukumaland an *itongo* is the abandoned homestead or stockyard site which is used for the cultivation of maize and vegetables. Naturally such sites are to be found on all the

[1] See Sukuma glossary, p. 202.

higher (*higuria*) lands where houses and stockyards are usually situated, and this fact may have given rise to the use of the word *matongo* in northern Sukumaland to denote the home fields on the ridge.

Crops. Being very heavily manured land, the *matongo* are the most favourable places for the cultivation of maize, gourds, cowpeas, grams, tobacco, and sesame. They are also occasionally used for sorghums. They are said to be less favourable for groundnuts and useless for bambarra groundnuts and potatoes. They cannot be cultivated until three or four years after the site has been abandoned by cattle.

Flora. There is no flora peculiar to *matongo* or *shilugu* other than that which is typical of the higher land and the various soils on which the houses and cattle-pens are built. *Lugobe* grass (*Cynodon plectrostachyum*) is, however, fairly common in *matongo*, as is *zunzu* (*Leucas martinicensis*), but *malamata* (*Setaria verticillata*) is common and grows luxuriantly.

C. *Longa*

This is a depression or valley and not a soil. Just as *itogolo* in its primary meaning is open space, *matongo* has come to mean the arable fields on high ground, *ikungu* in Nera means open bush country, so *longa* may be said to indicate the 'lower ground' and could be translated 'down there' or 'below in the valley'. In fact, it is one of a number of locality names which have been confused with soil names.

D. *Ilambo* or *Itaba*

These two names are synonymous, as both refer to depressions which fill with water during the rains, and both may dry out later, though *ilambo* is usually used when deep water is present. These depressions are found in practically all Sukumaland soils including the light and sandy types, where, however, they are rare. They are most common along the main seasonal river systems and the tributaries, and may be the 'ox-bows' or old river-channels which have been cut off by an alteration of the river-bed. They are also common in the *ibambasi ya mkomangwa* hardpan country. The deep 'ox-bows' may hold water long into the dry season, but the smaller depressions, particularly in *ibambasi*, dry up quickly.

Crops. They are used only for the cultivation of rice.

Trees, shrubs, and herbs

Aeschynomene Pfundii	In *Commiphora campestris* hardpan country:
Water lilies and aquatic plants	*Echinochloa haploclada* (reddish purple grass)
	Hygrophila spinosa (in the pond)
Gardenia Thunburgii	*Aeschynomene telekii*

E. *Italwa* or *Italu*

This is the name given to the patches of soil near the rivers on which an efflorescence of salts is visible. There is little flora and no crops can be grown. The salts called *magembia*[1] are extracted from the *italwa* soil by placing the earth on grass tables and running water through it into trays below. The water is then evaporated. The salts thus obtained are used for human consumption though salt from Lake Eyasi is preferred when obtainable. In some areas considerable village industries exist operated by the women producing *magembia* in this way.

F. *Ibumba*

This is a clay used for making pots; it is found under *kikungu*, *itogolo*, and *ibambasi* soils. Only the women know the surface indications which show them where to dig for the clay which is not obtainable on the surface (cf. *Itaka ly' ebumba* in Zinza).

G. *Ndoba*[2]

This is the Sukuma name covering both the white granite grit with calcareous cement, and also the calcareous nodules in a clayey matrix. *Ndoba* very frequently underlies *mbuga*, *ibushi*, *itogolo*, and some of the hardpans, and it is the fact that it has proved impervious to a high degree that has made the construction of surface-water catchment works possible over the vast majority of the waterless plains of Sukumaland.

H. *Sands and muds*

Misengelelwa
Mseni
Misengwa
} These are some of the names given to river sand in various parts of Sukumaland.

Masalu. This is the generic name for all sand from anywhere. Thus one can say *masalu gaza* = red sand. *Masalu gwa mongo* = river sand.

Ludefu. This is a quicksand.

Kadondolio. Deep alluvium deposits left by a receding river in which a traveller can sink as in a quicksand.

Bololo. Sloppy wet mud which squelches between the toes.

Bubumbila (south). Drier mud which sticks to the feet.

Bugado (north). Drier mud which sticks to the feet.

---

[1] Analysis made by the Geological Department shows 'some earthy insolubles, a trace of sulphates and phosphates, some nitrates and much iron, alumina, lime and magnesia'.

[2] Commonly known as 'white *changarawe*'.

8. WATER AND SOILS

The *isanga* and *kikungu* groups are generally speaking the only soils below which springs and seepage areas occur. This is due to the fact that they form a very thin covering of superficial material over the solid rock. It is also possible to obtain water from below, or at the outcrop of laterite sheets,[1] particularly where these overlie granite. Water is less commonly found in connexion with the metamorphic rock occurrences in Sukumaland. As water is found very frequently below *luseni*, a soil map gives a good general impression of natural water supplies if the sandy river-beds, in which water is almost always found, are marked. More important still, such a map will show the definitely waterless areas, as springs and wells are never found in the hardpan, *ibushi*, and *mbuga* soils, and only very rarely in the *ndoba* subsoils.[2]

9. SUITABILITY OF VARIOUS SOILS FOR CROPS

This is a rough guide to the selection of soils in their order of preference by a self-constituted agricultural committee of the village of Nyashimba:

Crop	Most suitable soils
Sorghums (*Busiga*)	1. Mbuga 2. *Ibushi* and *Itongo* 3. *Itogolo* (low land) 4. *Kikungu*
Cotton (*Buluba*)	1. *Ibushi*
Sweet Potatoes (*Mandolo*)	1. *Ibushi* 2. *Ilago* 3. *Kikungu* 4. *Isanga*
Groundnuts (*Nhalanga*)	1. *Kikungu* 2. *Isanga* 3. *Mabushi* (a sandy variety) 4. *Nduha* (very red = *ikurusi*) 5. *Itogolo* or *Nhogolo*
Maize (*Mandege*)	1. *Itongo* 2. *Ibushi* 3. *Kikungu* and *ikurusi* 4. *Ilago* with *mbuga*
Bambarra groundnuts (*Mhande*)	1. *Isanga* 2. *Kikungu* 3. *Ikurusi*

---

[1] Cf. the *Biliga* (pl. *Bilisé*) wells through murram in the northern Gold Coast.
[2] The soil map covers some of the more important waterless areas of Sukumaland.

Suitability of Various Soils

Crops	Most suitable soils
Cowpeas (*Shili*)	1. *Itogolo* or *Nhogolo* / *Itongo* 2. *Kikungu* 3. *Ikurusi*
Grams (*Ndulu*)	1. *Itongo* 2. *Ibushi* 3. *Itogolo* or *Nhogolo*
Cassava (*Maliwa*)	1. *Luseni* 2. *Ikurusi* 3. *Ibushi* (sour) 4. *Kikungu*
Rice (*Bupunga*)	1. *Ilago* 2. *Mbuga* with *isanga-luseni* (delta deposits)
Tobacco (*Itumbati*)	1. *Itongo* 2. *Kikulu* 3. *Ibushi* 4. *Kikungu*
Sesame (*Bunyonya*)	1. *Itongo* 2. *Isanga* 3. *Kikungu* 4. *Ikurusi* 5. *Ibushi* 6. *Itogolo* or *Nhogolo*

And the following soils are less favourable for crops:

1. *Italwa* or *Italu*.
2. *Ibambasi* bare patches which will not even grow grass, though crops can be grown if there is an admixture of other soil in sufficient quantity or if the pan has been broken up by tie-ridging.[1]
3. *Lukele* and *Ikelege*, unless sufficient water is present to make an *ilago*, when rice can be grown.

VEGETATION

SOME SUKUMALAND GRASSES AND PASTURE PLANTS

Sukuma name	Botanical name
Muhululang'hang'ha	*Achyranthes aspera*
Huruda ndo	*Aristida adscensionis* (Annual)
Cheyu	*Aristida stendiliana* (Foxtail) (Annual)
Yiinza	*Blepharis acanthoides*
Huruda ntale	*Bothriochloa insculpta*

[1] Experience at Lubaga Experimental Farm with tie-ridging *ibambasi*, and at Nyalikungu with irrigation beds, &c., has shown that if run-off can be prevented and water can be retained long enough to penetrate, *ibambasi* has great potentialities, the importance of which will be realized from the soil map, p. 175, which indicates the prevalence of this soil type.

Vegetation

Sukuma name	Botanical name
Huruda ndo	*Chloris gayana* (Annual or Perennial)
Galu moso	*Chloris pychnothryx* (Annual or Perennial)
Uwele wa kuli	*Chloris virgata* (Annual)
Ouibila	*Corchorus olitorius* (Spinach)
Lugobe	*Cynodon dactylon* (Perennial)
Lugobe	*Cynodon plectrostachyum* (Perennial)
Samata	*Cyphocarpa orthocantha*
Bugimbi	*Dactyloctenium Aegyptium* (Annual or Perennial)
Lambolambo	*Digitaria perrotteti?* (Annual)
Lambolambo	*Echinochloa*, cf. *Haploclada* (Perennial)
Nduko	*Eleusine indica* (Annual)
Ndindindi	*Eragrostis aspera* (Annual)
Ndindindi ndo?	*Eragrostis chalantha*
Ndindindi ndo	*Eragrostis chapelieri*
Gagurunya ndo	*Eragrostis* sp. (Perennial)
Ndindindi sp.	*Eragrostis ?tenuifolia*
Igunguli	*Heleotropum zaylanicum*
Dasa	*Heteropogon contortus* (Spear grass) (Perennial)
Ifa ilulu	*Hyparrhenia* sp.
Nhelengu	*Hyparrhenia rufa*
Mikuli	*Indigofera viscosa*
Lusuunga	*Lactuca taraxacifolia* (Sow thistle)
Zunzu	*Leucas martinicensis*
Fweya	*Loudetia* sp.
Ndululu	*Panicum maximum* (Perennial)
Gurunya	*Panicum* sp.
Legi	*Pennisetum racemosum* (Perennial)
Maswa nyanzige	*Rhynchelytrum repens*
Busiga wa kuli	*Rhynchelytrum roseum*
Mabembere	*Rottboellia exaltata*
Ilendi	*Sesamum angustifolia* (Foxglove)
Ilamata (pl. *Malamata*)	*Setaria verticillata* (Annual)
Ikumbo	*Sida grewioides*
Supyu	*Sporobolus arginatus*
Bushiku	*Sporobolus indicus*
Keduma	*Tephrosia elegans*
Bayanda ba nyasauci	*Tragus racemosus* (Annual)

Note. As in the case of soils, these Sukuma names will show dialect variations, and further investigation is required.

USEFUL INDIGENOUS SUKUMALAND TREES

The following species of trees found in this area are valuable for the reasons shown against each and are usually protected from felling during bush clearing.

Sukuma name	Botanical name	Uses of tree
Nshingisha	Boscia Fischeri (Pax.)	Tembe roofing; shade; leaves are valuable for cattle fodder
Mondo	Entandrophragma Bussei (Harms.)	Medicine; shade
Nshishi	Tamarindus indica (L.)	Edible fruit; shade; walking sticks made from roots
Mgunga	Acacia spirocarpa (Hochst.) Acacia tortillis	Valuable for poles; hoe handles; shade
Ngumo	Ficus nigropunctata (Warb. ex Mildbr. & Burret p.pt.)	Medicine; fruit edible
Nkuyu	Ficus sonderi (Miq.)	Vegetative reproduction; planted as gate posts to stockyards
Male	Lonchocarpus eriocalyx (Harms.)	Medicine for coughs made from bast (phloem)
Nkola	Afzelia quanzensis (Welw.)	Used for doors, beds; shade
Mpogoro bongole	Albizzia amara (Boiv.)	Medicine; bark is used instead of tea
Nkonze	Mimusops densiflora (Engl., non Bak.)	Medicine from bast or roots; valuable for shade
Igwata	Acacia Senegal (Willd.)	Gum
Ng'wandu	Adansonia digitata (L.)	Fruit and leaves edible; string from bark; harbours bees—therefore honey and wax
Mlangali	Euphorbia candelabrum (Trém. ex Kotschy)	Used for making beds and slates for use in village schools
Ng'hongwa	Sclerocarya birrea (Hochst.)	Edible fruit
Ngongwa	Acacia rovumae (Oliv.)	Shade; a good hardwood
Ngazu	Tricalysia cacondensis (Hiern.)	Aperient medicine from bast and roots

Bibliography

THE following is an abridged list of books and papers relevant to the subject-matter of this study, some of which have been referred to in the text.

AGRICULTURAL RESEARCH CONFERENCE. Nairobi, 29–31 July 1947. *East African Agricultural Journal*, October 1947.

BAKER, E. C. 'Administrative Survey of Uzinza.'[1]

BAKER, S. J. K. 'The Distribution of Native Population over East Africa', *Africa*, January 1937.

BALL, R. S. 'Mixed Farming in East Africa', *East African Agricultural Journal*, March 1936.

BÖSCH, R. P. FRIDOLIN. *Les Banyamwezi*. Münster, 1930.

BOURDILLON, SIR BERNARD. 'The Future of Native Authorities', *Africa*, July 1945.

BRAYNE, F. L. *Socrates in an Indian Village*. Oxford, 1929.

BUELL, R. *The Native Problem in Africa*. Macmillan, 1928.

CAMERON, SIR DONALD. *A note on Land Tenure in the Yoruba Provinces*. Lagos, 1933.

CAMPBELL, SIR GEORGE. 'The Tenure of Land in India', in *Systems of Land Tenure*, 1881.

CHARLESWORTH, J. B. 'Notes on Usukuma.'[1]

COBDEN CLUB. *Systems of Land Tenure in various countries*. Cassel, Petter, Galpin, 1881.

CORY, H. 'The Usule Chiefdom, Shinyanga District.'[1]

—— 'Tribal Constitution'[1] (Draft).

CURRIE, SIR JAMES. 'The Educational Experiment in the Anglo-Egyptian Sudan. 1930–1933.' Reprinted from the *Journal of the African Society*, 1934, 1935.

DARLING, M. L. *The Punjab Peasant in Prosperity and Debt*. Humphrey Milford, 1925.

—— *Rusticus Loquitur*. Humphrey Milford, Oxford, 1930.

DE KAT ANGELINO, A. D. A., *Colonial Policy*, trans. G. Renier, The Hague, Martinus Nijhoff, 1931.

DIXEY, F. *A Practical Handbook of Water Supply*.

DOWSON, SIR ERNEST. 'Report of an Enquiry into Land Tenure and Related Questions.' el'Iraq, 1931.

EAST AFRICAN AGRICULTURAL JOURNAL. Editorial 'Soil Fertility', July 1945.

ERNLE, THE RT. HON. LORD. *English Farming Past and Present*. Longmans, 1922.

GILES, L. C. 'The Hausa Village and Co-operation.'[1]

GILLESPIE, J. A. 'Notes on Pack Transport amongst the Baggara of the Sudan', 1938.[1]

[1] Unpublished.

Bibliography

GILLMAN, C. 'Problems of Land Utilisation in Tanganyika Territory', *South African Geographical Journal*, April 1938.
—— 'Man, Land and Water in East Africa', *East African Agricultural Journal*, March 1938.
—— *Water Consultant's Report*. Government Printer, Tanganyika.
GILLMAN, H. 'Bush Fallowing on the Makonde Plateau', *Tanganyika Notes and Records*, June 1945.
GRABHAM, G. W. 'Water Storage in the Anglo-Egyptian Sudan', 1927.[1]
GRIFFITHS, A. W. M. 'Land Tenure and the Wachagga.'[1]
—— 'Land Tenure in Bukoba.'[1]
GUISE-WILLIAMS, O. 'Memorandum on Village Organisation in Usukuma.'[1]
—— 'The Village Constitution in Usukuma.'[1]
HAILEY, THE LORD. *An African Survey*. Oxford University Press, 1938.
—— *Native Land Tenure in Africa*, C.M. No. 10. Colonial Office, 1945.
—— 'Native Administration in Africa', *International Affairs*, July 1947.
HALL, SIR DANIEL. *Review of Improvement of Native Agriculture in Relation to Population and Public Health.*
HARRISON, E. *A Memorandum on Soil Erosion*. Crown Agents for the Colonies, 1937.
HARTLEY, B. J. 'Land Tenure in Usukuma', *Tanganyika Notes and Records*, April 1938.
HONE, E. D. 'Memorandum on Redistribution of Population between the Nyanza Chiefdoms and Zinza.'[1]
HORNBY, H. E. 'Some notes on Pack Transport.'[1]
HOWARD, L. E. *The Earth's Green Carpet*. Faber & Faber.
HUXLEY, E. Articles on Soil Erosion in the *Geographical Magazine* and elsewhere.
KANTHACK, F. E. *Report on the Control of the Natural Waters of Tanganyika*, &c. Dar-es-Salaam, 1936.
KERKHAM, R. E. 'Grass Fallow in Uganda', *East African Agricultural Journal*, July 1947.
KING, J. G. M. 'Memorandum on Soil Erosion and Reafforestation in Shinyanga District',[1] 1937.
—— 'Mixed Farming in Northern Nigeria',[1] 1938.
LEAKE, H. M. *Land Tenure and Agricultural Production in the Tropics*. W. Heffer and Sons, 1927.
LEWIS, A. D. *Small Earth Dams across Streams*. Dept. of Irrigation, Pretoria, 1935.
LIVERSAGE, V. 'The Tenure of Native Land in East Africa; the Economic Aspect', *East African Agricultural Journal*, March 1936.
LONGLAND, F. 'Development of Water Supplies in the Western Province.'[1]
LYNN, C. W. *Report on a Visit to Northern Nigeria to study Mixed Farming*. Accra, 1937.

[1] Unpublished.

Bibliography

MAHER, C. Review—'Erosion in the Punjab'—*East African Agricultural Journal*, April 1947.
MAIR, L. P. 'Native Land Tenure in East Africa', *Africa*, July 1931.
MAKWAIA, NTEMI. 'Notes on Land, Cattle and Water in Shinyanga District.'[1]
—— 'Notes on the Banghonghogongho of Busiha.'[1]
MALCOLM, D. W. *Report on Gum and Gum Arabic*. Dar-es-Salaam, 1936.
—— 'Report on Economic Conditions in Ukara Island.'[1]
MAYNARD, THE REV. W. J. 'Notes on the Basukuma inhabiting Shinyanga District.'[1]
MILNE, G. 'Soil Reconnaissance Report.'[1]
NYANGA, MAKANI. 'Notes on the Banangoma and Basumba Batale.'[1]
OOSTHUIZEN, E. A. 'The Safe Discharge of Flood Waters at Antisoil-erosion Works', *East African Agricultural Journal*, July 1938.
PERHAM, M. *Native Administration in Nigeria*. Oxford University Press, 1937.
PIM, SIR ALAN. 'British Protectorates and Territories', *United Empire*, May 1934.
PRENTICE, A. N. 'Tie-Ridging', *East African Agricultural Journal*, October 1946.
REVINGTON, T. M. 'The Banangoma and Basumba Batale Societies of the Bukwimba Wasukuma', *Tanganyika Notes and Records*, April 1938.
RICHARDSON, R. B. 'Peasant Holdings in the Western Province and the Certificate used at Kingolwira.'[1]
SAMPSON, H. C. 'Soil Erosion in Tropical Africa and Problems connected with it', *Empire Cotton Growing Review*, January 1936.
SCUPHAM, MAJOR W. E. H. 'Sukuma Society', in notes commenting on Mr. Guise-Williams' memoranda.[1] 101/1/49 of 30/4/31.
SHIJA, NTEMI. 'Notes on the Banghonghogongho of Salawe.'[1]
SHOKA, NTEMI. 'Notes on the Banghonghogongho of Buduhe.'[1]
SPEKE, J. H. *The Source of the Nile*. William Blackwood, 1863.
STANLEY, H. M. *Through the Dark Continent*. Sampson Low, 1878.
—— *In Darkest Africa*. Sampson Low, 1890.
STAPLETON, R. G. *The Land Now and To-morrow*. Faber & Faber, 1935.
STEBBING, E. P. 'The Man-made Desert in Africa', *Journal of Royal African Society*, January 1938.
STOCKDALE, SIR FRANK. 'Notes on Soil Conservation Work in America.'[1]
SWYNNERTON, C. F. M. 'An Experiment in Control of Tsetse-Flies at Shinyanga, Tanganyika.' *Imperial Bureau of Entomology*, 1925.
—— 'Tsetse-Flies of East Africa.' *Royal Entomological Society*, 1936.
THOMAS, H. B. 'An Experiment in Native Land Settlement', *Journal of the African Society*, April 1928.
—— and SCOTT, R. *Uganda*. Oxford University Press, 1935.

[1] Unpublished.

VAN RENSBURG, H. J. 'The Role of Pasture Development in Soil Conservation, Tanganyika Territory', *East African Agricultural Journal*, July 1947.
WAKEFIELD, A. J. 'Mixed Farming and Peasant Holdings in Tanganyika', *E.C.G.C. Review*, April 1934.
—— Address on Peasant Holdings given to the B.M.A. Dar-es-Salaam, 1936.[1]
WARD-PRICE, H. L. *Land Tenure in the Yoruba Provinces.* Lagos, 1932.
WORTHINGTON, E. B. *A Development Plan for Uganda.* Government Press, Entebbe, 1946.

Reports of Departments, Committees, &c.

Agriculture in India. Report of the Royal Commission. Cmd. 3132. 1928.
Agricultural Department, Tanganyika. *Annual Report* 1935 et seq.
The Soils, Vegetation and Agricultural Systems of North Western Rhodesia. Report of the Ecological Survey by C. G. Trapnell and J. N. Clothier. Lusaka, 1937.
Enquiry into Grievances of the Mukama and People of Toro. Uganda, 1926.
Livestock Enquiry Report. Kenya. Summary in *East African Agricultural Journal*, July 1937.
Land Tenure in Uganda Protectorate. Report on Uganda. 1906 and 1907.
The Kibanja System in Bunyoro. 1931. Report of the Committee. 1932.
Native Land in the North Kavirondo Reserve. Report of the Committee. 1930, 1931.
Native Land Tenure in the Kikuyu Province of Kenya. Report of the Committee. 1929.
Northern Nigeria Lands Committee Report. Cmd. 5103. 1910.
Minutes of the First Meeting of the Standing Committee on Soil Erosion. Dar-es-Salaam, 1931.
South Africa. *The Official Year Book of the Union.* 1933-4 et seq.
Tsetse. Report of the Tabora Conference.[1] 1937.
—— Research Department. 'The Provision of Water.' Scheme No. 19.[1]
Veterinary Department. *Annual Report.* 1935 et seq.
Zinza Settlement. Minutes of Inter-Departmental Meeting in Mwanza.[1] January 1938.

Memoranda and Correspondence

Land Tenure and Peasant Holdings in the Western Province. Memoranda and Correspondence[1] by H. C. Baxter (D.O.), D. Sturdy (S.A.O.), L. H. L. Foster (Ag.P.C.), F. J. Bagshawe (P.C.).
Peasant Holdings and Resettlement. Memoranda and Correspondence[1] by G. F. Webster (P.C.), F. J. Bagshawe (P.C.), H. C. Baxter (D.O.), W. S. Marchant (Ag.P.C.), A. J. Wakefield (D. of A.).

[1] Unpublished.

Glossary

Abanyampala (Kiz.)[1]	Old men, cf. *Banamhala*.
Babuta	The father's family or ancestors.
Badakama	People of the south.
Badrilili	The snake society (also called *Bagoyangi* and *Bayeye* q.v.)
Bafumu	Doctors. Sometimes but not necessarily members of religious societies.
Bagalu	A dance society.
Bagika	A dance society.
Bagikulu	Old women; an age grade with a society or association.
Bagoyangi	The snake society (also called *Badrilili* and *Bayeye* q.v.)
Bagumha	A dance society which also organizes collective agricultural work for members.
Bahabi	Those who have no cattle, cf. *Basabi*.
Bajaha	Men 40–50 years of age.
Bambilija	Sub-chiefs; judicial assistants.
Bana ba nda ya bu	'Children of the pregnancy of the bush.'
Banamhala	Old men; an age grade with a society or association.
Banamhala ba Ibanza	Court elders.
Banamhala ba Igunguli	Village elders.
Banang'oma	'Councillors of State', see *Munang'oma*.
Banangwa	Village headmen, see *Ng'wanangwa*.
Bang'hong'hogong'ho (Kinyamwezi)	See *Munang'oma*.
Banhya	Young women.
Baniki	Girls up to puberty.
Banunguri	Porcupines; a dance society of porcupine hunters.
Basa ya ndugu wane yatema kunu	'My family's axe cut here.'
Basabi	Cattle-owners (from *kusaba*—to become rich), cf. *Bahabi*.
Bashike	Women 40–50 years of age; an age grade with a society or association. Women who have been married and have had children but who have left their husbands or whose husbands have died.
Basumba batale	Village leaders of the young men's societies.
Baswezi	A secret society.

[1] (Kiz.) = Kizinza or *Olunyabuzinza*.

Glossary

Basumba batale balonda	Junior *Basumba batale* in charge of sections of villages (Maswa). *Mlonda* means follower.
Batemi bado	Subordinate chiefs.
Bayanda	Boys up to puberty.
Bayanda ba nyasauci	*Tragus racemosus.*
Bayeye	The snake society, cf. *Badrilili* and *Bagoyangi.*
Biliga (*Bilisé*) (Gold Coast)	A well.
Bisanzu (Kiz.)	Young men of the *Nsumba Ilika* who hold no office in the society.
Bizukuru	Grandsons (of chief), cf. *Ng'wanangwa* and *Munang'oma.*
Bololo	Sloppy wet mud which squelches between the toes.
Bubiti	Ostracism; *kufunyiwa bubiti*—to be ostracized (Shinyanga, Zinza).
Bubumbila	Mud which sticks to the feet (South Sukumaland).
Bufumu	A religious society connected with ancestor worship.
Bugado	Mud which sticks to the feet (North Sukumaland).
Bugimbi	*Dactyloctenium Aegyptium.*
Buluba	Cotton.
Bumanga	A religious society connected with ancestor worship.
Bunyonya	Sesame.
Bupunga	Rice.
Bushiku	*Sporobolus indicus.*
Busiga (*Masiga*)	Sorghum; *Durra.*
Busiga wa bukula	The red sorghums.
Busiga wa kuli	*Rhynchelytrum roseum.*
Buta	Bow.
Butende	Marriage without bride-price.
Butundo	Pig iron.
Butwale	Area comprising the villages under an *Ntwale.*
Changarawe (Kiswahili)	Gravel; murram.
Cheyu	*Aristida stendiliana.*
Dasa	*Heteropogon contortus* (Spear grass).
Do	Little.
Doto (*Madoto*)	Small basket used for carrying seed when broadcasting.
Fweya	*Loudetia* sp. The best thatching-grass.
Gagurunya ndo	*Eragrostis* sp.
Galu moso	*Chloris pychnothryx.*

Glossary

Ganana (Maganana)	Grass basket mainly used for carrying sorghum heads, &c., at harvest. Also used for earth or manure transport.
Gurunya	*Panicum* sp.
Higuria (Maguria)	The higher lands on which houses are built.
Huruda ndo	*Aristida adscensionis*; also used of *Chloris gayana*.
Huruda ntale	*Bothriochloa insculpta*.
Ibambasi (Mabambasi)	Generic name of a group of the grey hardpan soils.
Ibambasi ya mahushi	Hardpan soil with *Acacia Fischeri* predominant.
Ibambasi ya malula (gapi)	Hardpan soil with dark gall acacias dominant.
Ibambasi ya masagala	Hardpan soil with *Anisotes dumosus* as the plant soil-indicator.
Ibambasi ya mitinje	Hardest hardpan soil with *Lannea humilis* as the plant soil-indicator.
Ibambasi ya mkomangwa	Hardpan soil with *Commiphora campestris* as the plant soil-indicator.
Ibumba	Clay used for making cooking pots, not found on the surface, cf. *Itaka ly'ebumba*.
Ibushi	Calcareous chocolate-coloured loam or friable plateau *mbuga*; the best soil for cotton on the lower slopes.
Ibushi lyapi	A variety of *ibushi* which is black and friable.
Idimilo (Madimilo)	Grazing area, pasture.
Ifa ilulu	*Hyparrhenia* sp.
Ifuma (Mafuma)	A large woven basket containing up to 2½ tons of grain, generally made with withies, bark string, and lined with cow dung.
Iginya	A society, the members of which do their hair like Swahili women. (South Busiha.)
Igunguli (Magunguli)	1. A village area. 2. *Heliotropum zaylanicum*.
Igwata (Magwata)	*Acacia Senegal*.
Ihyu	Ostracism (Maswa, Bukwimba, Mwanza), cf. *Bubiti*.
Ikela (Makela)	Grass fallow in arable land (Shinyanga).
Ikiri (or Lukili)	Pale-coloured powdery form of *Nduha* (or *Ikurusi*) (Msalala).
Ikumbo	*Sida grewioides*.
Ikungu	Bush (North Sukumaland).
Ikurusi	Rich red to orange loam from metamorphic rocks.

Glossary

Ilago (*Malago*)	1. Damp fields usually on dark grey to black soil, watered by springs, in which rice or potatoes are grown (Maswa—near rivers).
	2. The flood plains of a river.
Ilago lya ikelege	Area watered by springs or seepage situated on *isanga* soils higher up the hillsides.
Ilala (*Malala* or *Milala*)	1. A crack; often used of cracks in *mbuga*.
	2. Stubble fields. (Maswa. Much the same meaning elsewhere and confused with *Ikela* q.v.).
Ilale (*Malale*)	Fallow arable land before cultivation, cf. *Ikela*.
Ilamata (*Malamata*)	*Setaria verticillata*; grass often found growing in abandoned stock yards.
Ilambo (*Malambo*)	An earth tank, natural depression or an excavation in a stream bed to water cattle.
Ilendi	*Sesamum angustifolia* (Foxglove).
Ilika (*Malika*)	A society, association or club.
Ing'ong'ho	Any hill without large boulders (includes dolorite, banded ironstone, &c.), cf. *Isoso*.
Isalenge	Collective cultivation by members of the village association of *Basumba* for contract work. Indicates the collection of hoes. (Not used in central Sukumaland but used in Shinyanga and known elsewhere.)
Isanga	1. Sandy soil derived from granite.
	2. Marshy sandy lake-shore potato soil (Kiz.).
Isanga ya ikelege	Damp sandy soil.
Isanga ya kinele or *shinele*	Damp sandy soil (moving water).
Isanga ya luselela	Damp sandy soil, often near a seepage area.
Isoso	Any hill without boulders, cf. *Ing'ong'ho*.
Itaba	1. Natural depression filling with water during the rains, often an old ox-bow of a river-bed, cf. *Ilambo*.
	2. Tobacco (Kiz.).
Itaka ly'ebumba (Kiz.)	Clay for making cooking pots, cf. *Ibumba*.
Italu	Patches of soil near rivers on which an efflorescence of salts is visible, cf. *Magembia*.
Italwa	Similar to *Italu* q.v.
Itogolo (or *Itogoro*)	1. Open space.
	2. Sandy clay loam capable of pan formation. The surface is very soft when wet.

Glossary

Itongo (Matongo)
1. Home fields (outside enclosure) usually behind the homestead, as the cattle go out in front (Maswa, Bukwimba).
2. Abandoned house and cattle-pen sites, not yet cultivated (Bukwimba).
3. Fields, usually of maize, &c., on old house or cattle-pen sites (Shinyanga, Zinza, Nzega, &c.).
4. Name given to soil of old habitations and cattle kraals.

Itumbati — Tobacco.

Itunu — Areas, including *Ngitiri* between *manala* hedges enclosing family group of huts. Used for reserve grazing of calves, &c., and for stacking fuel (Central Sukumaland).

Iwe lya bujeje (Mawe ga bujeje) — A granite boulder which has begun to decompose on the surface.

Iwe lya gembe (Mawe ga gembe) — Dolorite. *Gembe* means 'ebony'.

Kadondolio — Deep alluvium deposits of *mbuga* mud left by receding river floods.

Kanumba
1. Assistant to *Nsumba ntale* in South Sukumaland; does the work of the *Nsumba ntale* in S.W. Shinyanga. In Maswa and Bukwimba means anyone who cooks the meat of the *Basumba*, cf. *Ngati*.
2. A small house.

Kaya (Makaya) — A family group of houses, 'homestead', cf. 1. *Itongo*—deserted *Kaya*. 2. *Kilugu*—an abandoned *Kaya* site when cultivated (Central Sukumaland).

Keduma — *Tephrosia elegans*.

Kibanda (Shibanda) — A section of a village—under the control of an *Nsumba ntale* or *Nsumba ntale mlonda* for *Ilika* activities including collective work.

Kibandagulu — Low or flat termite mound, made by *nswa gwa kaserere*, generally calcareous.

Kiganga (Shiganga) — A granite boulder.

Kigulu (Shigulu) — A fairly high termite mound made by *nswa gwa matine*. It forms a valuable source of lime fertilizer.

Kikungu
1. The point at the top of a house used for mounting the ostrich egg.
2. Red sandy laterized soil (South Sukumaland).

Glossary

Kilaba (*Shilaba*)	1. Fields cultivated by unmarried dependants, usually children. 2. Fields cultivated by women alone for their own benefit.
Kilugu (*Shilugu*)	An abandoned *Kaya* site when cultivated.
Kubirisa	To lend—used mainly of cattle deposited with a friend who will look after them.
Kubola (Kinyamwezi)	To marry without bride-price (Shinyanga), cf. *Butende*.
Kukwa	To pay bride-price.
Kulagula	To practise divination.
Kusenga	To clear bush for cultivation.
Kusesa	To remove grass with a hoe (also used of flat as opposed to ridge cultivation).
Kutindula	To cultivate for the first time in a treeless valley.
Kutobanga	1. To stir up. 2. To stamp flat—used of intentional heavy stocking practised to improve coarse rank pasture.
Lambolambo	*Digitaria perrotteti*, also used of *Echinochloa*, cf. *Haploclada*.
Legi	*Pennisetum racemosum*.
Longa	1. Lower slopes. 2. A depression above the headwaters of a river and between hills.
Ludefu	Quicksand.
Lugobe	*Cynodon dactylon*, also *Cynodon plectrostachyum*.
Lugundiga	Seasonal grazing.
Luguru (*Nguru*)	A hill with granite boulders.
Lukele	A soil uncultivable except when sufficient water is present, when it can be used for rice, &c. Similar to *Ilago lya ikelege*.
Luliki	Synonym for *Ikiri* q.v.
Lusanga	A sandy to gravelly soil of a light reddish colour derived from granite, cf. *Isanga*.
Luseni	A pale-coloured fine sandy gritty soil similar to *Isanga*.
Lusuunga	*Lactuca taraxacifolia* (Sow thistle).
Mabambasi	Hardpan soils.
Mabembere	*Rottboellia exaltata*.
Madimilo	Grazing areas, pastures.
Madoto	Small grass baskets, cf. *Doto*.
Mafuma	Baskets for storing grain, cf. *Ifuma*.
Magaganika	Tussocks, lumps.

Glossary

Magaka	An aloe with red or orange flowers used by the Sukuma for the demarcation of boundaries of cattle tracks, roads, &c. It can be transplanted any time of the year without water.
Maganana	Grass baskets, cf. *Ganana*.
Magembia	Salt extracted from *Italu*.
Magitiri	Grazing reserves, cf. *Ngitiri*.
Mahushi	*Acacia Fischeri*.
Malago	Plural of *Ilago* q.v.
Malale	Plural of *Ilale* q.v.
Male	*Lonchocarpus eriocalyx*.
Malika ga mbina	Dance societies.
Maliwa	Cassava.
Malula (gapi)	'Black' gall acacias *A. drepanolobium* *A. formicarum* *A. malacocephala*.
Malula gape	'White' gall acacias *A. seyal* *A. seyal* var. *fistula*
Manala	*Euphorbia tirucalli*.
Mandege	Maize.
Mandi	Earth ridges burying weed growth.
Mandolo	Sweet potatoes.
Mang'ong'ho gape	A limestone deposit. *Gape* means 'white'.
Manonho	Tussocks, lumps.
Manyara (Kiswahili)	*Euphorbia tirucalli*.
Masagala	*Anisotes dumosus*.
Masalu	Generic name for all sands.
Masalu gaza	Red sand.
Masalu gwa mongo	River sand.
Maseni	Plural of *Luseni* q.v.
Mashishiwe (or *Masikiwe*)	Sharp decomposing granite or rubble.
Mashororo	Round stones which can be thrown, often granite rubble.
Maswa nyanzige	*Rhynchelytrum repens*.
Matinde	Tussocks.
Matogoro	Plural of *Itogolo* q.v.
Matongo	Arable fields on high ground, cf. *Itongo*.
Mawe ga bujeje	Plural of *Iwe lya bujeje* q.v.
Mawe ga gembe	Plural of *Iwe lya gembe* q.v.
Mbale	Banded ironstone; stone from which iron is smelted.
Mbuga (Mabuga)	Valley; usually dark heavy clay soils good for sorghums.
Mbuga ya bololo	Synonymous with *Mbuga ya bubuni*. *Bololo* means wet mud.
Mbuga ya bubumbila	Similar to *Mbuga ya bololo*.

Glossary

Mbuga ya bubuni	Light grey *mbuga* flat with fine powdery ash-like sodium dust; very viscous when wet.
Mbuga ya iwawa	Synonymous with *Mbuga ya bubuni*.
Mbuga ya lunongu	'The ostrich flats'; friable *mbuga* showing lime nodules. A form of *Ibushi*.
Mbuga ya majinje	Synonymous with *Mbuga ya matinde*.
Mbuga ya malula	Similar to *Mbuga ya milala*, but where cracking is not so marked. *Malula* means gall acacias.
Mbuga ya matinde	Seasonal swamps in the lower-lying areas and depressions in *mbuga* flats. *Matinde* means tussocks.
Mbuga ya milala	All *mbugas* where cracking is considerable. *Milala* means cracks.
Mbuga ya mwilago	Riverine flood basins; means 'in the *ilago*'.
Mbuga ya ndago	A small strip of alluvial *mbuga* within the old river banks, characterized by *ndago* reeds.
Mbuga ya nseseko	Alluvial *mbuga* deposited with some sand. The best *mbuga* for sorghum crops.
Mchenya	A fine of two arrows, tobacco, or a spear imposed by the village society for failing to turn out to collective labour (Maswa).
Mgunga	*Acacia spirocarpa*
	Acacia tortillis.
Mhande	Bambarra groundnuts.
Mikuli	*Indigofera viscosa*.
Miombo (Kiswahili)	*Brachystegia/Isoberlinia* woodland.
Misengelelwa	River sand.
Misengwa	River sand.
Mitinje (pl.)	*Lannea humilis*.
Mkomangwa	*Commiphora campestris*.
Mlamji	Sub-chief, cf. *Ng'wambilija*.
Mlangali	*Euphorbia candelabrum*.
Mondo	*Entandrophragma Bussei*.
Mongo	River.
Mpogoro bongole	*Albizzia amara*.
Mseni	River sand.
Muhululang'hang'ha	*Achyranthes aspera*.
Munang'oma (*Banang'oma*)	A member of the Council of State of a chiefdom chosen from grandsons and great-grandsons of former chiefs, when old, cf. *Bizukuru, Ng'wanangwa*.
Mwanangwa	Kiswahili spelling of *Ng'wanangwa*.
Ndago	Reeds used for making sleeping mats.
Ndindindi	*Eragrostis aspera*.

Glossary

Ndindindi ndo	*Eragrostis chapelieri*; also used of ?*Eragrostis chalantha*.
Ndoba	An impervious detritus of granite often found as a sub-soil underlying *mbuga* clays.
Nduha	A red sandy soil (North Sukumaland), cf. *Kikungu*.
Nduko	*Eleusine indica*.
Ndulu	Grams.
Ndululu	*Panicum maximum*.
Nfumu (*Bafumu*)	A doctor of any society.
Ngati (*Bagati*)	The assistant to the *Nsumba ntale* in North Sukumaland (Bukumbi).
Ngazu	*Tricalysia cacondensis*.
Ngegu	River banks.
Ngese	The first weeding.
Ng'hongwa	*Sclerocarya birrea*.
Ngitiri (*Magitiri*)	Reserved grazing, personal or village.
Ngole ntale or *Ngole w'igembe*	The first wife of the chief. Her round house is ornamented at the apex with a cooking pot surmounted by a hoe, which is her insignia. Formerly it was the custom that, on the death of a chief, his *Ngole w'igembe* could not marry again, but this custom appears to be dying out; e.g. the wives of the late Chief Seni of Kanadi have all been inherited and have married again.
Ngole w'ihanga	A girl of a certain clan who is chosen at the same time as the new chief. She does not become his wife but participates in all the major ceremonies such as his original installation, the benediction of the seed, the periodical haircutting of the chief, when her hair is also cut. The chief supports her in a house of her own at some distance from his headquarters. She never marries. If the chief is deposed by the Council of State, she ceases to be his queen.
Ngongo	The back.
Ngongwa	*Acacia rovumae*.
Ngumo	*Ficus nigropunctata*.
Nguru (pl.)	Hills with granite boulders.
Ng'wambilija (*Bambilija*)	Assistant; sub-chief (Maswa).
Ng'wanangwa (*Banangwa*)	1. A chief's son, cf. *Munang'oma* and *Bizukuru*. Thus—
	2. A village headman.

Glossary

Ng'wandu	*Adansonia digitata*, baobab.
Nhalanga	Groundnuts.
Nhelengu	*Hyparrhenia rufa*, thatching-grass.
Nhogolo	Synonymous with *Itogolo* q.v.
Nkola	*Afzelia quanzensis*.
Nkonze	*Mimusops densiflora*.
Nkuyu	*Ficus sonderi*.
Nsango	1. Judgement. Thus—
	2. Payment (usually of two head of cattle) on the birth of each child in a *Kubola* or *Butende* marriage.
Nshingisha	*Boscia Fischeri*.
Nshishi	*Tamarindus indica*.
Nsumba (*Basumba*)	Young man.
Nsumba ntale (*Basumba batale*)	Head and representative of the association of young men within a village.
Nsumba ntale mlonda (*Basumba batale balonda*)	Junior *Nsumba ntale* in charge of a *Kibanda* (Maswa).
Nswa gwa kaserere	A small species of termite.
Nswa gwa matine	Another species of termite.
Nsweda	Assistant, messenger.
Ntale	Great.
Ntemi (*Batemi*)	Chief.
Ntemi ndo (*Batemi bado*)	Subordinate chief.
Ntemi nhoja	A chief appointed by the *Banang'oma* or Council of State exactly like the chief himself. The *Ntemi nhoja* is given a section of the chiefdom by the chief in which area he used to obtain labour, tribute, and the salutation accorded to chiefs. The *Ntemi nhoja* has no court, no judicial or administrative power or functions, is not invested with the *Ndeji* shells ornamenting the wrists of chiefs and he can be dismissed by the chief if he abuses his position. His main duties are in connexion with tribal ceremonies such as the benediction of the seed.
Ntwale	Regional headman or sub-chief; previously a military rank.
Nyangogo	A leader of the *Bufumu*. The nearest approach to a high priest in Sukumaland.
Nzala ya mitundu	The famine of 1900, when the phloem of *Brachystegia spiciformis* was chewed.
Nzubile	The second weeding, cf. *Ngese*.

Glossary

Nzukuru (*Bizukuru*)	Grandson or great-grandson (of a former chief).
Omukama (Kiz.)	Chief.
Ouibila	*Corchorus olitorius* (Spinach).
Samata	*Cyphocarpa orthocantha*.
Sekule	Tribute formerly payable to the chief, usually a small basket of sorghum.
Sesa	Flat cultivation, i.e. without ridges, cf. *Kusesa*.
Shiganga	Granite boulders.
Shilaba	Personal fields of either women or children.
Shili	Cowpeas.
Shillingi jitobialaga	'Shillings do not breed.'
Shilugu	Abandoned *Kaya* sites when cultivated.
Supyu	*Sporobolus arginatus*.
Uwele wa kuli	*Chloris virgata*.
Wakili (Kiswahili)	Chief's deputy.
Wilu	White varieties of sorghums.
Yaza	Red.
Yiinza	*Blepharis acanthoides*.
Zunzu	*Leucas martinicensis*.

INHERITANCE TABLE

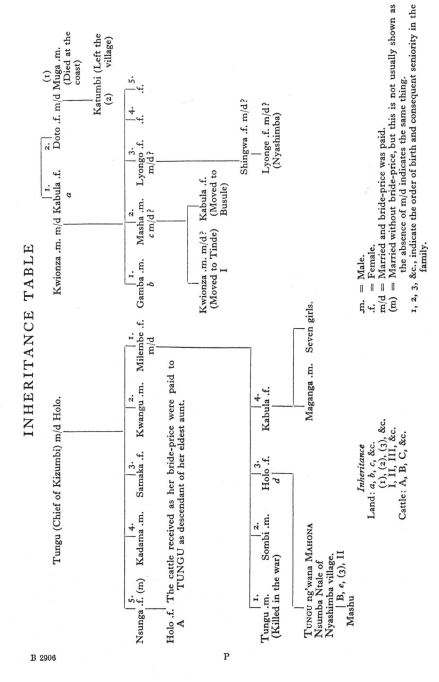

Planned Group Farming

PLANNED GROUP FARMING IN NYANZA PROVINCE, KENYA[1]

1. The urgency of the need for a radical change in land utilisation to save the soil and to improve or even to maintain the returns from African peasant cultivation is now generally appreciated.

2. The possible means of attaining this change are the development of mixed farming small-holdings, large farms with employed labour, collective farms, or through some form of co-operative farming under acceptable local land authorities.

3. It is felt that the change cannot be attained by the development of individual mixed farming small-holdings with all the difficulties of economics and efficient usage, and existing systems of land tenure—with fragmentation. Such holdings have been developed for experimental and demonstration purposes on the Agricultural Department's Farm at Bukura.

The economic shortcomings are apparent and there has been no real spread of practices thence to the neighbouring African lands.

4. The evolution of large farms with employed labour would in general be too gradual a process and open to doubt ethically, particularly as sufficient industrial development to absorb the surplus population is most unlikely.

The possibility of collective farming has been mooted, but seems to be too dependent on drastic coercion of the sluggard to be considered. Effective management is unlikely to be forthcoming, and from many points of view, the idea would be abhorrent to the African.

5. Co-operative effort would appear to be the right approach, and the Agricultural Officers of Kenya passed the following resolution at a Conference in 1947:

> The policy of the Department for the Native Lands shall in general be based on encouraging co-operative effort and organisation rather than individual holdings. It is considered that only by co-operative action can the land be properly utilised, and the living standard of the people and the productivity of the land be raised, and preserved. While this involves a change from the modern trend towards individualism, it is in accord with former indigenous methods of land usage and social custom.

6. With heavy intensities of rainfall drainage type terraces are generally required in Nyanza, and it is necessary for the land to be treated in drainage units for conservation and proper utilisation.

7. Lack of planning can be seen everywhere in the siting of villages, the haphazard planting of fruit and timber trees, in the use of steep land for annual, and flat land for perennial crops. Difficulties of access to

[1] Extract from the Monthly News Letter of the Agricultural Department, Kenya. Seventh issue. September 1949.

Planned Group Farming

grass leys prevented by neighbours' crops, in contour ploughing, and in siting drainage ways and the like, are concomitant with individualism, fragmentation, and lack of planning. To overcome these difficulties a method termed 'Planned Group Farming' was advocated.

8. Basically this entails initial planning by the members of a group, and similar use of contour strips by neighbours, as the boundaries between holdings normally run from the top to the bottom of the slopes.

The use of each strip from drainage way to drainage way would be decided, based primarily on soil and topography. A strip would be chosen for housing, others, depending on the slope, for bananas, fuel or timber plantations, or permanent grazing, and the flatter land for alternate husbandry, arable and grass leys, in accordance with an agreed rotation.

There would be no interference with the individual's tenure of his holding, but he would have to use each contour strip within that holding in conformity with the edicts of the group or its committee.

9. Permanent hedges or fences would be allowed only round the perimeter of the group farm and on the contour, and in cases where permanent pasture is necessary, for the rotational grazing of such pasture. Normally where soil, climate, and topography permit, alternate husbandry should be adopted, though this may take time. Any fencing between holdings for grazing must be removable, so that, for the arable courses of the rotation, the implements can traverse all holdings on the contour.

10. With individuals owning scattered holdings, it may be necessary for some to be members, at any rate initially, of more than one group, and there is nothing to preclude this, though consolidation by exchange would be encouraged and expected.

11. Mutual trust is essential between members of a group, who would normally be relatives, and there is no limit either way to the numbers of members or to the size of a group farm, which would be bounded on each side by drainage ways. Natural drainage ways are preferable, but grassed channels can be made where necessary. As group farms develop they may combine with others to form Unions for marketing produce, acquiring dips, dams or other improved water supplies, and farm machinery.

12. The system permits the use of mechanical equipment and economies in oxen and implements, and can progress through co-operative better farming societies, controlling their members, obtaining loans, acquiring their own implements, and marketing their own produce. It provides scope for specialisation, since the groups will, as they develop, require stockmen, dairy experts, marketing clerks, and perhaps tractor drivers and the like. It is hoped that the groups will select

youngsters for training on these lines, who will return and be their specialists. It is also hoped that membership of a group will provide the necessary insurance without which salaried Africans cannot be expected to leave the land. Above all Land Authorities in the form of Group Farm Committees would develop, and some form of such authority is deemed essential, if any real and lasting progress is to be made.

13. The adoption of dipping and limitation to carrying capacity for the improvement of livestock is difficult, while stock have free range over all fallow land, and are regarded more as a social than as an economic asset. Group farms and their committees should assist with this development, and with improvement through the group ownership of improved bulls and, as they develop, through having their stock specialist. In certain over-populated areas group farming with mechanisation should assist by allowing the use of all the limited grazing for the production of milk.

14. Safeguards will be needed to ensure compliance with group edicts, and it is thought that this can best be attained through by-laws after registration of the groups, as Co-operative Better Farming Societies. These would not, however, cover withdrawal from a group by a member or his successor, after due notice, and rules under the African District Councils' Ordinance are envisaged to ensure that all users of land in a group farm follow the farming practices, and use of contour strips as decreed by the majority of the members, or the committee on their behalf.

15. Such a change in farming trends is not one that can be imposed by Government Order alone, and it is clearly understood that we must have the African with us, and make him realise that the group is his, and that he must produce his ideas and views when he seeks our guidance. Group farming is really only a modernised version of much of the old indigenous system of land control and usage.

It is felt that it is a method of attaining good farming with its proper balance between crops and stock, and by which, where topography permits, the use of mechanical equipment as an aid to hand labour is feasible, and which should be acceptable to the African.

Index

Abuse of land, 60–61.
Acacia-Adansonia vegetation complex, 5–6.
Acacia Arabica, planting by Native Authorities, 54.
'A' Courts, powers of, 94.
Acquisition of land, 50–51.
— of stock, 64–67.
Administration of Local African Government, 83–106.
Administrative functions of Native Authorities, 87–90.
Administrators in India, 84.
Advances to individuals, 126–7.
Advocates in court cases, 95.
Afforestation, 141–2.
African Land Rights, 110.
— Local Government in Sukumaland, 83–107.
— — — lightweight structure, 99–100.
Agricultural indebtedness, 113.
— specialization, 112, 119.
Agriculture, capitalization of, 116.
— static, 55.
Allocation of land, 17–19, 22, 25, 26, 30–31, 38, 51.
Aloes (*magaka*) for permanent demarcation, 162.
Ancestor worship, 50, 67–69.
Annual cash income, 49, 108–9.
— crops, 115.
Anti-famine measures, 58–60.
Anti-soil-erosion, 120, 127.
Ants (*see also* Termites), 142.
Appeals, venue of, 94.
Arable land for grazing, 75.
Arbitration, 25–26, 85, 93.
Arthur Young, 124.
Authorities, *see also* Native Authorities.
— contact with people, 86.
— unrecognized indigenous, 101.

Babuta, father's ancestors, 68.
Bahabi, stockless people, 75, 80–81, 133.
Bahi, hunters, 20.
Baker, E. C., *Administrative Survey of Uzinza*, 14, 24, 43–44.
Bambarra groundnuts, 56, 190.
Bamigongo, mother's ancestors, 68.
Banamhala, village elders (*see also* Village Elders), 40–41.
Banana plantations, sale of, 55.
Bananas, planting of, 54, 112.
Banang'oma, Councillors of State (*see also* Council of State), 23.

Banangwa, sons of chiefs, 23.
— village headmen (*see also* Village Headman), 23.
Baobabs, 5, 6, 53.
Bariadi river, 64.
Bark rope, 53.
Barter, 16.
Basabi, people with stock, 75.
Basumba, young men's society, 34.
Basumba batale, collaboration with village headman, 43.
— — grazing control, 76.
— — history in Shinyanga, 34–35.
— — mouthpiece of people, 100.
— — rights and duties of, 37–38.
— — village labour leader, 34–40.
'B' Courts, powers of, 94.
Beer, payment in, 81.
Beeswax, 53.
Benediction of seed, 23, 28.
Binza Council of Chiefs, meeting of, 88, 90–91.
Birds, damage to crops by, vi, 6, 141.
Birth blood-price, 45, 66.
Bizukuru, grandsons of chiefs, 23.
Block reserves, 139–40.
Borers in grain, 71.
Borrowing of fields, 7, 18, 31, 51, 59.
Bösch, Rev. P. Fr., *Les Banyamwezi*, 21.
Boundaries of village, 30.
Bourdillon, Sir Bernard, *The Future of Native Authorities*, 103.
Brachystegia-Isoberlinia vegetation complex, 6.
Breaches in dams, mending of, 157–58.
Bride-price in cattle, 65.
— in hoes, 69.
— influence on inheritance, 45.
— marriage with, 29.
— payment of, 44.
— withdrawal of, 65–66.
British Administration, Sukumaland, at beginning of, 83–84.
Bubiki, village work on water supply, 33.
Building houses, 18, 33.
— — collective labour for, 37–38.
— materials, 47–48.
— — collection of, 53.
Bulking of manure, 80.
Bureaucracy, 99.
Burials, organizing of, 38.

Index

Bush clearing, cutting of regenerating bush, 40.
—— importance of soils, 174–5.
—— method of land acquisition, 51.
———— of redistribution of people, 150.
—— reclamation of tsetse-infested land, 132, 137.
—— right of occupation, 46.
— fallow, block reserves under, 137.
—— land abandoned to, 13.
—— regeneration of, 6, 140–1.
—— reoccupation of land under, 131.
—— reversion to, 13–14, 15.
—— rotation of arable land with, 55, 108, 113.
— grazing, 64, 72–73.
— indestructibility of, 6.
— products, 53.
— regeneration of, 54–55, 76, 78.
Busiha system of rotational grazing, 76, 122.
— water tanks, 16.
Butende, marriage without bride-price (*see also* Marriage), 44.
Butter, clarified, 70.
By-products from cattle, 70–71, 72.
———— ownership of, 71, 72.

Cameron, Sir Donald, G.C.M.G., K.B.E., 83–85.
—— *My Tanganyika Service*, 85.
Campbell, Sir George, K.C.S.I., M.P., *The Tenure of Land in India*, 115.
Capital, cattle as, 70.
Capitalization of agriculture, 111, 116, 129.
Cases, recording of, 85.
Cash crops, 52, 108.
— economy, 83, 112.
— incomes, 61.
—— annual, 49, 108–9.
Cassava plots, 58.
Cassia Siamea, planting of, 54.
Catena, 4, 174, 175–6.
Cattle and Water, 133–5.
— as invested capital, 133.
— as wealth, 16.
— by-products from, 70–71, 72.
— disposal of chiefs', 67.
— distribution of, 64.
— heritable wealth, 45.
— introduction of, 63.
— lending of, 72–73, 75, 123.
— markets, introduction of, vi.
— ownership, 123, 127.
— pens, burial in, 50.
— population, 63–64.
—— statistics, 62–63.
—— total, 1.

Cattle, redistribution of, 64, 133–5.
— rights, 62–82.
— sales, 61, 99, 109.
— slaughter of, 42, 81.
— tracks, 122, 140.
— training of, 126.
— unit, definition of, 1, 62.
— used for sealing dam basins, 157.
— watering of, 78–79.
— Zebu, 63.
Chairman of Sukumaland Federation, 88.
Check dams, 171.
Chickens used for divination, 68.
Chief Alexander of Karumo, 24, 28, 43.
— as representative of people, 96.
— authority of, 100.
— Balele of Nera, the late, 90, 97.
— candidacy for post of, 101–2.
— deposition of, 25.
— Jimola of Bugarama, 90.
— Kidaha of Busiha, M.L.C., 89, 97, 98.
— leadership of, 103.
— Majebere of Ng'wagala, 89, 146.
— Makwaia of Busiha, the late, 16, 28, 98.
— Ndaturu of Ntuzu, 89.
— popular approval of, 98.
— recognition by Government of, 98.
— tenure of office, 96.
— termination of office, 96.
— William Nhumbu of Ng'unghu, 89.
Chief's advisors, 103.
— cattle, disposal of, 67.
— court, constitution of, 94–95.
—— powers of, 93–94.
—— recognition of, 85.
— deputy, 87.
Chiefs, graves of, 50.
— misrule of, 105.
— rights of, 25–28.
— selection of, 97–98.
— strangers appointed as, 22, 24, 25.
— subordinate, 29.
Chiefdoms, reorganization of, 83–84.
— subordinate, 25.
Chieftainship and democracy, 95–98.
— as anachronism, 102–3.
— circumscription of authority, 94–95.
— inheritance, 44.
— matrilineal succession, 22–23.
— origin of, 20–22.
— patrilineal succession, 23.
— transmission of, 23–25.
Children as herdsmen, 71.
— as wealth, 69.
— fields of, 52.
Citizens as advisors, 103.
Clan elders, rule by, 21.

Index

Clarified butter, 70.
Clay for cooking pots, 189.
Collective bargaining, 36.
— cultivation, 37-38, 41-42, 127.
— herding, 79.
— labour, 12, 58.
— village sorghum field, 58, 128.
— work, 126.
Community control of land, 112, 114, 118-19, 124.
Compensation, 30, n. 1; 93, 95.
— for unexhausted improvements, 116, 119, 143.
Compulsion, 137, 138, 139.
Congestion of population, 11, 12.
Constituent federations, 91.
Constitutional development in India, 84.
Contour cultivation, 60, 127, 142.
— hedges, 117, 124.
Control of pasture, 114-15.
— of use of land, 137.
Co-operation of Native Authorities in dam construction, 150.
— of people, 144.
— with Native Authorities, 144.
Co-operative organization, 115, 127.
— societies, 101, 126.
Corruption, danger of, 118, 139.
Cotton as cash crop, 61.
— borrowing fields for planting, 17, 18.
— burning of plants, 100.
— delay in planting, 124.
— doubling of crop, 128.
— interplanting of, 56, n. 1.
— planting, effect on grass fallow, 56.
— planting of, 99.
— plots, 58.
— sale of, 52.
— soils for, 190.
— yields, 128, 129.
Cotton, Sir Henry, 85.
Council meeting of federations, procedure, 86, 88-90.
— of State, constitution and functions of, 22-25.
— — control of chief's cattle, 67.
— — duties of, 23.
— — powers of, 25, 26, 96.
— — religious functions of, 23.
— — selection of, 23.
— — — chief by, 97-98.
Court, conduct of, 99-100.
— elders, 94-95.
— fines, 94.
— houses, 95.
— of chief, recognition of, 85.
— of sub-chief, powers of, 93-94.
— procedure, 95.
— supervision of, 93.

Crops, cash, 122, 125.
— interplanting of, 56.
— on hardpan soils, 181, 182.
— on *ibushi* soil, 179.
— on *mbuga* soils, 183-6.
— on red fossil soils, 178-9.
— on sandy soils, 176-7.
— on termitaria, 186-7.
— permanent, 112, 116, 124.
— property of man, 52.
— — of woman, 52.
— residues of, 52, 77.
— — for fodder, 56.
— rotation of, 55-57, 129.
— sale of, 51.
— suitability of various soils for, 190-1.
Cultivation by contract, 28.
— collective (*see also* Collective), 37-38.
— dry, 124, 128.
— first, 46.
— mechanical, 127-30.
— of hardpan soils, 181.
— of *ibushi* soil, 180.
— of *mbuga* soils, 184, 185.
— of red fossil soils, 179.
— of sandy soils, 176-7.
— on contour, 60.
— shifting, 14, 108, 113.
Custom, law and, 81-82.
— modification of, 40.
— variation of, viii.

Dam banks, consolidation of, 172.
— — planting of grass, 172.
— basins, sealing of, 157-60.
— breaches, 157.
— building, 93.
— — aid to resettlement, 17.
— catchment area, 154, 160, 163.
— check, 171.
— construction of, 99, 132, 150.
— — on instalment system, 162.
— definition of, 152.
— hand made, number of labourers, 172.
— layout of, 160-2.
— Malya, 154.
— Ng'wamapalala, 160, 162.
— Nhomango, 160, 162.
— reasons for breaches in, 173.
— — for leaks in, 173.
— scoops, 172.
— Shishiyu, 154.
— siting of, 160.
— size limits population, 154.
— Sola, 160.
— spillways, 160, 162-5.
— sub-surface, 136, 171.

216 Index

Dance Societies, collective labour for members, 41, 126.
— — power of, 41.
— — religious, 41, 67–68.
— — varieties and activities of, 41–43.
Darling, M. L., *The Punjab Peasant in Prosperity and Debt*, 8, n. 1; 112, n. 1.
— — *Rusticus Loquitur*, 8, n. 1.
Delegation by chiefs, 22, 29.
Democracy, 84, 85.
— chieftainship and, 95–98.
Democratic system, 105–6.
— — of government, 103.
Density reduction, 135, 139.
Depopulation, 136, 137.
Desiccation, vi, 3.
Development, British constitutional, 83–85.
— federal, 86–87.
— funds, 107, 111.
— of Native Authorities, 101–6.
— of Sukuma land tenure, 114–19.
— political, 85–86.
— Schemes, 132.
— team, vii, 107, 144.
Dialect variations, field names, 57.
Disease, 108.
Disposal of stock, 64–67.
Distribution of population, 11–14.
District Commissioners, educative supervision by, 85.
Divorce, 52.
Dixey, F., *A Practical Handbook of Water Supply*, 171, n. 1.
Doctor, indigenous, 68.
Donkey, transport by, 16, 130.
Drainage of soil, 60.
— system of rivers, 7.
Dust storms, vi, 7, 8.
Dutt, *Economic History of India*, 84.

East coast fever, 73, 74, 122.
Economics, 61.
Edition, first, 107.
Education of sons of chiefs, 97.
— political, 102.
Efficiency of Native Administration, 99–102.
Elders, court, 94–95.
— judicial work of, 87.
— of village, 40–41.
Elected authorities, 33–43.
Elphinstone, Lord, 84.
Emigration from Nyanza Federation, 15.
— from South Maswa, 15, 19.
— from Sukumaland, 15.
Entrance fee to *Banamhala*, 40.
Epizootics in cattle, 71, 72.

Ernle, The Rt. Hon. Lord, *English Farming Past and Present*, 22, 60, n. 2.
Erosion, aeolian, 6.
— attitude of Sukuma to, 60–61, 78.
— caused by over-stocking, 73.
— — by run-off from rocks, 121.
— *donga* or gully, 4, 60–61, 171.
— — — caused by ploughing, 126.
— reason for movement of population, 15.
— sheet, 4, 5, 122.
Estimates, preparation of, 91.
Euphorbia hedges, 12, 15.
European influence on appointment of chief, 24.
— — on closed economy, 108.
— officers, difficulty of, 91.
Evaporation, losses from, 154.
Eviction from land, 26–27, 51.
Evolution, political, 104–5.
Exchange of cattle for grain, 66, 71.
Executive Committee of Sukumaland Federation, 89, 91.
— functions of chiefs, 87.
Exotic trees, ownership of, 54–55.
Expenditure of federations, average yearly, 92.
— of Native Treasury money, 92.
Exploitation of newly inhabited areas, vi.
Export of ghee, 71.
Expulsion from land, 26–27.
Extracts of information from field investigation, v, viii.
Eyasi depression, 3.
— Lake, 7.

Fallow, adjunct of balanced husbandry, 120.
— as grazing land, 56.
— reduction of, 107–8.
— rotation of crops and, 55–57.
Family, as security in old age, 69.
— elders, division of inheritance, 65–66.
— group, extension of, 43–44.
— head of, 65, 66.
Famine, control of population increase by, 107–8.
— in 1900, 12.
— possession of cattle as insurance against, 71–72.
— risk of, 130.
Farm mechanization, 109, 125–6.
Farming, Planned Group, 119, 145, 210–12.
Federal Appeal Court, 147.
Federal councils, work of, 86.
— union, 86–87.

Index

Federation court, powers of, 94.
— executive committee, 147.
— formation of, 146.
— of Sukumaland, vii.
— process of, 86–87.
Feed for stock, 130.
Fencing of fields, 31.
— of land, 48.
Fertility losses, 60–61, 108.
Fields, borrowing of, 47, 51, 114.
— manuring of, 79–80.
— names of, 57.
— of children, 52.
— of wives, 52.
Fig trees, planting of, 54.
Finance, Native Treasury, 86, 91–93.
— supervision of, 92–93.
Fines, court, 93–94.
Fire, making of, 39.
Fishing industry, 18.
Food shortage, vi, 15, 16, 64, 67.
— stores, 38.
Forde, Prof. Daryll, Ph.D., *Social Development in Africa*, 86, n. 1; 104.
Forest reserves, 121.
Fragmentation of holdings, danger of, 47, 48, 113, 118.
Franchise, broadening of, 101.
Freehold, 110.
Fruits of baobab and tamarind, 53.
Fuel, crop residues as, 52.
— manure as, 59, 71.
— shortage of, 141.
Furrows, intake, 168–71.
— on contour, 60.

Game, 12, 14, 21.
Ganda invasions, 15.
Geology of Sukumaland, 3–4.
German Administration, 12, 29, 47, 110.
Gerontocratic rule, 20–21, 24, 41.
Gezira, 111.
Ghee, 70–71, 72, 79, 90.
Government, influence of, 100–1.
— local, 84–85.
— recognition of chiefs, 96.
— — of officials, 101.
Grain as tribute, 85.
— as wealth, 52.
— from collective field, 58.
— sale of, 71.
— storage, 16, 129.
— store in village, 118.
— — manure lined, 71.
— — of chief, 27.
Granite, 3, 4.
— outcrops, 121.
Grantham, Dr. D. R., Geologist, 4, n. 1; 174.

Grass, collection of, 53.
— fallow, blocks reserved under, 137.
— — individual reservation of, 73.
— — resting periods under, 120.
— — rotation with crops, 55–56.
— — use in Busiha system of grazing, 77.
— for thatching, 73.
— leys, 141.
Grasses on *mbuga* soils, 183–6.
— on red fossil soils, 178–9.
— on sandy soils, 176–7.
— Sukuma names of, 191–2.
Grassland in Sukumaland healthy for cattle, 72.
— deterioration of, 122.
Graves, land rights and, 50.
Grazing, cattle rights and, 62–82.
— heavy, 73.
— open commonage, 76–77.
— reservation, 72–78.
— — Busiha system, 76.
— reserves, 90–91.
— — renting of, 50.
— — rotational, 114, 124, 133.
— seasonal, 72.
— shortage of, 72.
Groundnuts, 52, 128, 129.
— bambarra, 56, 190.
— planting, effect on fallow, 56.
— soils for, 190.
Guise Williams, O., *Memorandum on Village Organisation*, 22.
— — *The Village Constitution in Maswa*, 22.
Gum, collection of, 53.
Guns, muzzle-loading, 36.

Habitable area, increase of, 109.
Haboobs, dust storms, 7.
Hafir, built on instalment system, 162.
— construction of, 150, 165.
— definition of, 152.
Hailey, the Lord, G.C.S.I., G.C.M.G., G.C.I.E., 115.
— — *Native Administration in Africa*, 102, 106, n. 1.
Hall, Sir John Hathorn, K.C.M.G., D.S.O., O.B.E., M.C., Foreword to *A Development Plan for Uganda*, 125–6.
Hamitic people, 21.
Hardpan soils, 181–2.
Harrison, E., C.M.G., formerly Director of Agriculture, 126, n. 2.
Hay, making of, 122.
— standing, 77.
Head porterage, 130, 131.
Hedges, euphorbia, 12, 15.

Index

Herding, collective, 79.
— by children, 71.
Herds, size of, 71.
Herdsmen, professional, 72, 133.
Heavy grazing, 73.
— stocking, 73.
Hides, 71, 72.
Hills, and rocks, Sukuma names of, 175.
Hives, 53.
Hoes as bride-price, 69.
— hand-, 124-6.
Holdings, no division of, 46-47.
— scattered, reasons for, 59-60.
— size of, 113.
Honey, 53.
Houghton, Sir Bernard, 84.
House and Poll Tax, 85, 92.
— building, 18, 33.
— collective construction of, 37-38.
— moving, 135.
— mud brick, 47.
— permanent, 116.
— property, 47-49.
— sales, 47-49, 116.
— — danger of, 49.
— sites, 48.
Housing improved, 48-49.
Howard, L. E., *The Earth's Green Carpet*, 20, n. 2; 56, n. 2.
Huma, introducers of cattle, 69.
— invasion, 14, 24.
Hunters, Bahi, 20.
Hunting, 14, 69.
Husbandry, improved, 61, 108, 122-31, 142-3.
— — means of, 124-6.
— — propaganda, 138.

Ibambasi soil, 37, 181-2.
Ibushi soil, 6, 179-81.
Ifuma, grain store, 27.
Immigration into North Maswa, 13.
— into Zinza, 13, 15.
— of Hamitic people, 21.
Implemental tillage, 126-7.
Importation of food, 16.
— of seed, 16.
Imprisonment, 93-94.
Incomes, rise in, 61, 108-9.
India, local government in, 83-85.
— settlement report, viii, n. 1.
Indigenous institutions, recognized, 85.
Indirect rule, 83.
Individualization, 112-14.
Inheritance, 44, 45-47.
— by women, 52.
— effect on ancestor worship, 68.
— of cattle, 64-67.
— of land, 50.

Insurance against famine, 71.
Intelligentsia, growth of, 101.
Intermediate courts, powers of, 93-94.
Internecine war (*see also* Tribal war), 24.
Interplanting of crops, 55-56.
Investment in cattle, 71-72.
Irrigation, 107, 124.
Isanga river, 64.
Isanga soil, 37.

Judicial assistance, 29.
— functions of sub-chiefs, 87.
— work, 99.
Justice, 93-95.
— honesty of, 99.

Kanumba, cook for collective labour, 36.
Kibanda, section of village, 34.
Kimberlite, 3.
King, J. G. M., Agricultural Officer, ix, x, 107, 174.
Kordofan, Sudan, 8.
Kubirisa, lending cattle, 72-73.
Kubola, marriage without bride-price, 44.
Kukwa, marriage with bride-price, 44.
Kwimba Federation, 90.

Labour, collective (*see also* Collective), 12, 35-36.
— recruitment of, 32.
— saving devices, 143.
— — methods, 131.
Lake Victoria, 112.
Land, abuse of, 60-61.
— acquisition, 50-51.
— allocation, chief's right of, 22, 25.
— — delegation to *nsumbantale*, 37-38.
— — — to village headman, 22, 26.
— — in bush areas, 30.
— — right endangered, 117.
— — to newcomers, 18, 19, 51.
— community control of, 118.
— expulsion from, 26-27.
— fragmentation of, 48.
— gifts of, 25.
— holdings, control of, 113-14.
— lending of, 47, 51, 114.
— malutilization of, 120.
— occupation, 121-2.
— of absentees, 31-32.
— Ordinance, 111.
— ownership of, 20.
— policy, 110-12.
— — Government's, 109, 111-12.
— reallocation of, 30-32, 47, 51.
— reclamation of, 137.
— reserves, 132.
— resources, development of, 110.

Land, resting, 140-2.
— rights, customary indigenous, 51, 110.
— — recognition of, 110.
— rotational use of, 140, 143.
— sales, 12, 47, 50-51.
— tenure, 27, 43, 110-19, 144.
— — usufructory, 114, 116.
— utilization, 119-22.
Landless labourers, 113.
Landlord system, 111.
Language, Sukuma, 11.
Languages, 43-44.
Law, African customary, 140.
— and Customs, 81-82, 146.
Laws, co-ordination of, 94.
Leaks, mending of, in surface-water catchment works, 155-7.
— reasons for, 155, 173.
Legislation, enforcement of, 138-9.
Legislative functions of federations, 87-88.
Lending cattle, 71, 72-73, 75, 78, 133.
Lions, 19, 64, 73.
— destruction of, 28.
Local self-government, 84-85.

Maine's *Ancient Law*, 113.
Maintenance of Water Supplies, 155-60.
Maize, soils for, 190.
Majebere, Chief, K.M., C.M., leader of Sukumaland Federation, 146.
Maldistribution of land, 119.
— of population and stock, v.
Malcolm, D. W., *Gum and Gum Arabic*, 53, n. 1.
Malika ga mbina, dance societies, 41-43.
Malutilization of land, 120.
Malya dam, 154.
Malya, headquarters of development team, vii, 145.
— — of federation of chiefs, vii, 105, 145, 146.
Mangoes, planting of, 54.
Manonga river, 17, 64.
Manure, bulking of, 80, 123, 141.
— by-product, 72.
— farm-yard, 70-81.
— in abandoned cattle pens, 50, 58-59.
— property of owner of stock-yard, 70.
— shortage of, 59.
— transport and, 130-1.
— use of, 127.
Manured land, rights in, 50.
Manuring, adjunct of balanced husbandry, 120, 142.
— advantages of, 130.

Manuring, necessity of, 12.
Manyara, euphorbia tirucalli, 15.
Marketing of livestock, 90.
Marriage, 44-45, 68-69, 69-70.
— influence on inheritance, 64-67.
— in Zinza, 44.
— polygamous, 45.
— with bride-price, 44, 45, 69, 80.
— without bride-price, 18, 44, 45, 69.
Masai, 10, 11, 14, 17, 24.
Matrilineal inheritance, 64-67.
— succession, 22-23, 97.
Mbuga areas, sub-division of, 134.
— grazing, 64, 72, 78.
— pastures, 133.
— soil, collective work on, 37.
— — cracks in, 5.
— — definition of, 3.
— — erosion of, 4, 6.
— — grass cover on, 5.
— — in Sudan, 8.
— — land sales of, 47.
— — varieties of, 183-6.
Meat production, 135.
— property of cattl -owner, 71, 72.
Mechanical cultivation, 127-30, 143.
— equipment, hire of, 143.
— implements, hire of, 127-8.
Mechanization of farming, 109, 125-6.
Medical services, 108, 123.
Medicine, plants as basis, 54.
Metcalfe, Lord, 84.
Methods of improved husbandry, 123-4.
Milk production, 135.
— property of herder, 70-71, 72, 79.
Milkweed, 15.
Milne, the late G., Soil Chemist, 4, 174.
— — Soil Reconnaissance Report, 134, n. 2.
Minutes of Sukumaland Federal Council meeting, 146.
Miombo woodland, 6, 17, 177.
Mirambo, the raider, 12.
Mixed cropping, 3.
— farming, 119, 130, 133.
Mlamji, sub-chief, 29.
Mortality from rinderpest, 72.
Movement in Mwanza District, 15.
— of people, reasons for, 17-18, 47-50.
— of population, 14-19.
Muds, Sukuma names of, 189.
Munro, Sir Thomas, 84.
Musoma District, clan elders, 20.
Mutual assistance, 16, 33-34.

Native Administration, adaptability of, 101-6.
— — efficiency of, 99-101.

Index

Native Authority Ordinance (*see also* Ordinance), 86, 140, n. 1.
— — — enforcement of enactments, 100.
— Authorities, 86.
— — legislative and administrative functions, 87–90.
— court fees, 90.
— Treasury estimates, 90.
— — finance, 85, 91–93.
Natural Resources Ordinance, 109, 139.
Nera chiefdom, description of, 2, 12.
Nfumu, doctor using divination, 68–69.
Ngitiri grazing reserve, 75.
Ngudu, 12.
Ng'wamapalala dam, 17.
Ng'wambilija, sub-chief, 29, 87.
Ng'wanangwa, village headman (*see also* Village Headman), 22.
Nhomango dam, 17.
Nigeria, Native Authorities in, 102.
— Northern, 8.
Nomination of successors by chiefs, 98.
Non-co-operation in collective labour, 38–39.
Nsango, birth blood-price, 45.
Nsumba ntale, rights and duties of, 37–40.
— — storage of grain by, 58.
— — tenure of office, 39.
— — translation of, vii.
— — village labour leader, 32, 34–40.
Nsweda, assistant, 31.
Ntwale, regional headman, 29.
Nyaisanga, shore dwellers, 44.
Nyamwezi tribe, 21.
Nyashimba village, survey of, vi, 46, 47.

Occupation of holding, after death, 45–46.
Occupations of people, 125.
Officials, unpaid, 101.
Oligarchy, danger of, 103.
Orders, enforcement of, 87, 94.
Ordinance, Native Authority, 86, 140, n. 1.
— — — Section 8, 87–88.
— — — 15, 88.
— Natural Resources, 109, 139.
Orthography, difficulty of, vii–viii.
Ownership of by-products from cattle, 70–71, 72.
— of land, 20, 25.
Oxcarts, 131.
Oxen for cultivation, 72, 126, 127.

Pack donkeys, 130.
— transport of manure, 59.
Panchayat, village council, 84.
Passive resistance, 36, 100.
Pastoralists, 71, 119.
Pasture control, 114–15.
— plants, Sukuma names of, 191–2.
— reservation, 77, 133.
— — by individuals, 73–76.
— reserves, renting of, 75.
Patrilineal inheritance, 64–67.
— succession, 23, 97.
Pawpaws, planting of, 54.
People, contact with authorities, 86.
— necessities of, 125.
Perham, M., *Native Administration in Nigeria*, 20, n. 1.
Permanent crops, of trees, 55.
Personal plots, wives', 52.
— reserves, difficulty of, 75, 76.
Persuasion to resettle, 138.
Planned Group Farming, 119, 145, 210–12.
Plantation, fuel, 141.
— of trees, 54.
— system, 111.
Planting of trees, personal, 54–55.
— season, 124, 129.
Ploughing, dangers of individual ownership, 126.
— effect on fallow, 56–57.
— legislation, 57, n. 1; 127.
— ox-drawn, 57, 126–7.
Policy of Indirect Rule, 83.
— Land, 110–19.
Political development, 85–86.
— organization, 111.
Popular approval of chief, 98.
— representation, 104.
Population, cattle statistics, 62–63.
— congestion, 11, 12.
— density control, 140.
— — reduction, 135, 136–7.
— distribution and density, 11–14.
— expansion of, 12, 131.
— increase of, 107–8.
— — race against, 109.
— Land and Production, 107–10.
— movements, 14–19.
— pressure, 137.
— — relieving of, 132.
— redistribution, 123, 131–40.
— statistics, 9–10, 108.
— total, 1.
— trends, 108.
Porcupine destruction, 41.
Potatoes, soils for sweet, 190.
Precedent, breaches of, 102, 105.
Pre-emption, right of, 119.
Primogeniture, 97.

Index

Problem, basic, 107.
Problems of Sukumaland, 107–45.
— positive approach, 142.
Produce of land, 51–52.
Production, economic unit of, 111.
— increase of, 109, 142.
— methods and means of, 109, 122–31.
Products from bush, 53, 193.
Progress of Native Administration, 104–5.
Provincial Commissioners, estimates submitted to, 92, 93.
Public opinion, 98, 100.
— speaking, 95.
Punjab, 8.
Purchase of cattle, 67.

Queens, 23.

Rainfall, Sukumaland, 6–7.
Reallocation of land, 31–32, 51.
Rebate of tax to Native Authorities, 85, 92.
Reclamation of land, 120, 137.
Recognition of chief, withdrawal of, 96.
— of indigenous institutions, 85.
Recording of cases, 85, 93.
Redistribution, external, 136–7.
— internal, 135–6.
— methods of effecting, 138–40.
— of population, 131–40.
— of stock, 120, 134–5.
— provision of water supplies for, 150.
Reduction of density, 135.
Reforms, unpopular, 99.
Regenerating bush, 54-55, 73.
Regents, selection of, 102.
Regional headman, 29.
Religion, 23, 41, 50, 67–69.
Reorganization of chiefdoms, 83.
Reservation of grazing, 50, 72–73.
Reserve blocks, 139–40.
— — supervision of, 140.
Resettlement, details of movements, 150.
— of population, 33, 72–73, 131–42.
Resolutions of Sukumaland Federal Council, 105.
— unanimous, 89.
Resting of land, 140–2.
Revenue, average yearly, 93.
— collection of, 93.
— from ghee, 71.
Rice, interplanting of, 56, n. 1.
— soils for, 191.
Right in cattle, 64–67.
— of collection of honey, 53.
— of pre-emption, 119.
Rights, definition of, 81–82.
— in land, recognition of, 110.
Rights of absentees, 32.
— of chiefs, 25–28.
— of inheritance, 45–46.
Rinderpest, elimination of, v, 11, 72.
— epidemic of, 13.
Rites of ancestor worship, 68.
River beds, sandy, 79, 136.
— silting of, 4.
Road construction, 4, 13.
Rocks, Sukuma names of, 175.
Rongo customs in Zinza, 66.
Rope from bark, 53.
Rotation of crops and fallow, 55–57.
Rotational grazing, 114, 122, 142.
— use of land, 143.
Rural economy, 110.

Salaries, payment of, 92.
Sale of cattle, 61, 67, 99.
— of crops, 51.
— of grain, 71.
— of houses, 116–17.
— — sanction for prearranged, 118.
Sand, eating of, 75, 77.
Sands, Sukuma names of, 189.
Sandy soils, 176–7.
— — manuring of, 81.
Sanga river, 17, 64.
Scattered holdings, reasons for, 59–60.
Scupham, Brigadier W. E. H., C.M.G., M.C., 22.
Seasonal grazing in *mbuga* areas, 64, 134.
— — lending of stock for, 72, 77.
— — organized, 133.
Seasons, contrast of, 1–2.
Seed benediction, 23, 28.
— ownership of, 52.
— sowing of, 40.
Seeding of grasses, 73, 77.
Seepage areas, 136.
Sekule tribute to chief, 27–28.
Selection of chief, 96–98.
Self-government, 84.
Semu river, 17.
Serengeti National Park, 17.
Shaduf, use of, 136.
Shibiti river, 17, 64.
Shifting cultivation, 14, 108, 113.
Shilaba, children's fields, 34, n. 1.
Shimiyu river, 16, 17, 19, 78.
Shinyanga federation, 86, 89.
Shrubs on hardpan soils, 181.
— on *ibushi* soils, 180.
— on *mbuga* soils, 183–6.
— on red fossil soils, 178–9.
— on sandy soils, 176–7.
Siting of houses, 48.
Slaughter of cattle, 67–71, 81.
Sleeping sickness, 136.
Smallpox, 90.

Index

Small stock as bride-price, 69.
Smith Sound, 19.
Snakes, 41.
Social insurance, 58, 128–9.
— organization, 111–12.
— services, development of, 92–93.
— structure, 83.
Societies, dance, 41–43.
— village, 33–34.
Society, secret, 43.
Soil catena, 4, 174, 175–6.
— crumb structure, 120.
— damage by cattle, 122.
— — by flat cultivation, 60.
— drainage, 60.
— exhaustion, 15.
— fertility damage, reasons for, 121–2.
— — deterioration, v, vi.
— — maintenance of, 134.
— — restoration of, 140.
— — *sine qua non* of land use, 119–20.
— — static agriculture, necessity for, 115.
— — Sukuma attitude to, 78.
— *ibushi*, 179–80.
— names, dialect variations, 174.
— pulverization of, 73.
Soils, grouping of, 174.
— hardpan, 181–2.
— less favourable for crops, 191.
— *mbuga*, 183–6.
— minor types, 186–9.
— pervious, 157.
— red fossil, 178–9.
— sandy, 176–7.
— suitability for various crops, 60, 190–1.
— Sukumaland, 4–5, 174–91.
— variety of, 59–60.
— where springs occur, 190.
Sorghums, 122, 124, 128.
— infested by *Striga helmonthica*, 57.
— soils for, 47, 190.
Spillway, size of, 162.
Springs, 79, 136.
Stalk borer in sorghums, vi.
Standard of living, rise in, 61, 107, 109, 125.
Stanley, H. M., journey through Sukumaland, 105.
— — *In Darkest Africa*, 2, 12, n. 2.
— — *Through the Dark Continent*, 2, nn. 1 and 2.
Stapleton, Sir R. G., *The Land Now and To-morrow*, 78, n. 1.
Starvation of cattle, 75.
State control of land use, 138.
Static agriculture, 55, 115.
Statistics, cattle population, 62–63.
— of area of Tanganyika, 132.

Statistics, population, 9–10, 108.
Stock distribution, 136.
— increases, 67.
— lending, 133.
— owning, reasons for, 67–72.
— maldistribution of, 120, 126.
— redistribution, 120.
Stock-yards, abandoned, 79.
— — cultivation of, 50.
Stocking, heavy, 73, 122.
Striga helmonthica, damage by, vi.
— — effect on rotation of crops, 57.
— — infestation of sorghums, 15, 57.
— — land abandoned due to, 15, 122.
— — legislation concerning, 90.
— — up-rooting of, 100, 138.
Strip cropping, 117, 142.
Structure of African local government, 99–100.
— of Native Authorities in future, 101–6.
Sub-chief, 29.
— court, powers of, 93.
— judicial work of, 87.
Subordinate authorities, 29.
— — origin of, 22.
Subsistence economy, 124.
Subsoil, *ndoba*, 189.
Sugar cane, 54.
Sukuma, agriculturalists, 10, 63.
— land tenure development, 114–19.
— — Utilization Report, v.
— language, 11.
— people, description of, 10–11.
— terms, spelling of, vii.
— — translation of, vii.
Sukumaland African local government, 83–106.
— description of, 1–2.
— development team, 107, 137, 144.
— Federal Council, 91.
— Federation, 86–87, 144–5.
— — advantages of, 149.
— — appeal court, 94.
— — legislative work, 88.
— — Native Treasury, advantages of, 93.
— — — organization of, 147–8.
— — — unification of, 92.
— — power of chiefs, 105.
— geology, 3–4.
— in relation to Tanganyika, 132.
— problems, 107–45.
— — positive approach, 142.
— rainfall, 6–7.
— river drainage system, 7.
— soils, 4–5, 174–91.
— topography, 3.
— vegetation, 5–6.
— wind in, 7–8.

Index

Supervision, educative, 104-5.
— of chief's court, 85.
— of courts, 93.
— of crops, 58.
— of finance, 92-93.
Surface Water Catchment works, 19, 33, 149-73.
— — — — Busiha, 28.

Tanganyika, statistics of areas, 132.
Tanks, cleaning of, 155.
— construction of, 150, 165-8.
— definition of, 152.
— water, Busiha, 16, 28.
Tax, 28.
— collection of, 92.
— rebate to Native Treasuries, 85, 92.
Taxation, cash crops, 52.
Team, inter-departmental, 107.
Tenure of land, 27.
Termitaria, 186-7.
Termites, 142.
Terminalia - Combretum vegetation complex, 6.
Terms of reference, 144.
Thatching grass, 73.
Thomas & Scott, *Uganda*, 22, n. 1.
Threshing floors, manure, 71.
Tick fever, 74-75, 78.
Ticks in grassland, 73, 122.
Tie-ridging, 61, 90, 121, 123, 127, 142.
Topography of Sukumaland, 3.
Tractor-drawn implements, 127.
Tradition, modification of, 102.
Traditional institutions, 84.
Trampling of grass, 75.
Transfer of people, 17-19.
Transport, 130-1.
— of manure, 58-59.
Treasuries, native, 85, 90, 91-93.
Trees, 53-55.
— acquisition by force, 54-55.
— advantages of, 142.
— exotic, ownership of, 54-55.
— on hardpan soils, 181-2.
— on *ibushi* soil, 180-1.
— on *mbuga* soil, 183-6.
— on red fossil soils, 178-9.
— on sandy soils, 176-7.
— on termitaria, 187.
— on plantations by Native Authorities, 6.
— planting of, 54.
— seed, touching of, 54.
— use of, 6, 54, 140-1, 193.
Tribal land, 110.
— war, 11-12, 24, 47, 64, 69, 108.
Tribute in grain, 85.
— to chief, 27-28.
Trustee of cattle, 65-66.

Tsetse fly, 13-14, 19, 64, 72, 73, 137, 141.
— Research Department, 8, 14.
Tusi pastoral people, 14.

Ukara Island, 130, 136.
Upper basement complex, 3.
Use of land, 55-57.
Utilization of land, 119-22.
Uzinza, *see* Zinza.

Vegetation, Sukumaland, 5-6.
Vermin, 73.
— danger of, 142.
Veterinary services, 108, 123.
Village associations, 144.
— boundaries, 30.
— chest for compensation, 118.
— community, 84, 124.
— co-operative organization, 101, 129-30.
— council, India, 84.
— elders, 22, 31, 40-41, 145.
— — judicial assistance, 40.
— — petty cases, 93.
— — religion, 40.
— field, 128.
— fortified, 12.
— growth of, 30-31.
— headman, eviction by, 27.
— — land allocation, 43, 51, 117.
— — manured land, 50, 79.
— — misrule, 47.
— — of new villages, 73.
— — pasture control, 76.
— — petty cases, 93.
— — rights and duties of, 29-32.
— — selection of chief, 98.
— — son of chief, 22.
— — labour leader (*see also* Nsumba ntale), 32.
— land tenure, 115.
— organization, new responsibilities, 143-4.
— societies, 28, 33-34, 128.
— sorghum field, 58.
— structure of, 43.
— woods, 140-2.

War measures, 99-100.
Water catchment pits, 33.
— cattle and, 133-5.
— collective labour, 32.
— Development Department, 149, 154.
— importance of permanent supply, 155.
— in bush areas, 72.
— maldistribution of, 122, 133.
— provision of, 121.
— rights, 78-79.

Index

Water shortage, 72.
— supplies, 13–14.
— — advantages of manual construction, 151.
— — amateur construction, 149.
— — construction of, 134.
— — digging of, 78.
— — failures, 15, 33.
— — *hafir* layout, 165.
— — importance of successful construction, 149.
— — intake furrows, 168–71.
— — leaks, 155–7.
— — limitation of, 140.
— — maintenance of, 155–60.
— — mechanical assistance with, 172.
— — minimum depth, 154.
— — Native Authority organization for, 150–2.
— — optimum capacity, 154.
— — — time for construction, 152.
— — policy, 150.
— — provision of, 131, 136, 138, 143.
— — requirements for survey, 151.
— — size of excavations, 165–8.
— — spacing of, 153–4.
— — tools for labour, 171.
— — transport of earth, 171–2.
— village supplies, 32–33.
Wealth, cattle as, 16.
— family as, 51–52.
Wealth, heritable, 45.
— in children, 69.
Weeds, inedible, 73.
— in pasture, 76, 78.
Wells, 32.
Wheel, introduction of, 131, 143.
Wheelbarrows, 131.
— advantage of, 59.
— subsidizing of, 131.
Whipping, 93–94.
Will of the people, chiefs responsive to, 98–99.
Williams, Dr. G. J., Geologist, 4, n. 1; 174.
Wind, velocity of, 8.
Witchcraft, 26.
Witchweed (*see also Striga helmonthica*), 15–16.
Woods, village, 117, 119, 140–2.
Worship of ancestors, 50.
Worthington, Dr. E. B., *A Development Plan for Uganda*, 109.

Young, Arthur, 240.

Zebu cattle, 63.
Zinza, 1, 13, 15, 18, 39.
— cattle movements to, 64.
— crops in, 52.
— customs of inheritance, 66.
— inheritance by women, 66.
— marriage in, 44.

PRINTED IN GREAT BRITAIN
AT THE UNIVERSITY PRESS, OXFORD
BY CHARLES BATEY, PRINTER TO THE UNIVERSITY